PETER
DISCIPLE—APOSTLE
MARTYR

PETER

DISCIPLE—APOSTLE—MARTYR

A Historical and Theological Study
by
OSCAR CULLMANN
Dr. Theol., D.D. (Edin.),
D.D. (Manchester)
Professor in Basel and Paris

Translated from the German by
FLOYD V. FILSON

Philadelphia
THE WESTMINSTER PRESS

The original edition
of this book was published in German under the title
PETRUS by Zwingli-Verlag, Zurich,
Switzerland

This edition
is published simultaneously in Great Britain and the
United States of America by the SCM Press Ltd.,
London, and The Westminster Press,
Philadelphia

First published in English
MCMLIII

PRINTED IN THE UNITED STATES OF AMERICA

To the
University of Manchester
And Especially
To its Theological Faculty
In Expression of Thanks
For the Conferring of the Degree of
Doctor of Divinity

"I believe in one holy catholic
and apostolic Church"

"You are 'Rock,' and on this Rock
I will build my Church"

"Built upon the foundation of
the Apostles and Prophets"

"I pray for those who believe
through the word of the Apostles"

TRANSLATOR'S PREFACE

PROFESSOR CULLMANN'S book on Peter deserves attentive reading by English-speaking Christians. We possess few thorough studies of Peter's career and position in the Church. Hundreds of lives of Jesus are available, and scores of lives of Paul, but there are few thorough presentations of the life and work of Peter, and none is up to date. This book therefore meets a definite need.

The usual discussion of Peter centres almost entirely on the question of his ecclesiastical office. Professor Cullmann gives a more balanced study; he includes also the significant role that Peter played in formulating the message of the Apostolic Church and in carrying out the missionary task of the first generation of Christians.

Recent excavations under St. Peter's Cathedral in Rome, and the explicit papal announcement that the burial place of Peter has been found, have caused increased attention to the subject of Peter's residence in Rome and his supposed martyrdom there. This book examines carefully the literary, liturgical, and archaeological evidence for the Roman residence and martyrdom of Peter.

No discussion of the work of Peter can ignore the claim that Peter was the first Pope, whose successors continue to hold the same ruling authority that he held. Professor Cullmann sketches the history of the interpretation of Matthew 16:17–19, which is the key passage on this subject. He then considers carefully the historical meaning of this passage, and goes on to state its theological significance for the Church today. His book is thus an important contribution to the ecumenical discussion of our time.

The author is constantly concerned to be fair to all sides. He is determined to go no further than the evidence permits. A few readers may wish that he had adopted a more polemic tone. Most of us, however, will be grateful for this calm and friendly spirit, and will find that it makes his argument the more compelling.

By reading the manuscript, offering suggestions, and answering

questions, Professor Cullmann has helped greatly in the preparation
of the English edition of his work. He has assured me that I have
understood his thought and rendered it faithfully. My hope is that I
have given it an effective English form, for the book has something
vital to say to students of the Bible, church history, theology, and
the ecumenical movement.

FLOYD V. FILSON

*McCormick Theological
Seminary, Chicago
January 15, 1953*

CONTENTS

Translator's Preface   7

Foreword   11

Part I

THE HISTORICAL QUESTION

Chapter One: PETER THE DISCIPLE   17

  1. Name, Origin, Call   17

  2. Position in the Circle of Disciples   23

Chapter Two: PETER THE APOSTLE   33

  1. Leadership of the Primitive Church   33

  2. Mission in the Service of the Jewish Christian Primitive
Church   40

  3. The Question of the Apostolic Commission   56

  4. The Theological Views of the Apostle   65

Chapter Three: PETER THE MARTYR   70

  1. The Problem   70

  2. History of the Debate Whether Peter Resided in Rome   71

  3. The Literary Sources   77

  4. The Liturgical Sources   123

  5. The Excavations   132

Part II

THE EXEGETICAL AND THEOLOGICAL QUESTION

THE PROBLEM   155

Chapter One: THE EXEGETICAL QUESTION CONCERNING
MATTHEW 16:17–19   158

  1. History of the Leading Interpretations of the Passage   158

  2. The Narrative Framework   170

  3. Genuineness and Meaning of the Saying   184

9

10 CONTENTS

Chapter Two: THE DOCTRINAL AND THEOLOGICAL
QUESTION OF THE APPLICATION OF
MATTHEW 16:17–19 TO THE LATER
CHURCH   213

1. The Laying of the Foundation of the Church   215
2. The Leadership of the Church   223

Index of Authors Cited   239
Index of Biblical Passages   248

FOREWORD

BEFORE I decided that in order to pay a debt of thanks, as well as to express respect and friendly fellowship in a common task, I should dedicate this book to the University of Manchester and especially to its theological faculty, I had intended to dedicate it to my Roman Catholic friends, and particularly to the theologians among them. With them I sincerely feel myself united not only on the basis of general human esteem but also in questions of our Christian faith. However, I gave up this intention, because the final section of my work quite naturally will fail to win the approval of their Church, and so I feared that this dedication might in some way be misunderstood. I can assure them, nevertheless, that during the preparation of the final chapter I recalled many a conversation that I had had with them. I also kept in mind new objections that my discussions might evoke in them. Thus while writing that closing section I often found myself carrying on a silent discussion with them as absent members in a personal conversation.

My previous publications concerning Primitive Christian theological thought have found much genuine understanding even in Roman Catholic circles. Therefore I dare to hope and wish that my discussion of the very thing that separates us—for in the present investigation this comes quite frankly to expression, along with much that may win their assent—may do no harm, but may rather render a service to the conversation that Christian confessions have with one another.

This discussion must be continued in spite of the papal encyclical *Humani Generis*, and perhaps particularly as a result of it. If I am well informed, the admonitions of that document do not have in view those discussions with non-Roman Catholic Christians in which each side clearly represents its own standpoint. Indeed, we promote mutual and improved understanding only if we do not pass over in silence that which separates us. Where men, fully aware that they invoke the same name, make a sincere effort to listen to one another, they need not fear to speak also concerning the themes on which, as far as human eye can see, agreement is not possible. I often note, in discussions between representatives of the various confessions, that both parties take anxious pains to speak only concerning those questions regarding which there exists a common basis of discussion. The other questions are studiously avoided, even though as a rule the conversation necessarily reaches a point where it should move on to precisely those other questions for which the common basis is lacking. When this point it reached, one should go back to the reason for this lack of a common basis, not—let me repeat—to fight for one's position and not, indeed, with the illusory purpose of converting one's partner, but rather to listen to him. My purpose would not be furthered if certain things which I say were to be used as a polemic against the Roman Catholic Church. For I hold that in addition to the ecumenical achievements of recent decades it is precisely the simple discussion between Roman Catholic and Protestant theologians that is one of the encouraging events in the church history of our time.

It is in this spirit, and on the basis of the exegetical and historical principles which control the entire work, that I have written the latter part of this book. I hope that it will call forth numerous utterances, from both camps, concerning the fundamental questions over which Christendom is divided. In earlier times there was much discussion of them. Since then, however, men on both sides have become so accustomed to the fact that they do not agree in their point of departure that they often consider it unnecessary to speak about the matter at all—and what is worse, they neglect even to think about it. Apart from the fact that under these circumstances such discussions of individual questions or doctrines as have taken place in recent years are more or less futile, this procedure gives rise on both sides to prejudices and misunderstandings. Their removal should be our first aim, and indeed as much for reasons of scientific study as of faith. A resumption of the discussion concerning the primacy of Rome is also advisable because the arguments are no longer the same as they were in the sixteenth and seventeenth centuries.

In the present study I have purposely avoided raising the doctrinal question until the final chapter. This book as a whole is meant to be *a contribution to the science of history*, and in particular to that part which deals with the beginnings of the Christian faith and the Christian Church. If a librarian should be in doubt as to how to catalogue it, I should like to help him out of his perplexity at once. In spite of the sub-title and in spite of my personal interest in the theological question concerning Peter—an interest which I, even as a historian, make no attempt to conceal—this book belongs neither in the field of dogmatic theology nor in the literature of ecumenical debate nor even in the field of apologetics, but in that of the history of Primitive Christianity.

It is a historical study concerning the Apostle Peter that I here present.[1] But the history of Peter runs on without a break into the *evaluation* of this history which occurs in the continuing *historical* development. This evaluation, however, is likewise theological in nature, and the history of Peter has become the object of a dogmatic pronouncement by the Roman Catholic Church. Thus in a historical study which seeks to deal with Peter, the theological problem, on the one hand, is not to be avoided; yet this theological problem, on the other hand, can only be studied in the closest connection with history.

May the faithful application of strictly historical methods, which I have taken care to use in dealing with this question, furnish a basis for the debate on the one hand between non-Christian and Christian historians, and on the other hand between Christian theologians of separate denominations who join in confessing One Catholic and Apostolic Church, but differ in the way they believe it is realized at the present time.

Oscar Cullmann

Easter, 1952

1 This seemed to me the more necessary since we have but few scholarly works on Peter. Monographs on Paul are much more numerous. Recent *general* works on Peter include, on the Protestant side, F. Sieffert, *Realenzyklopädie für Theologie und Kirche*, 3rd ed., Article on "Peter," Vol. 15, pp. 190 ff.; F. J. Foakes-Jackson, *Peter, Prince of Apostles: A Study in the History and Tradition of Christianity*, 1927; W. Brandt, *Simon Petrus*, n.d. (popular in character); E. Fascher, *Realenzyklopädie des klassischen Alterthums*, Pauly-Wissowa, Article on "Peter," columns 1335 ff.; on the Roman Catholic side, C. Fouard, *S. Pierre et les premières années du christianisme*; L. Fillion, *Dictionnaire de la Bible*, Article on "S. Pierre"; A. Tricot, *Dictionnaire de Théologie catholique*, Article on "S. Pierre," 1935; M. Besson, *S. Pierre et les origines de la primauté romaine*, 1928 (beautifully illustrated); M. Meinertz, *Lexikon für Theologie und Kirche*, Article on "Petrus," 1936.

Part I

THE HISTORICAL
QUESTION

THE SOURCES for our knowledge of Peter consist mainly of the writings of the New Testament. For the final period of his life we shall have to use both archaeological and liturgical evidence and texts of the Apostolic Fathers and the Church Fathers.

We can group the information we have concerning Peter under the following headings: (1) Peter the Disciple; (2) Peter the Apostle; (3) Peter the Martyr. In the section that deals with the Apostle we shall speak also of his theological views; in that dealing with the martyrdom we shall have to raise the radically important question concerning the stay of Peter in Rome.

Chapter One

PETER THE DISCIPLE

1. *Name, Origin, Call*

As SOURCES concerning Peter the Disciple only the canonical Gospels are to be considered. The apocryphal gospels add only legendary material.

The fantastic attempt to deny the historical existence of Peter and to explain "the Christian Peter as the humanized form of the Persian Petros or Mithra" needs no refutation. It deserves mention only as a curiosity.[1]

We begin with the question as to the *name* of Peter; it is linked with the question of his role in the circle of the Twelve.

The original name of the apostle is Symeon or Simon. Symeon[2] is a Hebrew name much used among the Jews. We find this Semitic form used of Peter, however, only in Acts 15:14 and II Peter 1:1.[3] The Gospels use the Greek name Simon. This did not originate, as has been supposed, by rendering into Greek the Hebrew name. It is rather "native Greek"[4] and is already attested by Aristophanes. It is probable that the original Hebrew name Symeon was later replaced by the Greek name of similar sound. However, it does not seem to me at all impossible that Peter, like his brother Andrew, had been given a Greek name from the outset, especially since this is true of Philip, who according to John 1:44 comes from the same place, Bethsaida, and Hellenistic influence, moreover, is attested precisely for this region.[5] It is not impossible, therefore, that Peter, as was

---

[1] See A. Drews, *Die Petruslegende*, 1924. [2] שמעון.

[3] In Acts 15:14 this form is purposely used, since the speaker is James. In II Pet. 1:1 the reading "Simon," Σίμων (B) is almost certainly secondary. The latest scholar to oppose identifying Symeon (Acts 15:14) and Peter is E. Fuchs (*Zeitschrift für Theologie und Kirche*, 1951, p. 350).

[4] See F. Blass—A. Debrunner, *Grammatik des neutestamentlichen Griechisch*, 7th ed., 1943, Par. 53, 2, and Fick-Bechtel, *Die griechischen Personennamen*, 1894, pp. 30, 251. See also A. Deissmann, *Bibelstudien*, 1895, p. 184, note 1 (Eng. Tr., *Bible Studies*, 1901, p. 315, note 2).

[5] See below, p. 22.

customary in the Dispersion and as we probably must assume for
Paul-Saul, had been given from the outset both the Hebrew name
Symeon and the Greek name Simon of similar sound.

In addition to this name he has a descriptive title: *Kepha*. This is an
Aramaic word and means "stone," "rock." Thus *Kepha* is not, as we
might be inclined to believe, a proper name.[6] It is not a given name
in ordinary use among the Jews, but is rather a common noun. In the
New Testament we find this title at times in its Aramaic form, that
is, merely *transcribed* in Greek letters; this is usually the case in Paul's
letters (Gal. 1:18; 2:9; 2:11,[7] 14; I Cor. 1:12; 3:22; 9:5; 15:5). At
times, however, it is *translated* into Greek: *Petros*. Paul writes *Petros*
only once, in Galatians 2:7, 8,[8] perhaps because he here cites an
official document, in the Greek translation of which the form *Petros*
was used. The Gospels say at times *Simon*, at times *Petros*, at times
Simon Petros.[9] The Syriac translations write *Simon Kepha*. Where in
Greek environment the word is preserved in its aramaic spelling, it
is supplied at the end with the Greek final -*s* in order to give it a
Greek ending: *Kephas*. According to the Septuagint of Jeremiah 4:29
and Job 30:6, the preferable Greek translation would be *Petra*,[10]

---

[6] This is wrongly asserted by Th. Zahn, *Kommentar zum Neuen Testament, Das
Evangelium des Matthäus*, 4th ed., 1922, p. 540; but he gives no example to support his view. M. J. Lagrange, in *L'Evangile selon S. Matthieu*, 5th ed., 1941,
p. 324, also considers it possible.

[7] The completely unfounded idea that Gal. 2:11 is talking about another Cephas,
who is entirely different from Peter and belongs to the Seventy disciples, appears
in ancient times in Clement of Alexandria, *Hypotyposeis*, V (Eusebius, *Ecclesiastical
History*, I, 12, 2), then in the lists of apostles (see Th. Schermann, *Propheten- und
Apostellegenden nebst Jüngerkatalogen*, 1907, pp. 302 ff.), and in recent times in
J. M. Robertson, *Die Evangelienmythen*, 1910 (German tr. of Part III of *Christianity
and Mythology*, 1900), p.103, and D. W. Riddle, "The Cephas-Peter Problem
and a Possible Solution" (*Journal of Biblical Literature*, 1940, pp. 169 ff.).

[8] In opposition to all the textual evidence A. Merx, *Die vier kanonischen Evangelien
nach ihrem ältesten bekannten Text*, II, 1, *Das Evangelium Matthäus*, 1902, p. 161,
regards "Peter" (Πέτρος) as secondary in these passages and assumes that in them
too "Cephas" (Κηφᾶς) was the original reading.

[9] The Fourth Gospel prefers to say: Simon Peter.

[10] Elsewhere in the Septuagint πέτρα translates צור and סלע. See Hatch-Redpath,
A Concordance to the Septuagint and the other Greek Versions of the Old Testament,
1897-1900. The Aramaic word בפא (Kepha) is translated by λίθος ("stone"), as
A. Dell shows, in his article on "Matthäus 16:17-19" (*Zeitschrift für die Neutestamentliche Wissenschaft*, 1914, pp. 19 f.), by the evidence of the Jerusalem Gospel
and the Sinaitic Syriac. Nevertheless, it remains true that *Kepha* in Aramaic
means both "stone" and "rock." Therefore the results that A. Dell draws from
the translation λίθος are to be rejected. See the following note.

which means "rock." Since, however, this word is feminine in Greek and has the feminine ending -a, the New Testament chooses for the translation a less usual Greek word which has the Greek masculine ending -os: *Petros* (John 1:42). There is no essential difference in meaning between *Petros* and *Petra*, for even if originally *Petra* designated live rock while *Petros* meant rather the detached stone, this distinction was not strictly observed.[11] The preference for the form *Petros* may have been due in part to the fact that in Aramaic there was a proper name *Petros*, which perhaps had the meaning "first-born."[12] This, however, is not certain.

In any event, the fact that the word *Kepha* was translated into Greek is significant. It confirms the fact that the word is not a proper name; proper names are not translated. The attempt has indeed been made to prove that even in pre-Christian times the name Peter existed as an abbreviation for the Latin Petronius and that it occurs in the Jewish author Josephus,[13] but the attempt at proof has failed.[14]

It is only because Peter has become for us today a familiar proper name that we are often tempted to forget that *Kepha* is a common noun. But this fact is important if we desire to judge rightly the bearing of the fact that Jesus gave Peter this title. It corresponds to Jewish custom to choose as titles words which somehow point to the promise in a particular situation and lay an obligation on their bearer. We know such examples from the Old Testament,[15] and in a similar way

---

11 In Homer, *Odyssey*, 243 ; Hesiod, *Theogony*, 675; and Wisdom 17:17 (LXX) πέτρα is used with the meaning "stone," "piece of rock." That the two words are interchangeable is said also by Galen, XII, 194. A. Dell, *op. cit.*, pp. 19 f., is probably wrong, therefore, in emphasizing that *Kepha* and *Petros* mean "stone" and not "rock."

12 J. Levy, *Neuhebräisch-chaldäisches Wörterbuch*, 1876 ff.; Dalman, *Aramäisch-neuhebräisches Wörterbuch*, 2nd ed., 1922; Strack-Billerbeck, *Kommentar zum Neuen Testament aus Talmud und Midrasch*, Vol. I, p. 530.

13 Josephus, *Antiquities*, 18, 6, 3. In reality what is involved here is a textual error for πρῶτος ("first").

14 The attempt has been made by A. Merx, *op. cit.*, pp. 160 ff. See also A. Meyer, *Jesu Muttersprache*, 1896, p. 51. It has been opposed by A. Dell, *op. cit.*, pp. 14 ff.: "The proper name Peter does not appear at all in pagan literature; it first appears in Tertullian." There was, on the contrary, as already mentioned (note 12), an Aramaic name פטרוס (Petros), which perhaps is to be connected with פטר (patar) "firstborn." The theory that the Greek *Petros* was first derived from it and gave occasion for a false retranslation *Kepha* into Aramaic is quite impossible, in view of the fact that in Paul's letters Cephas is already the usual designation and Peter clearly was only a later derivation from it.

15 Gen. 17:5 ff., 15; 32:28; Isa. 62:2; 65:15. See also on this point Justin, *Dialogue With Trypho*, 106, 3.

Jewish disciples also received from their Rabbi a title.[16] Jesus himself gave such a title not only to Peter but also to the Sons of Zebedee: *Boanerges*, which is explained in Mark 3:17 to mean "Sons of Thunder."[17] In order to understand what an impression the giving of a name to Peter must have made on him and on the other witnesses of this event, we would do well to translate the word *Kephas* not with the word Peter, which for us today is all too familiar and has become too rigidly fixed as a proper name, but with the English word "rock," and so call him Simon Rock.[18]

According to the unanimous witness of the Gospels, the giving of this name goes back to Jesus. It will not do to ascribe it to the fellow disciples, who supposedly gave him this name of honour only later, on the basis of the fact that he was the first who saw the risen Lord.[19] In saying this we have not yet said whether it was actually given to him in the situation described in Matthew, ch. 16. The agreement of the Evangelists concerning the basic fact is the more noteworthy in view of their absolute divergence about the circumstances in which the name was given. According to the basic passage, Matthew 16:18, with which we shall have to deal in detail, Jesus first gave Simon this title on the occasion when he likewise explained it more fully. This was at the moment when, according to Mark 8:27 ff., Peter uttered his famous confession of Jesus at Caesarea Philippi. There Jesus asks his disciples, "Who do men say that I am?"[20] The disciples report to him the various views current among the people. Thereupon Jesus asks, "And in your view, who am I?" Peter speaks up and says, "You are the Christ (Matthew adds: the Son of the Living God)." According to Matthew 16:17, Jesus answers, "Blessed are you, Simon son of Jonah! It was not a man but the Father in Heaven who gave you this revelation." Then he continues: "And I say to you, You are the Rock, and upon this Rock I will build my Church."

[16] See P. Fiebig, *Gleichnisreden Jesu*, 1912, pp. 53 ff.

[17] See on this point E. Preuschen, "Die Donnersöhne" (*ZNW*, 1917, pp. 141 ff.) and F. Schulthess, "*Zur Sprache der Evangelien*" (*ZNW*, 1922, pp. 243 ff.).

[18] H. Pernot, in his French translation of the Gospels (1943), rightly chooses the word *roc*, and it seems to me unjustified that this suggestion has been received with some scoffing.

[19] So K. G. Goetz, *Petrus als Gründer und Oberhaupt der Kirche und Schauer von Gesichten nach den altchristlichen Berichten und Legenden*, 1927, pp. 67 f. Further, E. Hirsch, *Frühgeschichte des Evangeliums*, II, 1941, pp. 306 ff.

[20] Instead of the pronoun "I" ($\mu\epsilon$), Matt. 16:13 writes "the Son of Man" ($\tau\grave{o}\nu$ $\upsilon\grave{\iota}\grave{o}\nu$ $\tau o\hat{\upsilon}$ $\dot{\alpha}\nu\theta\rho\acute{\omega}\pi o\upsilon$), according to the best textual witnesses, but since this reading awkwardly anticipates the answer, it is certainly secondary in comparison with Mark 8:27. See below, p. 175.

Thus in the same way that Peter gives to Jesus a name which later is regularly added to the name of Jesus, and finally becomes fixed as his proper name, "Christ" (in Hebrew "Messiah," that is, "Anointed One"), so, according to Matthew, Jesus gives to Peter a descriptive title: "Rock."

Did Jesus really give this title to Peter on the specific occasion indicated by this Gospel? We are justified in raising this question, for according to Mark 3:16 this event—without the addition of the explanation—took place upon another occasion, and John 1:42, moreover, places the giving of the name in still another setting. According to Mark 3:16 Jesus already called Peter "Rock" at the time of the call of the Twelve;[21] according to John 1:42 he did so even earlier, on the occasion of their first meeting in Judea, although Jesus here speaks in the future tense: "You *will be* called Cephas." From these variations, which one can harmonize if he is determined to do so,[22] we conclude that in the process of transmission the memory of the moment in which Jesus gave Peter the title had become lost; the same is true of the setting of many other stories in the Gospels.

We must keep this in mind when we come to the detailed exegesis of Matthew 16:16 ff. In itself the time when the name was given has no fundamental significance. What is important, however, is first of all *the fact* that according to the unanimous witness of the Gospels Mark, Matthew, and John, Jesus did give this name to Peter and, second, that according to a tradition handed down only by Matthew, Jesus *explained* this name on a special occasion by his purpose of founding his Church upon the Apostle whom he designated as the Rock.

*   *   *

We can derive from the Gospels the following additional *biographical notes*. According to Matthew 16:17, Peter is the son of Jonah—Aramaic *bar-yônâ*, which John 1:42 and 21:15 f. indicate is

---

21 M. J. Lagrange, in agreement with A. Loisy, J. Knabenbauer, etc., maintains in *L'évangile selon St. Marc*, 6th ed., 1942, p. 65, that this is the original occasion: "The time chosen by Mark is probably that which best accords with the facts, since from then on Simon becomes the corner stone of the building begun by Jesus." From this moment Mark consistently avoids the name Simon, which up to this time he has regularly used. Only in ch. 14:37, in the Gethsemane scene, does Jesus say to him: "Simon, are you sleeping?" Perhaps Mark purposely avoids having Jesus address Simon in this situation as "Rock."

22 See below, p. 177.

an abbreviation for John. Whether another explanation, which appeals to a Jewish lexicon, is correct must remain doubtful. According to it, the Aramaic *bar-yônâ* had no connection with the name John, but meant the same as "terrorist."[23] In that case Peter belonged to the party of the determined enemies of Rome, the so-called "Zealots," just as did Simon the "Zealot" (Luke 6:15; Acts 1:13[24]) and perhaps Judas Iscariot.[25]

According to John 1:44 Peter comes from Bethsaida ("fisherman's city"), which according to the view that is by far the most probable is to be sought on the eastern bank of the Jordan near the point where it empties into the Sea of Gennesaret.[26] Even if the place itself was Jewish, we must note,. nevertheless, that it was located in Gentile surroundings. This is indicated, indeed, as John 1:44 and 12:21 suggest, by the Greek name of his brother Andrew and of Philip, who likewise came from Bethsaida, as well as by the name of Simon himself.[27] "Anyone brought up in Bethsaida would not only have understood Greek, but would also have been polished by intercourse with foreigners and have had some Greek culture."[28] Thus is explained the fact that according to John 12:21 the Greeks turn to Philip, the native of Bethsaida. If the information of the Gospel of John that Peter came from that place is true, this could be related to the fact that in the account of Acts, chs. 10 and 11, Peter champions a universalistic point of view and, as we shall see, is not too far removed from Paul in his theology. This does not prevent Acts 4:13 from characterizing him and his companion John as "uneducated."[29] He had not "studied" either by Jewish or by Greek standards.

Later we find that Peter has moved to Capernaum and settled

---

[23] So Robert Eisler, *Jesous basileus ou basileusas*, 1929 f., p. 67, who follows Eliezer ben Jehuda, *Thesaurus totius hebraitatis*. In favour of this view might be the fact that Jonah is not attested elsewhere as a shortened form of Johanan.

[24] The reading is Κavavaîos in Mark 3:18; Matt. 10:4. This is not to be translated "Canaanite," but "Zealot," and the word merely transliterates the Aramaic word *qan'ânâ*.

[25] Iscariot would be derived from *sicarius* = "bandit." J. Wellhausen, *Das Evangelium Marci übersetzt und erklärt*, 1909, p. 23, mentions this interpretation, but does not consider it probable.

[26] See G. Dalman, *Orte und Wege Jesu*, 1919, pp. 158 ff. English translation, *Sacred Sites and Ways*, 1935, pp. 161 ff.

[27] See above, p. 17.   [28] G. Dalman, *op. cit.*, p. 163 (Eng. Tr., p. 165).

[29] ἀγράμματοί εἰσιν καὶ ἰδιῶται. F. J. Foakes-Jackson, *Peter, Prince of Apostles: A Study in the History and Tradition of Christianity*, 1927, p. 55, thinks that this judgment is to be ascribed to contempt for the Galilean accent.

(Mark 1:29 and parallels). It appears that Jesus often entered his home there, and perhaps actually lived with him for a short time (Matt. 8:14).

He was a fisherman by calling (Mark 1:16 and parallels: Luke 5:2 f.; John 21:3). He seems to carry on this work together with the two sons of Zebedee, who are described as "partners" (Luke 5:10).[30]

According to the testimony of the Synoptic Gospels (Mark 1:29 ff. and parallels) as well as of Paul (I Cor. 9:5), Peter was married. Later stories concerning his children[31] and the martyrdom of his wife, at which he supposedly was present,[32] are legendary.

The Johannine account (John 1:35 ff.) permits us to suppose that before he joined Jesus he, as well as his brother Andrew and the un-named disciple, had belonged to the inner or wider circle of the disciples of John the Baptist.[33]

2. *His Position in the Circle of Disciples*

We learn from the Synoptic Gospels that Peter actually occupies an unique position within the group of disciples. Together with the sons of Zebedee and his brother Andrew he belongs to the intimate circle of those who gathered about Jesus. According to Mark 1:16 and Matthew 4:18, he with Andrew is the first disciple whom Jesus calls. Mark 5:37 notes explicitly that Jesus permitted no one else to follow him into the house of the ruler of the synagogue except Peter and the sons of Zebedee. On other occasions also we find him to-gether with this pair of brothers (see Mark 9:2 and parallels; Mark 14:33 and parallels).

But even within this innermost circle it is almost always Peter who stands in the foreground. In the story of the miraculous catch of fish (Luke 5:1 ff.) he clearly plays the chief role, although at the very end the sons of Zebedee are included with him. According to Matthew 14:28, only Peter attempts to imitate his Master in walking on the sea. Almost always he appears as the spokesman for the

---

[30] κοινωνοί.

[31] Clement of Alexandria, *Stromateis*, III, 6, 52; concerning a daughter, see *Actus Vercellenses*.

[32] Eusebius, *Eccles. Hist.*, III, 30, 2, who quotes Clement of Alexandria, *Stromateis*, VII, 11, 63; concerning Peter's wife, see further the Pseudo-Clementine *Homily*. XIII, 1, 11; *Recognitions*, VII, 25, 36; IX, 38.

[33] The hypothesis according to which "bar-Jonah" designates Peter as a "disciple of John the Baptist" cannot be proved.

Twelve. We have already seen that it is Peter who answers when Jesus directs a question to *all* the disciples (Mark 8:29 ff. and parallels). Correspondingly, the close of this Markan narrative (ch. 8:33) says that Jesus *looks upon all the disciples* as he speaks to Peter the stern word, "Depart from me, Satan. Your thinking is not under divine but under human control." The reproach is obviously directed equally to all the disciples, because Jesus knows that even the words which Peter has addressed to him to hold him back from his path of suffering reproduce the Satanic desire of all the Twelve. Thus here, too, Peter appears as the spokesman of all the disciples.

The same conclusion results from the transfiguration story, Mark 9:2 ff. Here, too, it is Peter who proposes to Jesus that they erect tents (Mark 9:5). The sons of Zebedee play on this occasion little more than the role of extras.

It is Peter who in various situations turns to Jesus with questions which all the disciples want answered: "Lord, how many times shall I forgive my brother who sins against me? As many as seven times?" (Matt. 18:21). "Lord, do you speak this parable to us or also to all?" (Luke 12:41). "Behold, we have left everything and followed you" (Mark 10:28 and parallels).

It also occurs that in one Gospel all the disciples ask the question, while in the parallel passage of the other Gospel it is only Peter who asks (Mark 7:17 compared with Matt. 15:15; Matt. 21:20 compared with Mark 11:21).

In Luke 22:8 Peter and John are directed by Jesus to prepare the Passover.—In Mark 14:29 Peter promises to be loyal to his Master.—Again, in Gethsemane, according to Mark 14:37 (Matt. 26:40), Jesus turns to Peter with the reproachful question whether he cannot watch one hour; but again the sons of Zebedee, who are likewise present, are included in the address.—According to Matthew 17:24 Peter is regarded by outsiders also as the special representative of the group of disciples. The people who collect the tax address their question to him.

The lists of the disciples (Mark 3:16; Matt. 10:2; Luke 6:14; Acts 1:13) do indeed vary in detail, but it is common to all of them that they give Peter the first place. The list in Matthew actually emphasizes the fact that he is the first ($\pi\rho\hat{\omega}\tau o\varsigma$). Characteristic also is the expression "Peter and those with him,"[34] used to designate the group of disciples (Mark 1:36; Luke 9:32; 8:45 according to the best attested reading). Particularly striking is the word of the angel in

[34] $\Pi\acute{\epsilon}\tau\rho o\varsigma$ $\kappa\alpha\grave{\iota}$ $o\acute{\iota}$ $\sigma\grave{\upsilon}\nu$ $\alpha\grave{\upsilon}\tau\hat{\wp}$; $\Pi\acute{\epsilon}\tau\rho o\varsigma$ $\kappa\alpha\grave{\iota}$ $o\acute{\iota}$ $\mu\epsilon\tau$' $\alpha\grave{\upsilon}\tau o\hat{\upsilon}$.

Mark 16:7: "Go and tell his disciples *and Peter* that (Jesus) goes before you to Galilee."

With respect to this unique position, therefore, there is no such difference as has often been asserted between Mark and the other two Synoptic Gospels. Precisely in the Gospel of Mark, of which it has been said that although written in Rome it knows no claim for the authority of Peter,[35] he appears as the spokesman among the disciples. An examination of the passages already listed is sufficient to convince one that in reality each of the three Synoptic Gospels emphasizes in its own independent way the pre-eminent position of Peter. Even though Mark lacks the saying of Matthew 16:17 ff. concerning the Church, yet his entire presentation leaves not the slightest doubt as to the special role that this Evangelist ascribes to Peter. To try to derive a tendency hostile to Peter from the fact that he does not keep silence about Peter's weaknesses is to misunderstand the significance of these items.[36] We have seen above[37] that at times all the disciples speak in one of the Synoptic Gospels, while only Peter speaks in the parallel passage of the other one. But we must notice that when this occurs it is not always the same Gospel that puts Peter in the foreground. Rather, we find that this emphasis upon this one disciple is found now in one and now in another of the Gospels. Thus in the Gospel of Mark (Mark 11:21) Peter takes the place of all the disciples, whereas in the parallel passage in Matthew (ch. 21:20) they ask the question concerning the withered fig tree.

Moreover, it will not do to make a basic distinction between Luke and Matthew in regard to their attitude to Peter, as though only Matthew had a special ecclesiastical interest in a permanent primacy for Peter.[38] Even if it is true that Matthew alone has the saying of

[35] H. Strathmann, "Die Stellung des Petrus in der Urkirche. Zur Frühgeschichte des Wortes an Petrus, Matt. 16, 17–19" (*Zeitschrift für Systematische Theologie*, 1943, pp. 223 ff.).

[36] Above all, we cannot speak of a hostility of Mark towards Peter, such as R. Bultmann assumes in "Die Frage nach dem messianischen Bewusstsein und das Petrusbekenntnis" (*ZNW*, 1919–20, p. 170). See M. Goguel, *L'Eglise primitive*, 1947, p. 191: "There is no trace of an anti-Petrine attitude in Mark."

[37] See p. 24.

[38] Thus H. Strathmann, *op. cit.*, judges each of the Gospels on the basis of its attitude to the claim of authority for Peter, according to the somewhat artificial scheme by which he assumes that it belongs to this or that Church: Mark—Rome—no interest in the Petrine claim; Luke and The Acts—Pauline missionary area—a primacy of Peter for only a limited time; Matthew—Antioch (see B. H. Streeter) — permanent primacy; John—Asia Minor—anti-Petrine and pro-Johannine tendency.

Matthew 16:17 ff., and also the story of Peter's walking on the sea (Matt. 14:28 ff.), as well as the designation "first" in Matthew 10:2, we must place on the other side the verses in which only Luke shows a positive interest in Peter; this is especially true in the story of the miraculous catch of fish (Luke 5:1 ff.). Furthermore, we must note particularly that in Luke's special material there is a parallel to the saying about the Rock in Matthew 16:18. It clearly gives to Peter for the future a unique function among his brothers: "Simon, Simon, behold, Satan has asked for you in order to sift you like wheat. But I have prayed for you that your faith may not fail, and when you have turned again (according to another reading: turn again and[39]) strengthen your brothers" (Luke 22:31). This saying's genuineness cannot be contested with the same arguments that are used against Matthew 16:17 ff., since it does not contain the word "church" (ἐκκλησία),[40] which many find objectionable on critical grounds. Hence it should be cited in this debate much oftener than it is. In this verse, too, Jesus says to Peter that he stands in a perilously close relation to Satan, but in this he is expressly linked with the other disciples: "Satan has asked (God) for you (plural) in order to sift you (plural)." We have seen[41] that this is also the silent assumption in Mark, ch. 8, and yet in both places Jesus directs the saying only to Peter, and particularly in giving the charge he speaks only to Peter: "Strengthen your brothers." Accordingly, it is impossible to discern in any of the Synoptic Gospels a bias for or against Peter.

Thus according to all three Synoptic Gospels Peter indubitably played the role of spokesman among the twelve disciples. Furthermore, according to the Gospels of Matthew and Luke Jesus appointed him specially to carry out later the mission of strengthening his brothers. So the knowledge of a special distinction given to Peter within the circle of disciples is common to the entire ancient tradition behind the Synoptic Gospels. This is clear even without taking into account the controversial passage Matthew 16:17 ff., which we shall discuss in detail in Part Two of this work. This unique position, which is attested not only in Matthew but also in Luke and Mark, cannot and must not be denied or even diminished in support of any confessional or critical tendency. We must add, however, that while in all these passages Peter is given prominence in the total group of

[39] E. Stauffer, "Zur Vor- und Frühgeschichte des Primatus Petri," *Zeitschrift für Kirchengeschichte*, 1943-44, p. 18, note 58, gives various reasons for preferring this reading.

[40] See below, pp. 164 f., 186 ff.   [41] See above, p. 24.

disciples, he always appears as their spokesman in "dialogue with Christ"; apart from this relation to Christ he never plays, as he does in the later literature, a leading role.[42]

A somewhat different picture emerges when we turn to *the Gospel of John*. Here the outstanding role of Peter, which is unchallenged in the Synoptic Gospels, becomes a problem, since for this Evangelist the mysterious unnamed "Beloved Disciple" of Jesus enters into a certain competition with Peter. Thus here, in a way different from the Synoptics, a contemporary interest of the author concerning the position of Peter may have influenced the presentation. However, it is noteworthy that this Gospel, which manifestly wishes to emphasize the particularly close relationship between Jesus and the "Beloved Disciple," nevertheless nowhere attempts to deny directly the special role of Peter within the group of disciples.[43] It only has the tendency to lessen this role, in so far as it seeks to show that beside the unique position of Peter there is the somewhat different special role of the "Beloved Disciple."[44] This is certainly connected with the receding of the entire group of the Twelve as such, a tendency which is characteristic of this Gospel's view of the disciples and to which as a rule not enough attention is given. That in spite of this manifest tendency the Fourth Gospel nevertheless accepts as a fact the pre-eminence of Peter appears to me to be a particularly strong proof that this fact was so well known in the Primitive Church that it could neither be directly denied nor passed over in silence, but only minimized.[45] It is only the exclusive nature of Peter's unique position that is opposed; in other respects the different character of the role of the two men is emphasized.

This appears in a particularly clear way in the Passion story, for example in ch. 13:24 on the occasion of the Last Supper, where Peter must turn to the Beloved Disciple, who is lying on the breast of the Lord, in order to learn a secret of Jesus. It appears again in ch. 18:15, where the Beloved Disciple enters with Jesus into the court of the high priest, while Peter remains outside before the gate. But particularly in the most decisive moment, at the foot of the cross, it is not Peter but the Beloved Disciple who is present, and he is

[42] This is rightly emphasized by J. L. Klink, *Het Petrustype in het Nieuwe Testament en de Oud-Christelike Letterjkunde*, Dissertation, Leyden, 1947.

[43] Peter also appears as spokesman for the other disciples in John 6:66 ff. and 13:36.

[44] The Gospel of the Hebrews goes much further in opposing the special position of Peter.

[45] This is also recognized explicitly by D. F. Strauss, *Das Leben Jesu. Für das deutsche Volk*, 1864, p. 423.

distinguished in a quite special way by the word here directed to him by the Crucified One.[46] Furthermore, the author tells how the Beloved Disciple comes first ($\pi\rho\tilde{\omega}\tau\sigma\varsigma$, ch. 20:4) to the grave but does not enter, while Peter only comes after him but does go in. The Beloved Disciple enters the grave after Peter does, but on the other hand it is said only of this Beloved Disciple that he "believes" at once when he has "seen" (ch. 20:8).[47]

These facts throw light also upon ch. 1:41, where we find as the first disciples of Jesus two former disciples of the Baptist, an unnamed one and Andrew the brother of Peter. Thus here Peter is not the "first" disciple; he is not the $\pi\rho\tilde{\omega}\tau\sigma\varsigma$. Nevertheless, *after* these two, whose meeting with Jesus serves rather as a kind of prelude, Peter is the first one who comes to Jesus. In fact, the writer speaks also in verses 41 of a "first" one, and this could refer to Peter. Nevertheless, the manuscripts here differ with regard to the ending of the word. Some read "the first one" in the nominative case ($\pi\rho\tilde{\omega}\tau\sigma\varsigma$); Andrew is thereby designated as the first one, who as such finds his brother Peter. In this case it is emphasized that the honour of being "the first one" belongs to both former disciples of the Baptist, the unnamed one and Andrew. The other manuscripts read "the first one" in the accusative case ($\pi\rho\tilde{\omega}\tau\sigma\nu$). In this reading Peter receives the honourable rank of "the first one," yet only in so far as he is the first to be found and led to Jesus by his brother, the former disciple of the Baptist. This divergence of the manuscripts shows how it was recognized even in ancient times that the Fourth Evangelist was specially interested in this question; whether he himself wrote the nominative or the accusative case—and this is hard to decide—it remains a fact that thereby, exactly as in ch. 20, he intends to point to the remarkable relationship between Peter and that unnamed disciple, who is probably identical with the Beloved Disciple and who was a disciple of the Baptist when he first met Jesus. Here also, it seems, the evangelist did not intend to deny the pre-eminent position of Peter, but he did wish to show how the unnamed disciple is "first" in another respect, in the way he became Jesus' disciple.

This tendency is even clearer in view of the fact that here at the

[46] Ed. Meyer, "Sinn und Tendenz der Schlussszene am Kreuz im Johannesevangelium" (*Sitzungsbericht der preussischen Akademie der Wissenschaften*, 1924, p. 159), actually assumes that by the words directed to him and to the mother of Jesus the Beloved Disciple is so to speak accepted into the family of the Lord and adopted as his brother in the fullest sense.

[47] See O. Cullmann, "$\epsilon\tilde{\iota}\delta\epsilon\nu$ $\kappa\alpha\tilde{\iota}$ $\epsilon\pi\tilde{\iota}\sigma\tau\epsilon\nu\sigma\epsilon\nu$," in the volume in honour of M. Goguel, *Aux Sources de la Tradition Chrétienne*, 1950, pp. 56 ff.

very beginning Andrew utters the confession of Jesus as the Messiah, while Peter comes to recognize this only later (ch. 6:66 ff.). Yet, as we must say on the other side, the Gospel of John expressly recognizes that Jesus gave to Peter the title of honour, "Rock," and as we have seen,[48] the Gospel puts this event at the very beginning (ch. 1:42). We must also say that it reports the decisive confession of Peter with an emphasis all its own (ch. 6:66 ff.).

Exactly the same double attitude toward the unique position of Peter is found again in the supplementary chapter 21, which thus in this respect agrees with chapters 1 to 20. On the one side, that position is explicitly recognized, while on the other side, it is reduced by being confronted with the unique position of the Beloved Disciple. Thus, at the beginning of the narrative here reported concerning the appearance of Jesus at the Sea of Galilee, Peter is named first in the series of disciples listed.[49] On the other hand, the Beloved Disciple is the first to recognize the Lord, but Peter again is the first to go to him. Thus this paralleling of the two unique positions marks this chapter also. It finds its climax in the conversation which, following the miracle, occurs between the Risen One and Peter. This account is characteristic of the way in which the author of this chapter, who, no matter who he is, belongs to the Johannine circle, has grasped the meaning of the entire Gospel of John; he shows this grasp by putting at the end precisely this conversation as a sort of crown or climax. In doing so, he probably has emphasized much too strongly this purpose which the Fourth Evangelist certainly had. But on the other hand, he has correctly understood the Evangelist's conception; in a quite analogous manner he sets the two disciples face to face and shows how the Risen One assigns a unique position to each one of them for the future, but gives each of them a different role.[50] Peter is installed in the office of shepherd;[51] to the Beloved Disciple, who

[48] See above, p. 21.

[49] According to E. Stauffer, op. cit., pp. 13 f., there lies at the basis of this narrative an early report, mentioned in I Cor. 15:5, concerning the appearance of Jesus to Peter alone. On this matter see below, p. 60.

[50] M. Goguel, L'Eglise primitive, 1947, p. 200, takes another view. He assumes that this dialogue serves to glorify Peter at the expense of the Beloved Disciple, and so stands in opposition to chs. 1-20.

[51] To dispute this, as K. G. Goetz, op. cit., p. 15, attempts to do, seems to me impossible. Goetz is no doubt correct when he writes that Peter is reinstated in the position of disciple that he had lost by the three-fold denial. At the same time, however, more is involved here than merely the confirmation of the call of a disciple. The fact that Jesus no longer lives on earth necessarily has as its result a new task for the disciple.

here only "follows" Peter, which in Johannine idiom[52] may also imply a spiritual attachment, it is promised that he will outlive Peter. In this context this promise quite probably signifies that he will have to fulfil a task which, though similar, is nevertheless, as in the entire Gospel, of a somewhat different kind.[53]

Thus the Gospel of John, precisely because, in distinction from the Synoptic Gospels, it has the tendency to emphasize the Beloved Disciple, indirectly confirms the result to which we were led by the investigation of the Synoptic passages concerning the disciple Peter: *Among the disciples of Jesus Peter, according to the united witness of the gospel tradition, occupies a peculiarly representative position.*

This does not mean, however, that during the lifetime of Jesus he possessed the role of *leader* in relation to his fellow-disciples. He is rather at all times their *spokesman*, their *representative* in good as in bad action. But he gives them no commissions in the name of Jesus, and the Master nowhere entrusts to him such a function for the period of his own earthly life. The three passages, Matthew 16:16 ff., Luke 22:31 f. and John 21:15 ff., in which he is charged with a special obligation towards his brothers, all refer to the future, to the time after the death of Jesus. Thus the gospel tradition knew how to

---

[52] See O. Cullmann, "Der johanneische Gebrauch doppeldeutiger Ausdrücke als Schlüssel zum Verständnis des vierten Evangeliums" (*Theologische Zeitschrift*, 1948, pp. 360 ff.).

[53] Thus R. Bultmann, *Das Johannesevangelium*, p. 547, writes that the authority of Peter here passes over to the Beloved Disciple. E. Stauffer, *op. cit.*, agrees with this, but adds that this involves the authority not only of the Evangelist, as Bultmann thinks, but also of the church leader John. This, however, confuses the difference between the two unique positions, a difference emphasized in the entire Fourth Gospel and also in this twenty-first chapter. The Roman Catholic scholar R. Graber, in *Petrus der Fels. Fragen um den Primat*, 1949, pp. 37 ff., considers the meaning of John, ch. 21, to be as follows: The question of Peter: "Lord, but what will happen to this man (the Beloved Disciple)" reckons with the possibility that the Beloved Disciple might be his "successor;" but the answer of Jesus, "If I will that he remain," is meant to reject explicitly this opinion of Peter, because others are destined to be his successors. This artificial explanation is much less justified than the hypothesis, well worth considering, of the first part of Graber's work (see below, pp. 38, 41); it merely aims to find a Scriptural witness to warrant the transfer of the apostolic succession of Peter to the Roman bishops. Moreover, the assertion of Graber (p. 39) that the Beloved Disciple was undoubtedly still living at the time of writing of John, ch. 21, is by no means proved by the argument that after his death it would have been nonsense to refute the idea that he would not die. Cannot one say, on the contrary, that precisely then it was necessary to show that the saying of Jesus concerning "remaining" was not proved false by the death of that disciple?

distinguish between the position of Peter before and after the death of Jesus.

In view of this fact, we must consider improbable the assertion some have made, that the pre-eminence of Peter in the circle of Jesus' disciples is merely a pre-dating of the position which he actually held only in the Primitive Church, after the death of Jesus. He is ascribed no leading position at all in relation to the group of the Twelve; on the contrary, he appears only as the most representative of the disciples. What all of them represent, do, and think, comes to particularly strong expression in his person.

One might indeed be tempted to go further and ask how this pre-eminence is to be *explained*. Is it due to the fact that by giving the name mentioned Jesus strengthened greatly Peter's consciousness of being a disciple? Or on the contrary, is it, together with the giving of the name, to be explained on psychological grounds by the character of Peter? The latter possibility has often been considered.[54] It takes its clue from the fact that during the lifetime of Jesus Peter did not show himself a "rock" at all; on the contrary, his human weakness was very striking. The scene at the Sea of Gennesaret gives a concrete illustration of Peter's character. He is impulsive and enthusiastic; in the first burst of enthusiasm, he does not hesitate to throw himself into the sea when Jesus calls him, but his courage soon fades and fear grips him. So, too, he is the first to confess loudly his loyalty to his Master, but he is the first one who will deny him in the hour of danger. And yet, so one assumes, precisely this character, with its notable contradictions, makes Peter appear as the disciple with special psychological fitness to be the "rock" among the other disciples. The exuberant enthusiasm, the fiery zeal of this disciple are said to be in fact the human qualities that are necessary to deserve such a title of honour. His instability and weakness are said to be only the dark side of these qualities.

Nevertheless, it is hardly possible to give a psychological basis for the unique position of Peter and for the giving to him of this name. Indeed, we should not ask at all why Jesus singled him out as "rock" instead of choosing another disciple.[55] According

---

[54] So especially by F. Sieffert in *Realenzyklopädie für Theologie und Kirche*, 3rd ed., Article on "Petrus," Vol. 15, p. 190.

[55] K. L. Schmidt, *Festschrift für A. Deissmann*, 1927, p. 301, rightly rejects this question as to the Why of the choice of Peter as the "rock." He observes that it can no more be answered than can the question why God chose the people of Israel.

to our sources, we can only confirm the fact of this distinction.

Probably, however, it is also a mistake to say that the representative position of the disciple Peter and the qualities mentioned were derived only from the giving of the name. We can hardly say that only by this act did he become conscious that in his person he represented, so to speak, the totality of the disciples, even during the earthly life of Jesus. Again we can only state *the fact*: Peter lets us see clearly everything that the call to discipleship involves in human weakness and privilege.

To the question whether his pre-eminence is to be explained by the giving of the name, or the giving of the name, on the contrary, by his actual pre-eminence, there probably is no simple answer. In reality what is involved is rather a reciprocal action. Jesus knows better than anyone else the qualities of Peter, both the good and the bad ones, and he takes account of them in his view of the work he intends his disciples to do. On the other hand, however, the special distinction given this disciple as a rock-man rests on the Master's act of sovereign decision, an act which may have strengthened Peter in the representative role that his nature had already given him.

For the period following the death of Jesus the question concerning the unique position of Peter presents itself in another way. The disciple becomes the apostle of the crucified and risen Lord. In this capacity his unique position necessarily takes on another character. Of this we must speak in the next chapter.

Chapter Two

PETER THE APOSTLE

ACCORDING to the sources at our disposal, the death and resurrection of Jesus creates for Peter a completely changed situation. This is true in two respects. In the first place, from this time on his unique role appears no longer merely as that of a representative; in view of the physical absence of the Lord, it naturally appears also in the leadership of the small community of disciples. The character and the time limit of this leadership, however, must still be more exactly determined. In the second place, this unique position now rests upon a specific commission, which must be defined on various sides.

We begin with the first point.

1. *The Leadership of the Primitive Church*

In *The Book of Acts* we clearly note that Peter takes a unique position in the Primitive Church in Jerusalem. Apart from the letters of Paul, of which we speak later, The Acts is our only source. We investigate first the data of the first twelve chapters.

It is Peter who in ch. 1:15 ff. prompts the choice of the twelfth disciple.[1] It at once becomes evident here that the fact of his being spokesman for the others signifies likewise that whatever may be his authorization, in every case he presides over the little group of believers.

He it is who explains to the assembled multitude the miracle of Pentecost (ch. 2:14). "He stands up with the Eleven," we are told, but he alone speaks. In verse 37 the witnesses present at the miracle address themselves, as the author puts it, "to Peter and the rest of the apostles."

In ch. 3 he performs the healing miracle on the lame man. In this

[1] P. Gaechter, "Die Wahl des Matthias (Apostelgeschichte 1, 15-16)" (*Zeitschrift für katholische Theologie*, 1949, pp. 318 ff.), traces the choice back to a special commission given by Jesus. See below, pp. 215 ff.

narrative John is named with Peter in a most remarkable manner. All the manuscripts mention him. But the way in which he is introduced and plays little more than the role of an extra could lead us to suppose that his name was added subsequently to that of Peter. Particularly noteworthy in this connection is verse 4: "Peter looked on the lame man, with John."[2] If the unnamed Beloved Disciple of the Fourth Gospel had at this time already been identified with John, one could ask whether the mention of John with Peter does not correspond to a tendency similar to that which we confirmed in the Gospel of John.[3] Concerning this point, however, we can say nothing certain. That John actually did occupy a certain authoritative position after Peter in the Primitive Church is made certain by Paul, who in Galatians 2:9 reckons him together with James and Cephas among the "pillars" of the Church.[4]

In the further development of the story it is Peter who defends the cause of the Gospel when the authorities take action against the apostles (chs. 4:8; 5:29). After the healing of the lame man it is Peter alone who speaks, although we are told in chapter 4:1: "While they were speaking . . ." and although John is again named with Peter in verse 13. In the latter case, however, the mention of his name again limps noticeably and looks like an addition. Thus it cannot be denied that according to this entire narrative Peter as a member of the Jerusalem church occupies the place of leader.

Particularly in the case of Ananias and Sapphira, however, he exercises church discipline in the congregation (ch. 5:1 ff.).[5] Here his authority is especially noticeable. However we may judge concerning the genuineness or spuriousness of Matt. 16:16 ff., and whatever may be the meaning of the words "bind" and "loose,"[6] in this narrative it is Peter who, as the earthly authority, holds court in the name of God, and according to verse 2 he does this publicly in the presence of the other apostles. The narrative concerning Simon the magician (ch. 8:18 ff.) also presupposes that Peter makes the decisions.

Furthermore, The Book of Acts emphasizes the faith of the people

---

2 ἀτενίσας δὲ Πέτρος εἰς αὐτὸν σὺν τῷ Ἰωάννῃ.
3 See above, pp. 27 ff.   4 See below, pp. 42 ff.
5 Ph.-H. Menoud, "La mort d'Ananias, et de Saphira (Actes 5, 1-11)," in *Aux sources de la tradition chrétienne. Mélanges offerts à M. Goguel*, 1950, pp. 146 ff., assumes that the intent of the entire section is to explain by their sin the fact of the death of the first members of the Church to die, Ananias and Sapphira.
6 See below, pp. 204 f.

in the miraculous power of Peter in particular. They actually consider his "shadow" capable of effecting a healing (ch. 5:15). Although it is said also of the other apostles that miracles are done by their hands (ch. 5:12) and that they teach (chs. 2:42; 4:33), yet after the first chapters these same activities are carried on by Peter in a way which makes him appear, as he did in the days of Jesus, to be particularly representative. But this, in the changed situation after Jesus' death, can only mean that he thereby occupies a *leading* role in relation to the Church; he stands at its head.

This authority extends also to the missionary field in Samaria, which in the earliest days was dependent on Jerusalem. This land may be called the original field of the Christian mission. Its actual missionaries are the Christians who were driven from Jerusalem, most likely at the time of the martyrdom of Stephen; they probably represented a point of view similar to that of Stephen. In Acts 8:1 it is explicitly said that on that occasion the Twelve were *not* expelled.[7] Therefore we probably must seek the fugitives mainly among the Hellenists of the Church, and the Twelve appear to have taken an attitude different from that of those men; otherwise they could not have remained in Jerusalem. These church members driven from Jerusalem, accordingly, are mentioned as the first missionaries in Samaria (ch. 8:4), and among them only Philip is definitely named, although he probably shared this work with other Hellenistic fugitives whose names are not given. The missionary preaching of these men resulted in complete success: "Samaria has received the word of God" (ch. 8:14). It is so much the more astounding that the apostles who had remained in Jerusalem did not rest satisfied with this result, but later sent Peter and John to Samaria. The Book of Acts explains the necessity for this by saying that the Holy Spirit had not yet come upon the Samaritans (ch. 8:16), although, as previously said in verse 12, they had already believed and been baptized. So it was necessary that Peter and John subsequently lay hands upon those baptized, and only then did the converted Samaritans receive the Holy Spirit (ch. 8:17).[8] This clearly means that laying on of hands and giving of the Spirit were regarded as connected with the office of the Twelve; it shows that all missionary activity was at first considered completely dependent upon the Jerusalem

---

[7] πλὴν τῶν ἀποστόλων.

[8] See O. Cullmann, *Die Tauflehre des Neuen Testaments: Erwachsenen- und Kindertaufe* (*Abhandlungen zur Theologie des Alten und Neuen Testaments*), 1948, pp. 7 f. (Eng. Tr., *Baptism in the New Testament*, 1950, pp. 11 f.).

church.[9] This fact is also of importance for the questions which arise when Paul's mission begins.

This dependence is here plainly presupposed. The presentation of The Book of Acts is merely allusive; nevertheless, it permits us to glimpse the state of affairs clearly enough. It gives the impression that those men driven from Jerusalem and now active as missionaries are to be put firmly in their subordinate position. I do not consider it improbable that the Fourth Evangelist opposes this view; when in connection with the mission in Samaria, he gives a saying of Jesus concerning "the others who have worked," while the apostles "have entered into their work" (John 4:38), he probably intends to put in the right light the work of those mostly unnamed missionaries to Samaria.

For our problem it is important that on this occasion also Peter was delegated by the Twelve in Jerusalem to go to Samaria. It is true that here again John accompanies him, but his individuality does not emerge at all in the story.

The special mention of the Hellenists in The Book of Acts— their special views as well as the particular lot which befell them— proves that even in the Primitive Church itself there were different tendencies. Peter and the Twelve as a whole appear to have taken a mediating position between the Judaizers and the Hellenists. Peter, therefore, was able to hold together the different elements.[10] As soon as James appears at the head of the Church, this situation will change.

Following the events in Samaria, Peter likewise appears in missionary activity in Lydda, Joppa, and Caesarea, where he performs several miracles and baptizes the Gentile Cornelius (Acts, chs. 9 and 10). This shows that there was a Jewish Christian mission not only among the Jews, but also among the Gentiles; and according to this narrative, Peter takes the first position also as a missionary to Gentiles and explicitly justifies this mission. The role that The Acts assigns to

[9] P. Gaechter, "Jerusalem und Antiochia, ein Beitrag zur urkirchlichen Rechtsentwicklung" (*Zeitschrift für katholische Theologie*, 1948, pp. 1 ff.), rightly stresses the dependence of the missionary area on the Jerusalem church. The conclusions, however, which he draws for the cessation of the pre-eminence of this church from the fact that Peter, from a certain time on, left Jerusalem, cannot be defended. See below, p. 43, note 30; p. 44, note 31; p. 49, note 45. Ed. Schweizer, in *Geist und Gemeinde im N. T. und Heute* (now in press; to appear in *Theologische Existenz*), understands the connection with Jerusalem only in the sense of a connection in redemptive history.

[10] See W. Grundmann, "Das Problem des hellenistischen Christentums innerhalb der Jerusalemer Urgemeinde" (*ZNW*, 1939, pp. 45 ff.).

Peter in the Primitive Church in Jerusalem has not been seriously questioned by scholars. As we shall see, the letters of Paul indirectly confirm it. But a definite objection to this picture has been raised as far as Peter's missionary activity is concerned. It has been held both in earlier as well as in quite recent times that this story, which traces the Gentile mission back to Peter, is entirely or partly the creation of the author of The Acts, who follows the tendency to make Peter parallel with Paul in every respect. Nevertheless, in the more recent studies, the fact that the Gentile Cornelius was converted by Peter is recognized,[11] even if it is claimed that the author's editorial activity, determined by theological interests, plays a more or less sizable role.[12]

After his imprisonment by Herod and his liberation, and in connection with these events, Peter leaves the Holy City, but the Book of Acts gives no information concerning the place to which he goes. The author here expresses himself in a somewhat mysterious manner: He went "to another place" (Acts 12:17).[13] The Roman Catholic exegetes—though not all of them—are accustomed to identify this "other place" with Rome.[14] Indeed, an argument recently urged

[11] See the historical kernel which W. Grundmann extracts in "Die Apostel zwischen Jerusalem und Antiochia" (*ZNW*, 1940, pp. 132 ff.). He rejects the chronology of The Book of Acts and transfers the story into the period of the events that occur after Acts, ch. 12, when Peter has already left Jerusalem.

[12] Among recent scholars M. Dibelius goes the furthest, in "Das Apostelkonzil" (*Theologische Literaturzeitung*, 1947, pp. 193 ff.); and also in "Die Bekehrung des Cornelius" (*Coniectanea Neotestamentica in honorem Antonii Fridrichsen*, 1948, pp. 50 ff.). He accepts as historical only the essential fact of the conversion of Cornelius. The entire treatment of the basic questions concerning the admission of Gentiles into the Church and table fellowship with Gentile Christians are to be ascribed, he says, to the author of The Acts and his special tendencies. J. R. Porter, on the contrary, in "The 'Apostolic Decree' and Paul's Second Visit to Jerusalem" (*Journal of Theological Studies*, 1946, pp. 169 ff.), assigns to the original narrative the treatment of the question of table fellowship of Jewish and Gentile Christians, but not that of the admission of uncircumcised persons into the Church; this, he says, was first added by the author of The Acts. See also R. Liechtenhan, *Die urchristliche Mission: Voraussetzungen, Motive und Methoden* (*Abhandlungen zur Theologie des Alten und Neuen Testaments*), 1946; he connects ch. 11:4-18 with 15:7-11.

[13] εἰς ἕτερον τόπον.

[14] J. Dupont, *Les problèmes du livre des Actes d'après les travaux récents*, 1950, p. 88: "If the apostle went to Rome at this time, one could explain the fact that Luke did not want to mention so early the city which was to represent the terminus of his story of the expansion of Christianity." J. Belser, *Die Apostelgeschichte*, 1905, p. 156, cites another argument; he refers to Ezek. 12:3: "remove from your place to another," where Babylon is meant. U. Holzmeister, on the contrary, in *Commentarius in epistolas Sanctorum Petri et Judae* (*Cursus Scriptorum*

anew[15] could speak in favour of this identification; I refer to the parallel structure of the two parts of The Book of Acts. The first part (chs. 1 to 12) closes with the imprisonment of Peter; the second (chs. 13 to 28) with that of Paul. The second culminates in the arrival of Paul at Rome (ch. 28:14);[16] so one could ask whether it is not the journey of Peter to Rome that marks the climax of the first part: "he departed to another place" (ch. 12:17). Nevertheless, the wording does not permit the identification of the "other place" with Rome. That the name of Rome was omitted for fear of the pagan authorities, in order to keep secret the place where the head of the Church was staying,[17] might indeed be a possible explanation. Nevertheless, it is purely hypothetical, and would presuppose that The Book of Acts was written during the lifetime of Peter. Again, it is possible that Peter at this time went directly to Antioch, but the story does not say so. It is true that Galatians 2:11 speaks of his presence in Antioch, but concerning the time of his arrival in that city we learn nothing.[18] In reality, that "other place" can be identified with any city of the Roman Empire.[19] We must reckon with the possibility that even the author himself of the Book of Acts had no definite place in mind.[20] In that case, the statement would only mean that from this point on Peter gives up his fixed residence in Jerusalem, and so also his position

Sanctorum), 1937, p. 62: "No argument proves that Peter left Palestine in the year 42; how much more impossible it is to prove that he reached Rome as early as that same year." C. Cecchelli, Gli Apostoli a Roma, 1938, p. 100: "Certainly it seems impossible to admit the presence of Peter in Rome before 63."

[15] R. Graber, Petrus der Fels. Fragen um den Primat, p. 21.

[16] See also J. Dupont, op. cit. above in note 14. R. Graber, op. cit., p. 21, appeals to A. Harnack, Mission und Ausbreitung des Christentums, 3rd ed., 1915, Vol. I, pp. 95 f.

[17] This is the thesis of R. Graber, Petrus der Fels, pp. 16 ff.

[18] See below, pp. 52 f.

[19] S. G. F. Brandon, The Fall of Jerusalem and the Christian Church, 1951, pp. 211 f., 225, 232, 242, assumes that Peter went to Alexandria. Matthew, who was connected with Alexandria, magnified Peter for this reason, while for the same reason Luke, who plays Paul off against Alexandria, pushes Peter into the background.

[20] Thus A. Fridrichsen, "Sprachliches und Stilistiches zum Neuen Testament" (Kungl. Human. Vetenskaps-Samfundet i Uppsala, Aorsbok, 1943, pp. 28 ff.), assumes that it was a stereotyped manner of expression. D. F. Robinson, "Where and When Did Peter Die?" (Journal of Biblical Literature, 1945, pp. 255 ff.), proposes a theory that is doubtful but worthy of mention: εἰς ἕτερον τόπον would be identical with the "place of glory," that is, Peter died in Jerusalem at that time, in the year 44; this, Robinson says, is the historical kernel which lies behind the narrative of Acts 12:1-19.

in the church there; one aim, among others, was probably to escape Jewish persecution. After this point Peter appears again in The Acts only in ch. 15, at the so-called Apostolic Council, concerning which we must speak later; then, strange to say, he vanishes completely from the narrative. The above mentioned statement of Acts 12:17, "he went to another place," thus plainly marks a transition in the activity of Peter and also in his position in the Primitive Church.]

But first we must ask how far *the letters of Paul* confirm the data derived from the first twelve chapters of Acts concerning Peter's function as head of the Primitive Church in Jerusalem. In so doing we must note that the greater documentary value naturally belongs to the letters of Paul; they are a direct and earlier source. Since they nevertheless all belong to a later time than the events of Acts, chs. 1 to 12, we cannot expect to find in them many references to these earliest events in the Primitive Church. For the most part, Paul mentions Peter in connection with events that occurred only in the later period of Peter's life, events about which, except for the Apostolic Council, the Book of Acts tells us so strikingly little. As a direct parallel between Paul's presentation and that of The Book of Acts, we thus have to consider only the Apostolic Council, and we shall see what great problems result when we compare the two passages here involved.

Yet the letter to the Galatians, in which Paul gives auto-biographical statements in support of the theological thesis he there defends, does contain a short item which refers to that early period. It confirms, indirectly at least, what we have learned from the first chapters of The Acts concerning Peter's leading role in the Jerusalem church. We hear in Galatians 1:18 ff. that during Paul's first visit to Jerusalem, three years after his conversion, he desired to get acquainted with Cephas. It is true that according to this passage James the brother of the Lord, who as we shall see will later succeed Peter in the leadership of the church, is already in Jerusalem. However, when Paul first comes to Jerusalem, James plainly does not yet occupy an outstanding position. It seems likely that in his capacity as a physical brother of Jesus he already is playing a certain role *beside* Peter. For while Paul did not come to Jerusalem with the purpose of meeting James, yet he is the only one whom Paul sees apart from Peter. Obviously, even at this time, that is, three years after Paul's conversion, it was already impossible for a Christian believer to make a stay in Jerusalem without coming into contact with James.

For the position of Peter, however, it is significant that Paul, who does not yet know him personally, undertakes the journey only on his account. Quite possibly a contributing factor may have been Paul's wish to receive from Peter personal memories of his life with Jesus. Other apostles in Jerusalem, however, could have given him such reminiscences. If he nevertheless wanted to become acquainted with Peter in particular, the reason probably was that Paul, like all converts, knew that this man then stood at the head of the Mother Church in Jerusalem. To be sure, the leadership of Peter did not have as yet the character of the later "monarchical" episcopate. The authority of his colleagues in the group of the Twelve, and probably that of James also, was too great to permit this. The role of the Twelve in Jerusalem must not be confused with that of the group of Elders who later stand at the side of the Bishop. Of that role we should probably be reminded by the added mention of John in the passages cited in The Acts. Only with this restriction can we speak of the episcopal office of Peter in Jerusalem.

The recognition of Peter's authority by Paul has the greater weight because it occurs in Galatians, in a letter, that is to say, written by Paul under special circumstances which prompted him to demonstrate in other respects his independence of the Jerusalem apostles. This independence, indeed, is clearly shown in the narrative of the conflict that broke out between Peter and Paul in Antioch (Gal. 2:11 ff.).

By the time Paul wrote his letter to the Galatians, the situation in Jerusalem had changed. Peter had long since left Jerusalem, and was now charged with the leadership of the Jewish Christian *mission*, while in Jerusalem itself James had become his successor.[21] It is therefore the more significant that Paul, in his account of that first journey to Jerusalem, nevertheless lets us see that at that time Peter still stood at the head of the Jerusalem church.

2. *The Mission in the Service of the Jewish Christian Primitive Church*

We have seen that according to Acts 8:14 Peter occasionally went, even in the first years of the Primitive Church, to the missionary district of Samaria. Thus gradually—above all by reason of the experiences which Acts, chs. 9 and 10, report that he had in Lydda,

21 F. M. Braun, *Neues Licht auf die Kirche*, 1946, p. 170, already speaks in this connection of "succession to apostles." But on this point see below, pp. 43 ff., 244 ff., 230.

Joppa, and Caesarea—he may have recognized that his real apostolic task, and probably also his spiritual gift, lay less in the leadership of the established Church than in missionary activity.[22] At any rate, it is quite remarkable that the apostle who later is regarded as the personification of organized church government in reality exercised such a function for only a short time at the beginning, and then exchanged it for missionary work. Peter is not the archetype of the church official but of the missionary.[23] The two functions—church administration and missionary work—were separated. These functions James and Peter divided among themselves. The division probably was not connected with any definite decision or act, as one might believe from later tradition, which says that the apostles, in obedience to a command of the Lord, left Jerusalem twelve years after the resurrection.[24] Although this is not completely excluded, the division was probably made rather by gradual and natural development. To this conclusion points the fact that while Peter is still the head of the Church, James already plays, as we have seen in Galatians 1:18 ff., a somewhat leading role *beside* him. According to Acts 12:17, when circumstances force Peter to be absent, James is already so to speak his substitute, for in verse 17 Peter says: "Tell this to James and to the brothers," just as it previously was said in Acts 2:37, in a way that corresponds to the existing situation: "Peter and the rest of the apostles." Certainly the final transfer of the leadership to James is connected with the imprisonment and liberation of Peter, as a result of which the latter had to leave Jerusalem.[25]

Accordingly, the vague statement of the similar passage Acts 12:17, "he went to another place," is intended simply to point out that after the liberation of Peter his final transfer to exclusively missionary

---

[22] According to W. Grundmann, "Die Apostel zwischen Jerusalem und Antiochia" (*ZNW*, 1940, pp. 129 ff.), Peter first went, after the events reported in Acts, ch. 12, to Joppa, Lydda, and Caesarea. Thus on this view The Book of Acts places this journey in the wrong chronological position.

[23] This fact is retained in the *Pseudo-Clementina;* no teacher is authorized without warrant from James (*Recognitions*, IV, 35); Peter is sent to Caesarea at the command of James to oppose Simon. There is thus no mention here of a transfer of the central leadership from Jerusalem to Rome. P. Gaechter, "Jerusalem und Antiochia" (*Zeitschrift für katholische Theologie*, 1948, pp. 1 ff.), does not take account of the actual role that James plays in Jerusalem.

[24] *Kerygma Petri*, according to Clement of Alexandria, *Stromateis*, VI, 5, 43. A. Harnack, *Geschichte der altchristlichen Literatur*, II, 1, 1897, p. 234, regards this tradition as very ancient.

[25] So rightly R. Graber, *Petrus der Fels*, p. 23: also W. Grundmann, "Die Apostel zwischen Jerusalem und Antiochia" (*ZNW*, 1940, p. 129).

activity took place. Preparation for the transfer had already been
gradually made in the previous period.

In the later apocryphal Acts of Peter, probably the only point
which we should preserve as the historical basis is the fact that in
the second half of the exercise of his apostolic calling, Peter actually
undertook extensive missionary journeys.

We also find this new function of Peter confirmed in the letters of
Paul. In I Corinthians 9:5 he speaks of the fact that "the rest of the
apostles, the brothers of the Lord, and Cephas take" their wives "with
them" on their journeys. The comparison with Barnabas and Paul
shows what is to be supplied: "on their missionary journeys."[26] Thus
at a considerably earlier time Peter must already have begun to concentrate upon missionary work. Accordingly he, just like Paul and
Barnabas, interrupted his missionary travels to go to Jerusalem for
the so-called Apostolic Council.

At the time of this so-called Apostolic Council, as Paul presents it
—that is, at the time when the two missionary districts, the Jewish
Christian and the Gentile Christian, were separated on the basis of the
friendly agreement of Galatians 2:1 ff.—the assumption of the leadership of the Church by James the brother of the Lord must already
have been an accomplished fact. Already in this connection Paul
indirectly ascribes to him the presiding role among the "pillars."
According to the majority of the ancient manuscripts Paul here
enumerates the "pillars" in the following order: James, Cephas, John.
This could be mere accident. But in a text such as this one, in which
the authority of the negotiating partners is not unimportant, the
order does mean something. Indeed, the ancient copyists correctly
sensed this. Hence arose the textual variants concerning this very
point of order. The text designated by D places Peter before James
in this list.[27] According to the principle that the "more difficult reading" is the more ancient, we must regard as secondary this variant
attested by D. For we perceive that in later times one could take
offence at this putting of James before Peter.[28]

---

[26] Thus we cannot speak of a transfer of the see from Jerusalem to Rome, as
E. Stauffer, *op. cit.*, p. 32, suggests (see also P. Gaechter, in note 9 on p. 36).
Paul is speaking of missionary journeys, which may have taken Peter in every
direction, and so, of course, to Rome also. See below, pp. 77 ff.

[27] It might seem suspicious that D here, in agreement with verses 7 and 8, reads
Πέτρος and not Κηφᾶς, as is customary in Paul. But P[46] also, which moreover
correctly reads James in the first passage, reads Πέτρος.

[28] On the other hand, Codex Alexandrinus does not mention Peter at all. Perhaps
an anti-Petrine tendency could be at work here.

At all events we conclude, from the order in which Galatians 2:9 lists the "pillars," that at the time of the incident reported it was no longer Peter but James who was the authoritative leader in Jerusalem.[29]

As far as the Jewish Christian missionary work dependent on Jerusalem is concerned, Peter stood at its head. For this reason Paul, in the same passage, Galatians 2:7 f., mentions only Peter as the organizer of the Jewish Christian mission, just as he regards himself as the organizer of the Gentile Christian mission: "(The leaders) saw that I had been entrusted with the gospel to the uncircumcised just as Peter had with that to the circumcised; for he who was at work in Peter to make him an apostle among the circumcised was also at work in me for the Gentiles."

Nevertheless, in this position as leader of the Jewish Christian mission Peter was dependent upon *Jerusalem*. This explains the fact that according to Galatians 2:12 he has to fear the "party of James" and must "dissemble" on their account.[30] In this fact, among others, lies the difference between his mission and that of Paul; he is a missionary in the closest dependence on Jerusalem, while Paul—by an understanding, it is true, with the Jerusalem "pillars"—has more independence as he carries out his preaching among the Gentiles.

The account in the letters of Paul informs us that there exists, in accord with the Jerusalem agreement of Galatians 2:9, a rather loose tie even between the Pauline mission to Gentiles and the Primitive Church of Jerusalem. This was the collection which Paul loyally made for Jerusalem in all the missionary churches that he founded. This collection for the Primitive Church was not only a humanitarian enterprise; it was conceived first of all as a manifestation of the unity of the Church, just as in Judaism the tax for the Jerusalem Temple represented the outward bond of unity for the entire company of Jewish believers dispersed throughout the Roman Empire.

---

[29] Against E. Fascher, in Pauly-Wissowa, column 1342. That James really was the authoritative leader of the entire Church is confirmed by the *Pseudo-Clementina*. See on this point H. J. Schoeps, *Theologie und Geschichte des Judenchristentums*, 1949, p. 125; *Aus frühchristlicher Zeit*, 1950, pp. 120 ff.; H. v. Campenhausen, *Zeitschrift für Kirchengeschichte*, 1950–51, p. 137. See further below, pp. 224 f., and the literature listed there in notes 18 to 22.

[30] P. Gaechter, *op. cit.*, p. 42 ff., who is concerned in his article that the role of Jerusalem should cease with the absence of Peter and pass over to Antioch, attempts to separate the party of James from James and minimize their role in Antioch. Peter, he says, yielded to them only "for the sake of desirable peace." This, however, conflicts with the fact that, as Paul explicitly writes, Peter *was afraid* ($\phi o \beta o \acute{u} \mu \epsilon v o s$) of the circumcision party. He has to fear these people!

The Pauline mission, which seems to have had its centre in Antioch, nevertheless remains subordinated, at least to the extent of this tie, to the leadership in Jerusalem.[31]

The bond created by the collection was the more necessary because now, as a result of the agreement reached at Jerusalem, there were two missionary organizations.[32] According to Galatians 2:9 this was the decision the apostles reached in Jerusalem: *Paul and his fellow workers were to go to the Gentiles, while the missionaries from Jerusalem went to the circumcised.* Thus there occurred even in Primitive Christianity a decisive church split, even though it took place in a peaceful way. In opposition to the later divisions, especially the great ones that go back to the sixteenth century Reformers, this first one, in spite of the complete and mutually recognized independence, nevertheless expressed the common bond in that joint task of the collection.[33] If conflicts nevertheless occurred at a later time, this was

---

[31] The reference which P. Gaechter himself gives, *op. cit.*, p. 44, to the collection and especially to Rom. 15:16 f. runs contrary to his attempt to minimize the important witness the collection gives against his thesis, according to which Jerusalem had ceased to be regarded as the metropolis.

[32] See on this point J.-L. Leuba, *L'institution et l'événement*, 1950, pp. 62 ff.

[33] If we look at the history of Christianity as a whole, it may be permissible, in view of the historical framework which is normative for the present work, to ask whether today also the Roman Catholic Church and the great Christian Council of Churches independent of Rome, frankly renouncing hope of agreement in matters of church polity and doctrine, should not seek to establish a similar tie in a shared task, which both sides would undertake with conscious surrender of any higher aim, simply as a sign of the fact that the two great separated Churches nevertheless invoke the name of the same Lord. For the unavoidable abstention of the Roman Catholic Church from all ecumenical conferences proves that as far as man can foresee, even though the effort to reach common convictions in central questions must never cease, there can no longer be a real union, at least in the points that cause that abstention. In proposing a common work which shall explicitly proclaim the unity, a proposal that perhaps even in this modest form is still utopian, we of course do not mean that the situation today is the same as it was at the time of the Apostolic Council. The gulf between the two separated Churches is unfortunately very much deeper. For here the division has not taken place in peace and "with a handshake," as it did in Jerusalem. Nevertheless, there too, in that Primitive Christian discussion concerning circumcision, what was involved was a doctrinal, *unbridged* difference, which concerned a *central point*, that is, the conception of grace. In this important respect, as the actual separation and the continued doctrinal discussions on this theme in the letters of Paul show, the discussion even on that occasion did not issue in a shared conviction. If nevertheless the decision to undertake separate labours was made *"with a handshake,"* this fact should give us food for thought even today.

because the separation could not be carried out in practice; the reason was that all of the local churches probably were already of *mixed* membership at the time of their origin. There naturally were no churches that were solely Gentile Christian, for in all the larger centres there were Jews; indeed, we know that Paul regularly addressed himself to them first of all. On the other hand, there were no churches that were solely Jewish Christian, for everywhere former pagans joined the existing Jewish Christian churches. This had not been taken into account in the separation decided upon in Jerusalem, and therefore conflict inevitably arose at once in Antioch.

Thus Jewish Christian missionaries could always build upon the fact that there were Jewish Christian members in the churches founded by Paul. They could use this fact to justify their interference in Pauline churches. Paul could have done the same thing in the churches that the Jewish Christian missionary organization had founded. In Romans 15:20, however, he explains explicitly that to him it was a matter of honour not to do so. This no doubt corresponded to the spirit of the Jerusalem agreement, even if the letter of it permitted an intervention in mixed congregations. Paul therefore always considered it an unjustified "intrusion" by the Jerusalem mission when their representatives intervened in the churches he had founded, probably with the argument that they were responsible for the Jewish Christian elements that such churches contained. Paul made but *one* exception; this was with regard to the church at Rome. Therefore he feels compelled to justify urgently this step; he appeals to his need of having in the capital city a working base for his further activity in the far West—Spain. More than elsewhere he fears that this step may cause conflicts to arise in Rome, and we shall see how justified these apprehensions were.[34]

The fact that the Jerusalem agreement did not take into account the unavoidably mixed composition of the churches has been insufficiently considered, it seems to me, in recent studies. Only this fact, however, makes intelligible the entire tragic debate whose echoes we hear in all the letters of Paul. We should emphasize here without delay that in this entire debate *Peter himself no doubt stood nearer to Paul* than did the other members of the Jerusalem mission.[35]

---

[34] The circumstances in which the martyrdom of Peter took place ("jealousy," I Clem., ch. 5) find explanation on this basis. See below, pp. 90 ff., 105 ff.

[35] J. L. Klink, *Het Petrustype in het Nieuwe Testament en de oudchristelijke Letterkunde,* 1947, actually assumes that Peter had to leave Jerusalem on account of his free attitude to the Gentile mission.

This emerges clearly from the way in which Paul speaks of him, and especially where he must blame him. Peter, of course, was bound by his position as the commissioned leader of the mission sent out from Jerusalem.

As far as the question about Peter is concerned, we must in any case be clear that from the time of the Apostolic Council there were two missionary organizations. On the one side was the one at whose head Peter stood. It depended directly on the Primitive Church at Jerusalem, which was now under the leadership of James. On the other side was the organization of Paul and Barnabas. It was independent of Jerusalem, and henceforth had with the Mother Church only the loose external connection provided by their joint work on the collection. We have seen that the Primitive Church in Jerusalem, even while Peter himself was still there, had claimed the right to exercise supervision over the mission in Samaria. Looked at in this light, the agreement of Galatians 2:9 meant that the Jerusalem group renounced in principle this claim of oversight with reference to the Pauline mission. *They henceforth acted as head only of the Jewish Christian mission carried out by Peter.*

This, however, means that in principle Paul was independent not only of the Mother Church in Jerusalem—towards which, however, he had the obligation of the collection—but especially of Peter. So we understand that when the conflict concerning table fellowship with converted Gentiles occurred at Antioch (Gal. 2:11 ff.), Peter does not appear in any sense as Paul's superior, but on the contrary *must accept a rebuke from him.* It may be that the Reformers, in their polemic against Rome, emphasized much too strongly the significance of this reprimand of Peter.[36] On the other hand, even the Church Fathers recognized its importance.[37] It may also be correct that Paul, in spite of this conflict, did not cease to designate Simon by

---

[36] See K. Holl, "Der Streit zwischen Petrus und Paulus zu Antiochien in seiner Bedeutung für Luthers innere Entwicklung" (*Gesammelte Aufsätze*, III, 1928, pp. 134 ff.).

[37] Chrysostom (Homily on Gal. 2:1; Migne, *P. G.*, LI, Col. 371 ff.) and Jerome (Epistles 86–97 and Commentary on Galatians) were so offended by this event that they used the highly artificial explanation that Peter and Paul staged the whole conflict as a trick to instruct the believers! Even Augustine (Epistles 8–19) protested against this interpretation. See J. A. Möhler, "Hieronymus und Augustinus im Streit über Gal. 2, 14" (*Gesammelte Aufsätze*, edited by J. Döllinger, 1839, pp. 1 ff.); Fr. Overbeck, *Die Auffassung des Streites des Paulus mit dem Petrus bei den Kirchenvätern*, 1877; A. M. Völlmecke, "Ein neuer Beitrag zur alten Kephasfrage" (*Jahrbuch von St. Gabriel*, 1925, pp. 69–104).

his title Cephas, Rock.[38] Nevertheless, this passage proves that from the time when each begins to exercise his parallel mission, no one can speak of a "primacy" of Peter in relation to Paul, and in Corinth Paul will no more permit a Cephas party than he will any other party whatever.[39] Was it perhaps with particular reference to this Cephas —"Rock"—party that Paul wrote I Corinthians 3:11, that no one can lay any other "foundation" except that one which is laid, Jesus Christ?

In estimating the important event of the Apostolic Conference and the separation of missionary areas made there, we have based the preceding discussions exclusively upon the information Paul gives in his letter to the Galatians. As already mentioned, however, Peter appears but once in The Book of Acts in the period following the events of ch. 12. It is the last time before he completely vanishes from the narrative. This appearance is in ch. 15, on the occasion of the Apostolic Council there described. We must inquire whether the role that Peter here plays agrees with what we have learned from the letters of Paul.

Before doing so, however, we must ask whether the meeting of the apostles recounted in Acts, ch. 15, is the same as the one in Galatians 2:1 ff. At the outset we note one fact: the answer to this much debated question does not have for our study of Peter the same fundamental importance which it naturally possesses in the endless discussions that occur in special studies, as well as in general presentations of the history of Primitive Christianity.

The question must nevertheless be raised. The detailed circumstances in the two accounts are so similar that the assumption almost forces itself upon us that both accounts must deal with the same event. If we make this assumption, undeniable differences appear between the presentation of Paul in Galatians 2:1 ff. and that of The Acts in ch. 15. These differences are hard to reconcile. It will suffice to mention here two points. According to Galatians 2:1, Paul went to Jerusalem by reason of a "revelation"; according to Acts 15:1 ff., on the contrary, he went by commission of the Church. Furthermore— and this is the most important difference—according to Galatians 2:6, no ritual requirements of any kind are imposed on Paul for his

[38] This is stressed by F. M. Braun, *op. cit.*, p. 84.

[39] Wilhelm Vischer, *Die evangelische Gemeindeordnung*, 1946, p. 18, writes on this very point: "By this teaching (that Peter should have a successor in his unique office) the papal Church enlarged the schism of the Corinthian Peter party into a yawning cleft in the foundation."

Gentile mission.[40] The fundamental question concerning the necessity of circumcision is not settled at all; the only decision is the already
mentioned separation of missionary fields. The conference of Acts,
ch. 15, on the contrary, ends with the passing of the so-called
Apostolic Decree (ch. 15:19 f.); it requires of converted Gentiles the
observation of a minimum number of regulations, chiefly of ritual
character and having to do with meals.[41]

The difficulty that results from this last-named difference is further
increased by the fact that in The Book of Acts itself this same "decree" is reported to Paul at a much later time, when he comes to
Jerusalem for the last time (ch. 21:25). It is reported in a manner that
does not at all presuppose he had previously known of it or actually
taken part in deciding upon it. Moreover, it has been pointed out,
especially in recent studies, that we really have to do with two quite
different problems, which stand side by side in The Book of Acts
without being clearly related to each other. On the one side is the
question of the conversion of the Gentiles and so of the acceptance of
uncircumcised men into the Church; on the other side is the question
of table fellowship with them.

All these and other observations have long since stimulated the
most varied attempts at a solution. We need not report here concerning them. I mention only the main types of explanation into
which the most recent hypotheses can be divided.[42] According to one
theory there is in the The Book of Acts absolutely no parallel to
Galatians 2:1 ff. According to a second view, while the meeting of
Galatians 2:1 ff. is reported in Acts, it is reported not in ch. 15, but
in ch. 11:27; this passage tells of an earlier visit of Paul and Barnabas
to Jerusalem, on the occasion of which they brought help to the
Christian brothers who were suffering from famine. According to
the third explanation, the event of Galatians 2:1 ff. is indeed identical
with that of Acts, ch. 15, but on this view the differences must be
explained either through a chronological inaccuracy of The Book of
Acts, or by a conscious tendency of its author, or by the way he

---

[40] ἐμοὶ γὰρ . . . οὐδὲν προσανέθεντο ("for to me . . . they imparted nothing
additional").

[41] H. Schlier, Der Brief an die Galater (Meyer's Kommentar, 10th ed.), 1949, ad. loc.,
seeks to solve the contradiction by emphasizing "to me" (ἐμοί): only on Paul
personally was no further obligation placed.

[42] A good survey is given by Dom J. Dupont, Les Problèmes du livre des Actes
d'après les travaux récents, 1950, pp. 51 ff., and also by W. G. Kümmel, "Das
Urchristentum" (Theologische Rundschau, 1942, pp. 81 ff.; 1948, pp. 3 ff., 103 ff.;
1950, pp. 1 ff.).

combined various sources. We have mentioned here only the most important solutions; in reality there exist an innumerable mass of variations.[43] Indeed, it will hardly be possible to attain here to certainty, and we can proceed only by the use of hypothesis. The most probable one to me is still that one which sees in Galatians 2:1 ff. the same event reported in Acts, ch. 15; it furthermore considers correct its chronological location in Acts, ch. 15; but it transfers to a later time the passing of the Apostolic Decree, and assumes that the author of the Book of Acts erred in connecting the decree with his account of the Apostolic Council.[44]

This question is of interest to us only in its relation to our study of Peter. We must consider whether, on the assumption that in Acts, ch. 15, we have to do with the same event as in Galatians 2:1 ff., the role of Peter corresponds to that which he plays in the meeting Paul describes in Galatians 2:1 ff.

First of all, we note that Peter appears here in his capacity as missionary, and no longer as leader of the Church. This fits perfectly the picture we formed from the letter to the Galatians. In the narrative of The Book of Acts (ch. 15:7), Peter, it is true, stands up first to tell of his missionary experiences, before Paul and Barnabas begin to speak. But it is James, nevertheless, who plainly presides over the entire assembly, for he draws the conclusion from what has been heard and also formulates the "decree."[45] Even if the author of Acts was wrong in connecting this decree with this Council, he nevertheless clearly held that James then stood at the head of the Mother Church in Jerusalem, and this is the more important since in the earlier chapters of The Book of Acts this role always belongs to Peter.

We further note that in Acts, ch. 15, Peter speaks simply as the representative of the mission dependent on Jerusalem. This agrees

[43] Above all, in the third interpretation the event of Acts 11:27 ff. also is identified with that of Acts 15:1 ff., in which case, of course, the question arises whether the date of Acts 11:27 ff. or that of Acts 15:1 ff. is to be preferred.

[44] So on the whole, although again with various differences in chronology, H. Schlier, *Der Brief an die Galater*, 1949, pp. 66 ff.; M. Dibelius, "Das Apostelkonzil" (*Theologische Literaturzeitung*, 1947, pp. 193 ff.); M. Goguel, *La Naissance du Christianisme*, 1946, pp. 323 ff.; W. G. Kümmel (see especially *Theologische Rundschau*, 1950, pp. 27 f.). See also M. Dibelius—W. G. Kümmel, *Paulus* (Göschen), 1951, p. 118.

[45] James is thus not merely one of the "chief figures" of the Council, as P. Gaechter writes in "Jerusalem und Antiochia" (*Zeitschrift für katholische Theologie*, 1948, p. 41).

P.—4

entirely with the assumption which earlier considerations have already forced upon us, that Peter as well as Paul and Barnabas *interrupted his missionary activity* to go to the Council at Jerusalem.

Among the missionaries present, it is true, he plays the leading role, since his task here is to represent the mission that reaches out from Jerusalem. In this respect the opening words of Peter in Acts 15:7 are characteristic: "Brothers, you know that in the early days God made choice among you[46] that by my mouth the Gentiles should hear the preaching of the Gospel and believe." This fits the situation perfectly. Peter, as we also learn from Galatians 2:14, in his innermost heart stood much nearer to Paul than to James in the whole question of table fellowship with Gentile Christians, and probably also in his general attitude toward the Law. In this conference, where the question at issue is the position on the problem of circumcision, he refers not to his experiences as apostle to the Jews but to the less frequent cases where he has converted Gentiles. He can also claim, in spite of the presence of Paul and Barnabas, that he has been elected to preach the gospel to the Gentiles. The right to do this *within the Jewish Christian mission* we must almost certainly concede to him, unless we banish entirely into the realm of legend the history of the conversion of Cornelius or, following the "Tübingen School," ascribe it to the author's tendency to obliterate the opposition between Jewish and Gentile Christians. We must recognize in it at least a historical kernel. Thus even before the decisive separation agreed on in Jerusalem, Peter belonged to another missionary organization than did the more independent apostle Paul.

Nevertheless, he represents a standpoint not far removed from that of Paul. To fail to take this sufficiently into account introduces great confusion into our conception of Primitive Christianity and leads to the formulation of unnecessary hypotheses. While Peter in administrative relations was dependent on the Jerusalem authorities, and for this reason has to "fear" the "party of James," nevertheless, in his relation to Gentile Christianity and the Law, he stands fundamentally much closer to Paul than to James.[47] It certainly contributed much

---

[46] According to Foakes-Jackson and Kirsopp Lake, *The Beginnings of Christianity*, *ad loc.*, we should translate: "that God has chosen us." (According to Torrey the Aramaic ⊐ is the object.) See also II Esdras 19:7=Neh. 9:7: ἐξελέξω ἐν Ἀβραάμ: "Thou didst choose Abraham."

[47] The all too simple statement that Peter was nothing but a representative of the Jerusalem viewpoint is made under the influence of the "Tübingen school," whose influence still continues, for example, in H. Lietzmann, "Zwei Notizen zu Paulus" (*Sitzungsbericht der Berliner Akademie der Wissenschaften*, 1930, No. 8)

to the peaceful settlement of the conflict that Peter particularly, the missionary leader commissioned by Jerusalem, supported his colleagues Paul and Barnabas so powerfully at the Council.

That later at Antioch, contrary to his inner conviction, he "dissembled" due to fear (Gal. 2:11 ff.), may fit the psychological picture we get from the Synoptic Gospels—the picture of the impulsive disciple Peter, over-zealous in swearing loyalty to his Lord and yet denying him in the hour of danger. But on the other hand, it must be said in extenuation that as the missionary leader dependent on the Jerusalem church, he occupied in relation to the party of James *an infinitely more difficult position* than did the independent Paul. This conflict must have put Peter, the former and first head of the Church, in *a particularly painful dilemma*. Its difficulty we can only surmise, since we have no such extensive collection of letters from Peter as we have from Paul, and in addition, precisely by reason of his dependence on Jerusalem, he could scarcely speak so openly on this subject as Paul could.[48] We must keep this in mind in our interpretation of later events.

In any case, we dare not forget this aspect if we wish to form a correct picture of Peter the apostle. We must think of it particularly when we attempt to form a conception of Peter's apostolic travels, concerning which we know so little. Mediators always have a particularly difficult position, and Peter, as we have seen,[49] probably had to mediate between the Hellenists and the Judaisers from the very beginning of the Primitive Church.

With regard to the Apostolic Council, which falls in the first half of this activity, our conclusion is that the data of The Book of Acts

and also in his *Geschichte der alten Kirche* (Eng. Tr., *History of the Early Church*, 4 vols., 1937–51). See for the opposite view E. Hirsch, "Petrus und Paulus" (*ZNW*, 1930, p. 23). In ancient times this false picture was spread especially by the *Pseudo-Clementina*, and above all by the ancient source of the Preaching of Peter that they incorporated. See on this point H. J. Schoeps, *Theologie und Geschichte des Judenchristentums*, 1949, pp. 118 ff. I believe that especially in the conception of the atoning death of Jesus it was Peter in particular who stood very close to Paul. This is indicated by the fact that The Acts in the first chapters seems to have preserved the memory that Peter described Jesus as παῖς ("servant"), that is, as the Isaian Suffering Servant of God. See on this point below, pp. 66 ff.

[48] A recollection of this, however, could be preserved in I Clem., ch. 5, where it says that Peter "on account of unjustified jealousy had to suffer not one or two but manifold troubles." Is this not a reference to the way that Peter was *constantly* torn between the two positions? See below, p. 107.

[49] See above, p. 36.

concerning the position of Peter agree on the whole with the earlier observations which we made independently of Acts, ch. 15. This is true, no matter how we think in detail concerning other aspects of the relation between Galatians 2:1 ff. and The Book of Acts. In any case this very point confirms the assumption that the author of The Book of Acts placed the Apostolic Council (except for the decree) in its correct chronological location.

Concerning the entire second half of Peter's missionary activity we know, as has been said, practically nothing but the fact that it occurred. The introduction of I Peter (ch. 1:1) seems to presuppose that he did mission work in Asia Minor. Nothing definite concerning it is known. His name is chiefly connected, however, with three mission centres in particular: Antioch, Corinth, and Rome.

We have heard that at the time of the incident reported in Galatians 2:11 ff., Peter was at *Antioch*, where he had to submit to the rebuke by Paul. He may already have been there at an earlier time, but we have no certain information on this point. The Book of Acts only tells that those scattered as a result of the Stephen persecution came to Antioch (Acts 11:19). Since it is reported in ch. 8:1 that the apostles were not then dispersed with the others, the assumption that Peter founded the church at Antioch, while not explicitly excluded, is nevertheless hardly probable.[50] One could ask at the most whether Peter *subsequently* did not have to confirm the conversion of the Antioch Christians, and so indirectly confirm the foundation of that church, somewhat as he did in Samaria in the position he then held as head of the Primitive Church in Jerusalem. We possess no information, however, of any such role. In any case, the assertion that Peter founded the church at Antioch appears relatively early, in Origen, and then later in Eusebius, Chrysostom, and Jerome.[51] The church of Antioch can thus make a legitimate appeal to this rather ancient tradition. It must be emphasized that Antioch can thus raise in principle the same claim as Rome, since this Petrine tradition for Antioch is attested at least as well, if not better. We shall have to recall this in Part Two of this book, for this question is not without importance in reference to the exclusive claim that the Roman

[50] It is denied also by H. Katzenmayer, "Die Beziehungen des Petrus zur Urkirche von Jerusalem und Antiochien" (*Internationale kirchliche Zeitschrift*, 1945, pp. 116 ff.).

[51] Origen, *Homily on Luke*, VI, c (Migne, *P. G.*, XIII, Col. 1814 ff.); Eusebius, *Ecclesiastical History*, III, 36, 2 and 22; Chrysostom, *Homily on Ignatius* (Migne, *P. G.*, L, Col. 591); Jerome, on Gal. 2:1 (Migne, *P. L.*, XXVI, Col. 340); *De viribus illustribus*, 1 (Migne, *P. L.*, XXIII, Col. 637).

Bishop lays to Matthew 16:16 ff. Only from this point of view are we interested in the assertion that Peter founded the church at Antioch. As a historic fact, however, the claim cannot be supported.

We have already seen that it is arbitrary to identify the "other place" of Acts 12:17 with Antioch.[52] The only certain thing, accordingly, is that Peter made a stay in Antioch. He probably also maintained rather close relations with this church, as the incident of Galatians 2:11 ff. presupposes. Indeed, his position as leader of the Jewish Christian mission necessarily brought him into particularly close connection with this church, which by reason of its racial composition was the centre not only of the Gentile Christian but also of the Jewish Christian mission.

Did Peter visit *Corinth* during his missionary travels? Neither The Book of Acts nor Paul's Letters to Corinth say so, and in any case, The Book of Acts appears to know nothing of any participation by Peter in the *founding* of this church. Its narrative in ch. 18 speaks only of the conversion of the Corinthians through the preaching of Paul; it scarcely leaves room for a parallel activity of Peter. The statements of I Corinthians also exclude Peter's participation in the founding of the church. In I Corinthians 3:6 Paul writes: "I planted, Apollos watered, God gave the increase"; and in I Corinthians 4:15: "Even if you have countless masters in Christ, yet not many fathers. For in Christ Jesus I[53] became your father through the Gospel." Here Paul clearly considers himself the sole founder of this church.

In I Corinthians, however, there is support for the assertion often made that *later* Peter also came to Corinth and worked there as a missionary. In the first chapters of I Corinthians we are told of parties which were formed in Corinth, and ch. 1:12 mentions, in addition to a Paul party and an Apollos party and the uncertain "Christ party," a "Cephas party." Does not the existence of this Cephas party presuppose the presence and preaching of Peter at Corinth? The fact that this letter directed to the Corinthians makes special mention of the example of Cephas, who takes his wife with him in his missionary travel (I Cor. 9:5), could argue for this view; one could, if pressed for evidence, also cite the noteworthy fact that Paul, as he himself says (I Cor. 1:14 ff.), baptized only Gaius, Crispus, and Stephanas and his household. Could it be that he was of the opinion that to baptize with the Spirit was the business of the Twelve, as in Samaria (Acts 8:14 ff.)?[54]

On these brief indications, however, we can build at best only a

[52] See above, pp. 37 f.   [53] ἐγώ.   [54] See above, pp. 35 f.

hypothesis. The assertion that Peter was in Corinth has been made, as we have said, by the above named scholars. It has also found vigorous opponents.[55] In ancient times it first appears about the year 170, in the letter of Dionysius of Corinth to the Romans. Eusebius cites it: "By this exhortation you have united closely the tree of the Corinthians and that of the Romans—trees that were planted by Peter and Paul. For both (apostles) taught in the same way, in that they planted in our Corinth, and after they taught together in Italy they suffered martyrdom together."[56] The value of this testimony is lessened at once by the manifestly false assertion, refuted not only by The Book of Acts but also by Paul, that the church in Corinth was *founded* by Peter together with Paul.

Altogether apart from this assertion of Dionysius, however, we must take a stand concerning the deduction which draws from the existence of the Cephas party in Corinth the conclusion that Peter later made a stay in this city. This conclusion is in any event not convincing. For all Jewish Christian missionaries regarded Peter as the head of their mission; no doubt they took particular pleasure in setting him up against Paul as the "true apostle," and they probably appealed to his special relations with Jesus, as we can perceive indirectly in the letters of Paul. On this account Paul has to protest that he, too, has "seen Christ" (ch. 9:1). But Peter himself certainly did not belong to those against whom Paul turns with particular severity in his letters to the Corinthians. He is not one of those whom Paul elsewhere characterizes as "false brothers," who have followed him everywhere to discredit his person and above all his apostolic authority.[57]

---

[55] Among the defenders of the thesis that Peter made a stay in Corinth I name particularly Eduard Meyer, *Ursprung und Anfänge des Christentums*, Vol. III, pp. 441 (note 1), 498 ff.; A. Harnack, *Mission und Ausbreitung des Christentums in den ersten Jahrhunderten*, 3rd ed., 1915, p. 63, note 2; H. Lietzmann, "Die Reisen des Petrus" (*Sitzungsbericht der Berliner Akademie der Wissenschaften*, 1930, pp. 153 ff.); J. Zeiller, *L'Eglise primitive* (*Histoire de l'Eglise*, Vol. I, p. 227; Eng. Tr., *History of the Primitive Church*, Vol. I, 1942, p. 233); recently, H. Katzenmayer, "Das Todesjahr des Petrus" (*Internationale kirchliche Zeitschrift*, 1939, p. 85), and especially his article, "War Petrus in Korinth?" (*Internationale kirchliche Zeitschrift*, 1943, pp. 20 ff.). Among those who oppose this view should be named above all W. Bauer, *Rechtgläubigkeit und Ketzerei im ältesten Christentum*, 1934, p. 117; M. Goguel, "L'apôtre Pierre a-t-il joué un rôle personnel dans les crises de Grèce et de Galatie?" (*Revue d'Histoire et de Philosophie religieuses*, 1934, pp. 461 ff.); *La naissance du Christianisme*, 1946, pp. 335 ff.

[56] *Ecclesiastical History*, II, 25, 8.

[57] So rightly E. Hirsch, "Petrus und Paulus" (*ZNW*, 1930, pp. 63 ff.), in opposition to H. Lietzmann, *op. cit.*, in note 55 above. See also on this subject above, pp. 50 f.

In Galatians likewise the polemic of Paul does not have Peter in view. Here, too, there is no need to assume, as various historians have asserted, that Peter had been in Galatia. Nothing indicates that the incident at Antioch led to a breaking of the Jerusalem agreement and so to a break between Paul and Peter.[58] Peter himself, according to all that we have concluded concerning his attitude, is probably not directly responsible for the counter-mission of the "false brothers" who sought everywhere to sabotage the work of Paul. Presumably they took particular pleasure in appealing to the name of Peter, and probably represented in some way that he had sent them. But doubtless this was not so. It is sufficient, therefore, to assume that these people came into the Corinthian church that Paul had founded.

This, however, does not exclude the possibility that in the course of his journeys Peter once visited Corinth (and also Galatia). Since he stood at the head of the Jewish Christian mission, we certainly must reckon with this possibility. But it cannot be proved either from the existence of the Cephas party nor by any other indications.[59] The stay in Corinth, accordingly, can neither be definitely asserted nor denied, but it may be considered as possible.

We thus see that since our ancient sources give only extremely meagre reports, we can say nothing certain concerning this entire missionary activity of Peter. It is particularly significant that these sources, the Letters of Paul and The Book of Acts, are also completely silent concerning the stay of Peter in *Rome*, which later was universally accepted. This question, however, we shall consider in connection with the special chapter which we shall devote to Peter the Martyr.

Thus far, then, we have established that *the Apostle Peter, in the first period after the death of Jesus, leads the Primitive Church in Jerusalem; he then leaves Jerusalem, where the leadership passes over to James; and from then on, by commission of the Primitive Church and in dependence on it, he stands at the head of the Jewish Christian mission.*

---

[58] This is rightly emphasized by M. Goguel, against H. Lietzmann, *op. cit.*

[59] H. Katzenmayer, "*War Petrus in Corinth?*" (see above, note 55), uses among other things to support his argument I Clem., ch. 47, where it says that Apollos was approved by the apostles. It is claimed that he could have met Peter only in Corinth. Nevertheless, it is by no means established: 1. that Peter is here meant; 2. that he could have met Apollos only in Corinth.

3. *The Question of the Apostolic Commission*

It still remains to answer the question which we put at the opening of this chapter: does this apostolic activity of Peter—in its two successive expressions, the leadership of the Church and the missionary preaching—go back to a special commission which Peter received from Jesus?

We have seen that as far as the unique position of Peter *during the lifetime of Jesus* is concerned, we can no longer determine how far it has its basis in his peculiar character traits, and how far in the distinction Jesus gave him by bestowing on him the name "Rock." We have shown that both answers must be taken into account, and furthermore that at that time Peter's unique position did not yet take the form of setting him over the other disciples. For the period after the death of Jesus, however, where Peter for a time actually *led* the Jerusalem church, the question concerning his commission presents itself in another way.

The Primitive Church has the consciousness that everything which happens in it and to it belongs to the central redemptive action which is being fulfilled in Christ.; all these events are an integral part of the redemptive plan of God. Thus is explained the lofty apostolic consciousness of Paul, who does everything in the conviction that he is an instrument of the God-guided Christ Event. We are not so well informed concerning the consciousness of any other apostle, but in view of the fact that the first Christians always regarded themselves as the true people of God, we may assume without question that Peter also was conscious in his action of being specially commissioned by Christ.

Does this consciousness of Peter's also rest upon the experience of a special call, as we know it does in the life of Paul? Does not such an experience, in the Primitive Christian view, belong as a matter of course to the apostolic office?[60] If so, then with reference to Peter the further question arises: Did his actual call to be an apostle come through the *incarnate* Jesus, if it refers also to the time after his death? Or did it first come from the *risen* Christ? Or must we reckon with *both*?

The saying to Peter concerning the Church (Matt. 16:16 ff.) will be discussed in detail in Part Two of this book. It must be mentioned here merely in a preliminary way, in so far as it presents a basis for a

[60] See below, pp. 215 f., and the literature cited there; also, A. Fridrichsen, "The Apostle and his Message" (*Uppsala Universitets Arsskrift*, 1947).

commission from the historic Jesus which Peter must carry out after Jesus' death. The action of Peter in condemning Ananias and Sapphira (Acts 5:1 ff.) could be explained very well as the fulfilment of the promise there given.

Since, however, that passage is so vigorously disputed, we shall adduce it here, as we did in Chapter One, in a merely provisional manner. Here, as there, we must say that even if we make no use of this saying, the result remains on the whole the same; the less disputed commission of Jesus to Peter to "strengthen the brothers" (Luke 22:31 f.),[61] and furthermore, the undeniable fact that Jesus gave him the name "Rock" (even without the reason added in Matt. 16:17 ff.), are sufficient to trace the unique position of Peter as leader of the Jerusalem church back to a commission that the earthly Jesus gave.

Thus, even apart from Matthew 16:16 ff., we find it clearly possible that Peter's leading position in the Primitive Church rests upon the distinction or commission which Jesus gave to his disciple Peter even during his earthly life and which Peter has occasion to fulfil only after the Lord's death.

It has of course been asserted that the saying in Luke 22:31 f., as well as all the passages in the Synoptic Gospels which give Peter a place of distinction, were later creations of the Church; in this way, it is claimed, the Church later provided a legal authorization by the historical Jesus for the leading role that Peter had actually played in Jerusalem. But we have already seen that the distinction given Peter by the name Cephas can in no case be so explained. Altogether apart from the *confirmation* that Matthew 16:17 ff. gives, we have to do here with a fact which is not open to doubt.

More recent studies, on the other hand, do indeed assume a special commission, but transfer it into the period after the death of Jesus, when the *risen* Christ appears and gives a commission to Peter. This commission, it is claimed, the gospel tradition later transferred back into the life of Jesus. We shall have to return to this explanation with reference to its special bearing on Matthew 16:17 ff. For the time being, however, we must say of it that at least the giving of the name Cephas cannot thus be ascribed to the Primitive Church.[62]

We possess, it is true, trustworthy traditions which attest that the

[61] See above, pp. 26 f.

[62] K. Goetz, *op. cit.*, pp. 67 f., does indeed take even this final step; he considers it possible that the giving of the name is to be ascribed to the Primitive Church. See above, p. 20.

risen Christ gave to Peter a special distinction and a special commission. Here at any rate we stand upon solid ground, and although, as I am convinced, we must acknowledge that the historical Jesus had already given Peter a special distinction, so that the question does not confront us in the form of an unconditional alternative, nevertheless for the foundation of the apostolate of Peter a *greater and more direct significance* attaches to the commission from the *Risen* One. We recall that it was an important but not the exclusive[63] prerequisite of the call to apostleship that one had seen the *risen* Lord (I Cor. 9:1; Acts 1:22).[64] So a call to a special apostolic office by the *Risen* One appears almost a necessity, even if, as was doubtless true of Peter, a distinction had already been conferred by the earthly Jesus.

In view of the great significance which the appearance as such has for the call to apostleship, one can ask whether every appearance of the Risen One was not regarded in itself as a "call." In the case of Paul, at least, it is certain that the appearance of the Risen One, whom he sees on the way to Damascus, coincides with his call. As far as Peter is concerned, however, the two facts are reported separately; they are not combined in the sources we possess concerning the appearances of the Lord that he saw. We hear on the one hand, in I Corinthians 15:5 and in Luke 24:34, that Christ appeared to Peter; on the other hand, in John, ch. 21, we hear that on the occasion of an appearance at which, in addition to Peter, other disciples also are present, the special commission is given to him to "feed the sheep of Christ." It has indeed been asserted that these passages all deal with one and the same event. Before we decide concerning this hypothesis, we desire first to evaluate separately the fact reported in I Corinthians 15:5 and Luke 24:34, to see what it teaches as to the role of Peter in the Primitive Church.

First of all, it cannot be emphasized too strongly that according to I Corinthians 15:5 Peter is the *first* one to whom the Lord appeared.[65]

---

[63] H. v. Campenhausen, "Der urchristliche Apostelbegriff" (*Studia theologica*, Lund, 1948, pp. 112 f.), rightly emphasizes how unsatisfactory is the recent custom which simply identifies apostle and witness to the resurrection. Sufficient to prove it unsatisfactory is the fact, clear from I Cor. 15:3 ff., that not all whom Paul enumerates as witnesses of the resurrection became apostles. (Note the more than five hundred brethren in I Cor. 15:6).

[64] See K. H. Rengstorf, Article on ἀπόστολος ("apostle") in G. Kittel's *Theologisches Wörterbuch zum N.T.* See further on this question below, pp. 215 f.

[65] F. Kattenbusch, "Die Vorzugstellung des Petrus und der Charakter der Urgemeinde zu Jerusalem" (*Festgabe für K. Müller*, 1922, pp. 328 ff.), and "Der Spruch über Petrus und die Kirche bei Matthäus" (*Studien und Kritiken*, 1922,

The risen Christ thereby put the seal, so to speak, upon the distinction which during his lifetime he had given Peter by naming him Cephas. The passage I Corinthians 15:5, which names Peter as the first witness of the resurrection, is perhaps the earliest Christian text that we possess; it is older than the letters of Paul and he explicitly quotes it as a citation from the earlier tradition transmitted to him.[66]

It is noteworthy that the Gospels do not tell of this appearance to Peter alone. Even Luke gives no account of it, although he briefly mentions the fact. In his Gospel the Eleven report to the returning Emmaus disciples: "the Lord has really arisen, and he has appeared to Simon" (Luke 24:34).

Was this appearance perhaps reported in the lost ending of Mark? The question forces itself upon us when we note that in two passages, and indeed in the last verses preserved for us, this Gospel makes special mention of Peter in connection with the journey to Galilee which Jesus announces is to occur after his resurrection.[67] In the former passage, Jesus says: "When I have risen I will go before you to Galilee" (Mark 14:28). It is Peter himself who in the following verse continues the conversation with a reference to this promise. In the other passage the young man at the grave who is clothed in white announces: "Say to his disciples *and to Peter* that he goes before you to Galilee" (Mark 16:7). In view of this one can indeed ask whether we must not postulate that a narrative concerning an appearance of Christ to Peter stood at the end of the Gospel of Mark.[68]

p. 130), wrongly denies this; he attempts to take the εἶτα ("then") in a non-chronological sense. For the enumeration in I Cor. 15:5, however, the order is obviously significant. Hence A. Harnack, "Die Verklärungsgeschichte Jesu," (*Sitzungsbericht der Preussischen Akademie der Wissenschaften*, 1922, p. 68); K. Goetz, *op. cit.*, pp. 4 ff.; and E. Stauffer, *op. cit.*, pp. 6 ff., have given proper attention to the fact that Peter is the first one who saw the Risen One. K. Goetz rightly points out, in opposition to F. Kattenbusch, that the words "last of all" in I Cor. 15:8 make it impossible to dispute the chronological element in the enumeration.

[66] According to our previous discussion it is in any case impossible to assert with E. Stauffer, *op. cit.*, p. 6, note 14, that "here speaks no partisan but rather an opponent of Peter." Neither the authors of the formula cited nor Paul, who cites it, can be called an opponent of Peter.

[67] The view championed by E. Lohmeyer, *Galiläa und Jerusalem*, 1936, that the appearance to Peter occurred in Jerusalem, is improbable both for this reason and on other grounds.

[68] So E. Stauffer, *op. cit.*, pp. 11 f. K. Goetz, *op. cit.*, p. 73, also considers this possibility. So does N. Huffman, "Emmaus Among the Resurrection Narratives" (*Journal of Biblical Literature*, 1945, pp. 205 ff.); to be sure, he rather arbitrarily seeks also to identify the unnamed disciple of the Emmaus story with

To assume this implies that the conclusion of Mark is lost and that it contained the narrative of the appearance to Peter that I Corinthians 15:5 and Luke 24:34 mention. This naturally remains a hypothesis, but much speaks for its correctness. It is certainly noteworthy that we possess no story concerning an event of such importance as the first appearance of the Lord, especially since it concerned the very disciple who shortly before had denied him. It may also justifiably be asked whether that event has left in the texts *preserved* any other traces, in addition to the two brief notices in I Corinthians and the Gospel of Luke.

First of all, it is believed that we possess more than a trace, that we actually possess an expansion of the actual narrative of that appearance, in the supplementary Chapter 21 of the Gospel of John.[69] It is indeed striking how, in the second part of this story, Peter is pushed into the foreground, but then, in the same way as in the corresponding passages of the preceding chapters, is put parallel to the Beloved Disciple. The threefold assertion of love for his Lord and the threefold commission undoubtedly stand in intentional contrast to the three-fold denial.[70] It may be that the miraculous catch of fish which is reported in the first part of the story connects also with the story of Peter's call in Mark 1:16 ff., and is intended to indicate the fulfilment of the promise there given concerning the "fishers of men." In its present form the chapter certainly bears the "Johannine" stamp in both its parts, and especially in the second one; it may be, however, that a Marcan narrative concerning the appearance of Jesus to Peter lies at the basis of the story.[71] Nevertheless, it must be conceded that this assumption also is only a hypothesis, inasmuch as this entire

Peter and makes Luke responsible for the transfer of the scene to Jerusalem. On the other hand, K. L. Schmidt, *Kanonische und apokryphe Evangelien und Apostelgeschichten*, 1944, p. 27; N. B. Stonehouse, *The Witness of Matthew and Mark to Christ*, 1944, pp. 86 ff.; W. C. Allen, in *Journal of Theological Studies*, 1946, pp. 46 ff.; 1947, pp. 201 ff., deny that the original conclusion of Mark has been lost. They hold rather that the words "for they were afraid" (ἐφοβοῦντο γάρ) are the intended conclusion of the Gospel.

69 This was already the view of Arnold Meyer, *Die Auferstehung Jesu Christi*, 1905, p. 168.

70 This interpretation, which had already been given by Ambrose and Augustine, is rejected by M. Goguel, *L'Eglise primitive*, 1947, p. 192; *Jesus*, 1950, p. 390. See on the other side J. Bernard, *A Critical and Exegetical Commentary on the Gospel According to St. John*, 1928, Vol. II, p. 690.

71 E. Stauffer, *op. cit.*, p. 16, actually writes that "The author of John, ch. 21, knew and used the lost ending of Mark." See also A. Harnack, *Lukas der Arzt*, 1906 (Eng. Tr., *Luke the Physician*, 1907).

story, as it is preserved for us in the Gospel of John, deals neither with the first appearance nor with one supposed to have been granted to Peter alone. If, however, it should prove correct that the connection of the commission given to Peter with the words referring to the Beloved Disciple is due merely to the author of the supplementary chapter, then this hypothesis would have a greater degree of probability. This would be the more likely since later eastern sources also tell of an appearance of Christ to Peter connected with a special commission.[72]

We cannot here attain complete certainty. Nor can we do so with regard to the further assumption that the gospel tradition transferred the important event of Christ's appearance to Peter back into the earthly life of Jesus, so that this event now finds expression in the narrative of Luke 5:1 ff. concerning the miraculous catch of fish at the Sea of Gennesaret,[73] further in the narrative of Matthew 14:28 concerning the walking on the sea,[74] especially in the transfiguration story, [75] and finally—concerning this we shall have to speak further at a later point—in the saying to Peter concerning the Church in Matthew 16:17 f. and in the commission of Luke 22:32.[76]

Not without reason, moreover, have I Peter 1:3 and II Peter 1:16 ff. been connected with the vision seen by Peter.[77]

Even if all these hypotheses are correct, it still remains puzzling

---

[72] See below, p. 63, note 83.

[73] So J. Bernard, op. cit., p. 690, and E. Stauffer, op. cit., p. 17.

[74] H. Sasse, "Die erste Erscheinung des Auferstandenen" (Theologische Blätter, 1922, p. 59).

[75] Thus Wellhausen, Das Evangelium Marci, 1909, p. 71, already assumed, as did R. Bultmann, Geschichte der synoptischen Tradition, 2nd ed., 1931, p. 278, and K. Goetz, op. cit., pp. 76 ff., that the transfiguration story arose from the memory of a resurrection appearance. On the contrary, A. Harnack, "Die Verklärungsgeschichte Jesu, der Bericht des Paulus und die beiden Christusvisionen des Petrus" (Sitzungsbericht der Preussischen Akademie der Wissenschaften, 1922, pp. 76 ff.), and Ed. Meyer, Ursprung und Anfänge des Christentums, Vol. I, 1921, pp. 152 ff., hold that the transfiguration story is good tradition; they actually assume the opposite position, that this event from the earthly life of Jesus is the basis of the vision that Peter had after the Lord's death. E. Lohmeyer, "Die Verklärung Jesu nach dem Markusevangelium" (ZNW, 1922, pp. 185 ff.), also disputes the derivation of the transfiguration story from a resurrection appearance; nevertheless, he does not consider the transfiguration historical, but holds that this narrative arose from Jewish conceptions.

[76] See E. Stauffer, op. cit., pp. 20 ff., 18 ff.; R. Bultmann, Theologie des Neuen Testaments, 1948, p. 46 (Eng. Tr., Theology of the New Testament, Vol. I, 1951, p. 45).

[77] Usually an allusion to the transfiguration story is seen here. K. Goetz, op. cit., p. 89, is probably correct in opposing this view.

that the memory of the appearance to Peter has been preserved only in scattered traces. Hence an explanation has quite properly been sought for this remarkable gap in our tradition. What interest may have been present to push into the background this usually important event? Some have thought of a conflict between adherents of James and of Peter.[78] But this could hardly have occasioned the silence that exists in the writings in which one expects a narrative concerning this event. A more likely contributing factor could have been the inner compulsion not to be content with *one* witness for so important a fact as an appearance of the Risen One, but to introduce two or more (Deut. 19:15), so that the preference would be given to appearances before more than one witness.[79] In this connection, furthermore, one has recalled also the discussions between Jewish and Gentile Christians, such as are attested for us from the beginning of the second century and probably reach back into even earlier times. We learn from the *Pseudo-Clementina* that in Jewish Christian circles the apostolic rank of Paul was contested by pointing out that it rests only upon a vision.[80] Thus in this Jewish Christian writing the value of visions in general is denied by Peter himself.[81] If such considerations were already raised in the controversies between Paul and the Judaizers, then we definitely must reckon with the possibility that the Jewish Christian gospel tradition tended to prefer not to base the authority of Peter upon a commission given only by the Risen One. Connected with this could be the fact that the significance which in the later life of Peter attached to the appearances in general, and above all to that first appearance of Jesus, was curtailed. Recent scholars, indeed, believe that they find in Peter a special capacity for visions.[82]

[78] A. Harnack, *op. cit.*, p. 70.

[79] See Lyder Brun, *Die Auferstehung Christi*, 1925, p. 22; K. Goetz, *op. cit.*, p. 74.

[80] *Homilies* 17, 19. See O. Cullmann, *Le problème littéraire et historique du roman pseudo-clémentin*, 1930, pp. 248 f. C. Holsten, *Die Messiasvision des Petrus und die Genesis des petrinischen Evangeliums*, 1867, p. 120, already explained on this basis the suppression of the report of Christ's appearance to Peter.

[81] *Recognitions*, II, 62. Peter here tells that at the Sea of Gennesaret he believed in his spirit that he saw Jerusalem and Caesarea, and when he later came to Caesarea, the reality did not correspond at all to what he had seen in vision.

[82] K. Goetz, *op. cit.*, pp. 98 ff., recalls in this connection Acts, chs. 10 and 11; 12:9; in addition, he recalls the passage mentioned in the Pseudo-Clementine *Recognitions*, II, 62, and especially the Apocalypse of Peter, which likewise presupposes that Peter was regarded as a "seer" in a special sense; he also recalls the famous *Quo-vadis* story from the *Actus Vercellenses*, ch. 35. See also W. Grundmann, "Die Apostel zwischen Jerusalem und Antiochia" (*ZNW*, 1940, p. 135).

However that may be, and in spite of its meagre emphasis in the Primitive Christian writings,[83] the unshakable fact remains that Peter was the first to see the Risen One. In the earliest period this certainly must have contributed greatly to his *authoritative position* in the Primitive Church.[84] For at that time there certainly existed no reason to belittle visions as a basis of apostolic authority. The enumeration of the appearances, which constitutes the content of the oldest Christian document preserved to us (I Cor. 15:3 ff.), proves on the contrary what a great value was ascribed to these events as an attestation of the resurrection. Thereby the witnesses themselves also received special distinction. It is clear that he to whom had been given the dignity of being the *first* witness of that mighty fact was regarded, just because of this chronological preferment, as the one especially commissioned by Christ to hand on this witness. Accordingly, even this first appearance of Jesus, which has sufficient documentary proof, would suffice to give the foundation for the authoritative position of Peter as the leader of the Church.[85] There is the additional point, however, as we have seen, that in John, ch. 21, we actually possess a tradition according to which Peter was explicitly commissioned by the Risen One to "feed his sheep." Whether this deals with the same event or not, the deeper meaning of the special commission to Peter in John, ch. 21, is in any case already implied in the fact of the appearance to Peter that I Corinthians 15:5 reports.

We still must consider the wording of the commission as it is formulated in John 21:16 ff.: "Feed my sheep." It has rightly been

[83] As attestations from *later* times should be named here: The Gospel of Peter, the Ethiopic Apocalypse of Peter, Pistis Sophia, the Syriac Treasure Cave (translation by C. Bezold, 1883, p. 71), and especially the mediaeval writing of the Arab Asch Shahrastani on "Religious Sects and Philosophical Schools" (*Die Religionsparteien und Philosophenschulen*, German translation by Th. Haarbrücker, I, 1850, pp. 360 f.). See on this subject F. Haase, *Apostel und Evangelisten in den orientalischen Ueberlieferungen*, 1922, pp. 208 ff.; further, K. Goetz, *op. cit.*, pp. 89 f.—According to A. Harnack, "Petrus im Urteil der Kirchenfeinde des Altertums" (*Festgabe für Karl Müller*, 1922, pp. 2 ff.), even Celsus knew of the appearance of Christ to Peter. He holds that Origen, *Contra Celsum*, II, 55, refers to Peter.

[84] The importance of the first appearance of Christ for the Petrine question is also correctly understood by E. Seeberg, "Wer war Petrus?" (*Zeitschrift für Kirchengeschichte*, 1934, pp. 571 ff.). J. Klausner, *From Jesus to Paul*, translated from the Hebrew (1943), also emphasizes it strongly. In general, he ascribes to Peter the exclusive leading role in the origin of the Primitive Church.

[85] Therefore a special call separate from the appearance, such as is postulated by A. Fridrichsen, *op. cit.* (see above, p. 56, note 60), would not be absolutely necessary.

pointed out[86] that the Damascus Document discovered in 1910,[87] which in connection with the recent manuscript discoveries in Palestine takes on particular importance,[88] speaks of the leader of the fellowship as the "shepherd of the flock." His duty is to proclaim the word, explain the Scripture, and exercise community discipline (ch. 13:9).

The command to feed the sheep includes the two activities which we have shown to be the successive expressions of Peter's apostolate: leadership of the Primitive Church in Jerusalem and missionary preaching. We perceive from the conceptions which lie behind John, ch. 10, that not only the leadership of the Church but also the missionary work belongs to the office of shepherd. The linguistic usage, which there designates the Jews first of all as the "sheep," proves that both functions have primarily in view *the Jews*. In this sense Jesus speaks in the Synoptic Gospels of the "lost sheep of the house of Israel" (Matt. 10:6), to which he knows himself to be sent; this does not exclude but is in fact the foundation for his responsibility for the "other sheep" who do not belong to this flock (John 10:16).

We thus see that the commission given by the Risen One may be applied to the functions which the apostle Peter actually exercised successively in his relations with the Jewish Christian Primitive Church.

So we reach the conclusion that *his position probably rests in the first instance upon a commission from the risen Lord*; at the same time, however, the fact that the earthly Jesus gave him the special distinction of the name Cephas, and further the representative role of the former disciple of Jesus, helped to confer authority on him as leader of the Church and as missionary.

Even here, however, we must emphasize that in John, ch. 21, the commission to feed the sheep also has connected with it the prediction of the martyrdom of Peter. This, however, means that the commission to the Apostle Peter *has a time limitation*. That is, it is limited to *the period of the foundation of the Church*. We shall have

---

86 E. Stauffer, *op. cit.*, pp. 4 ff.

87 W. Staerk, *Die jüdische Gemeinde des neuen Bundes in Damaskus*, 1922; L. Rost, *Die Damaskusschrift*, 1933.

88 From the almost endless literature on this subject I cite A. Dupont-Sommer, *Aperçus préliminaires sur les manuscrits de la Mer Morte*, 1950; P. Kahle, *Die hebräischen Handschriften aus der Höhle*, 1951; and the survey articles of W. Baumgartner, "Der Palästinische Handschriftenfund" (*Theologische Rundschau*, 1948–49, pp. 329 ff., and 1951, pp. 97 ff.), which are quite complete down to 1951.

to take this aspect into account in Part Two of the present book.[89]

4. The Theological Views of the Apostle

In view of the nature of the sources it would be a rash undertaking to try to present a "theology" of the apostle Peter. Even if one holds that the First Epistle of Peter was written by the apostle himself, the basis for this undertaking is too small. However, some very important points can be established with a relatively high degree of certainty.

More than once I have pointed to the fact that Peter was not far removed from Paul in theology.[90] Indeed, I should go even further and definitely assert that within the circle of the Twelve he is the one who in this respect *stands closest to Paul*.

We have already emphasized his *universalism*. In opposition to a widespread error, this is definitely attested, not only by The Book of Acts, which since the days of the Tübingen School scholars have regarded as tendential in this respect and therefore have wanted to discard as a proof, but also by Paul. Precisely in connection with the conflict at Antioch, Paul expressly recognizes that Peter in theory represents the same universal viewpoint that he himself holds. Indeed, he reproaches Peter at Antioch only because he has been untrue to his conviction out of fear of the people from James. It may even be true that his origin in the city of Bethsaida,[91] with its Hellenistic influences, had much to do with shaping this broadminded attitude of Peter. But this attitude doubtless requires a deeper foundation.

Peter obviously learned from his Lord that the divine election of the Jewish people for a definite function does not mean that God's gracious working is limited exclusively to this one people. It was not in vain that Peter was an eye-witness. He understood Jesus' words concerning those who come from the East and the West to recline at table with Abraham, Isaac, and Jacob in the Kingdom of God (Matt. 8:11). He also understood the meaning of that scene with the centurion of Capernaum. Therefore later, in the Primitive Church at Jerusalem, he took a mediating attitude between the group of the

---

[89] See below, pp. 207 ff.
[90] See above, pp. 45, 49 f. On this subject, see E. Hirsch, "Petrus und Paulus" (*ZNW*, 1930, pp. 63 ff.).
[91] See above, p. 22.

Judaizers and that of the Hellenists, and he was able to hold the two sections together as long as he stood at the head.[92]

But his universalism seems to me to have a still deeper *theological* anchor. This was in the understanding he achieved that Christ's death was the atoning death. Perhaps he was the first one to grasp this after Jesus' resurrection. It is true that it has become common custom to regard the apostle Paul as the creator of the theology of the cross. Indeed, he did in a powerful way put his mighty spiritual gift of systematic thought at the service of the preaching of the cross, and Peter certainly never received the rabbinical training of a Paul. But I do not believe that Paul was the first one to understand the death of Jesus as an atoning death for the forgiveness of sins. On the contrary, I am inclined to ascribe to Peter this particular and fundamental insight. Although he was anything but a theologian, I think that here too he should be given the place of honour at the beginning of all Christian theology.

At this point we must keep in view the significance of the earliest Christology we possess, the explanation, namely, of the person and work of Jesus by the figure of the "Suffering Servant of God" prophesied by Second Isaiah. This explanation, in addition to the Son of Man Christology, certainly goes back to Jesus himself.

I believe, indeed, that this earliest Christological explanation can be shown to have the apostle Peter as its author.

The Book of Acts proves that in the earliest times of Primitive Christianity there existed an explanation of the person and work of Jesus which we may designate somewhat incorrectly as Christology of the "Servant of God," *ebed Yahweh*, in Greek *pais theou*; more correctly, we could call it "Paidology." We could even go further and assert that this is probably the earliest solution of the Christological question. The narrative concerning the conversion of the Ethiopian eunuch (ch. 8:26 ff.) is the chief evidence that Jesus was explicitly identified with this *ebed Yahweh* in the first century, and that the vivid memory was clearly preserved that Jesus himself so understood his divine mission.

Apart from this narrative, however, there are other passages in The

---

92 See on this point W. Grundmann, "Das Problem des hellenistischen Christentums innerhalb der Jerusalemer Urgemeinde" (*ZNW*, 1939, pp. 45 ff.), and "Die Apostel zwischen Jerusalem und Antiochia" (*ZNW*, 1940, pp. 110 ff.). W. Grundmann distinguishes, in partial dependence on E. Lohmeyer, *Galiläa und Jerusalem*, 1936, three groups in the Primitive Church: the Galilean, the Judaistic, and the Hellenistic.

Book of Acts which, while they do not all contain an actual quotation from the Book of Isaiah, are nevertheless of the greatest importance for our question. In them Jesus openly receives the very title *ebed Yahweh*, "Servant of God," in the Greek rendering, *pais tou theou*. In the Septuagint the latter phrase translates the expression which Deutero-Isaiah uses for the Suffering Servant of God who takes upon himself in a substitutionary way the sins of the people. There are four passages of this kind; it is significant that all four occur in the same section, in chs. 3 and 4, and that Jesus is called *pais tou theou* in no other book of the New Testament. He first appears in this capacity in Acts 3:13, where reference is made to Isaiah 52:13, then in chapter 3:26, where we really have to do with a Christological title. The expression here is Jesus—Pais, exactly as one will be accustomed later to say Jesus—Christ. Similarly one gets the clear impression in the next chapter, 4:27 and 4:30, that *pais* is used almost as a fixed term; it is tending to become a proper name, just as occurred in the case of the word Christ. This confirms the existence of a very early Christology on the basis of which Jesus was called *ebed Yahweh*. It will disappear in the following period, but its use must reach back into the very earliest times.

It is probably no accident that of those four passages, the only ones in the New Testament to designate Jesus as *pais, two stand in speeches which are ascribed to the Apostle Peter* and two in a prayer spoken in unison by the Jerusalem group of disciples when Peter is present. The Book of Acts, which has twenty-eight chapters, uses this expression in no other passage. It is probably not too bold to conclude from this fact that the author thus preserves the clear memory that it was the apostle Peter who by preference designated Jesus as the "Suffering Servant of God."[93] This agrees with what we know of Peter. According to Mark 8:32, he is the very one who at Caesarea Philippi showed so little understanding of the necessity for Jesus to suffer. He took Jesus aside to say to him: "This will not happen to you," so that Jesus, who saw in him the same tempter who already had tried once to turn him from his path, had to repulse him with the words: "Away, Satan!" We understand that the same apostle who later, according to I Corinthians 15:5, was the first to see the Risen One,

---

[93] For more detail on this, see O. Cullmann, "Jésus serviteur de Dieu" (*Le Dieu vivant*, No. 16, 1950, pp. 19 ff.). There is a tendency toward this view in W. Grundmann, *ZNW*, 1939, p. 53. According to R. Bultmann, *Theologie des Neuen Testaments*, 1948, p. 51 (Eng. Tr., *Theology of the New Testament*, p. 50), this passage suggests not the Suffering Servant but the Son of David (Acts 4:25).

thereafter in the light of the resurrection was also the *first* to preach the actual necessity of the suffering and the death of the Lord, concerning which during the lifetime of Jesus he wanted to know nothing. We understand the fact that he made the suffering and death of Jesus the very *centre* of his explanation of the earthly work of Jesus. The backward look to the denial likewise makes this easily intelligible, especially since as early as Luke 5:8 the story appears to presuppose a particular intensity in Peter's consciousness of sin.

In this connection it is interesting to recall the further fact that The First Epistle of Peter cites with emphasis the passages from the Book of Isaiah which refer to the *ebed Yahweh* (I Pet. 2:21 ff.). This observation remains of value for our study quite independently of the question whether this Epistle is genuine or not. For even if Peter did not write it, nevertheless the anonymous author who ascribed it to him was acquainted with the fact that Peter by preference applied to Jesus the conception of the Suffering Servant of God.

The Christology of the apostle Peter, if we may dare to use this expression, was quite probably dominated by the concept of the *ebed Yahweh*. If so, he who tried to turn Jesus from the way of suffering, and denied him at the decisive moment of the Passion story, was the first one who, after Easter, grasped the necessity of this offence. He could not express this conviction better than by using the designation *ebed Yahweh*; this was the more true since he must have known how great an importance Jesus himself had attached to the ideas connected with the phrase.

Thus of Peter's theological attitude we may say, though with some caution, that the rock apostle, who in Jerusalem was the leader of the first church and doubtless was the first to preach Christ there, was not merely the organizer with only practical interests, as we usually conceive him. Here too the picture of the Prince of the Church is incorrect. He certainly possesses a much greater significance in the foundation of Christian theology than we are accustomed to assume. If we had from him a large collection of letters, such as we have from Paul, it is certain that a different picture would result. It is true that he did not have the technical theological training of Paul, who studied with the Rabbis. But the great idea which Paul later worked out in systematic form very probably occurred first to the fisherman Peter.

This remains true although the same insight was revealed to Paul independently of Peter. For we must believe Paul when he writes in Galatians that he received his gospel neither from men nor through human mediation (Gal. 1:12). By the term gospel, Paul, in keeping with his whole theology, can only have meant its central point, the word of the cross.

Later times have often been unjust to Paul by putting him in the shadow of Peter. Theologically, however, scholars seem to me to be unjust to Peter when they put him entirely in the shadow of Paul, or regard him as Paul's antagonist devoid of understanding for the great Pauline insights.

Chapter Three

PETER THE MARTYR

1. *The Problem*

EVEN in our presentation of the missionary activity of Peter the fragmentary character of our sources drove us to inferences and hypotheses. Such measures are still more necessary when we undertake to determine definitely the circumstances of his death. It is noteworthy that the single ancient source from which we might expect information on this point, The Book of Acts, is as silent concerning the death of Peter as it is concerning that of Paul, and we have at our disposal no other ancient texts which report this event of such importance for the Primitive Church. We nevertheless must discuss the indirect witnesses from which conclusions concerning the martyrdom of Peter are drawn. The following sections must inquire whether or not these deductions are correct.

The question is the more important since it is closely connected with the problem of Peter's stay in Rome. The solution of this problem, in turn, is linked with the interpretation, so weighted with historical consequences, which the Roman Catholic Church still gives to the saying of Jesus in Matthew 16:17 ff. concerning the rock upon which the Church of Christ is to be built.

This explains also the violent emotion with which the whole discussion has been carried on ever since the stay of Peter in Rome was questioned, first by the Waldensians in the Middle Ages and in more recent times by Protestant scholars. All too often there slip into this debate, consciously or unconsciously, considerations of a confessional kind, which belong in the realm of Protestant-Catholic controversy. In opposition to such an attitude it must be emphasized at the outset that we are dealing here with a purely historical question, which can be handled only with the objective methods of scientific historical study. To proceed thus is the more important since the question whether the papal claim of power over the Christian Church is justified is much too complex for us to answer simply by solving the problem whether Peter ever made a stay in Rome. In reality the decision can only be reached by explaining Matthew 16:18 ff.

If indeed it could really be proved that Peter never set foot in Rome at all, as many have often asserted and still assert, then of course the papal claim could not be *historically* defended at all; it would have to rest content with a purely dogmatic justification,[1] which has often been declared sufficient from the Catholic standpoint.[2] Only in this respect is the theological and ecclesiastical question linked with the result of historical study. The opponents of the papal claim may always be greatly tempted to make the matter easy for themselves by thinking that perhaps in this radical way the entire problem can find a relatively quick solution. On the other hand, however, we must say that if scientific reasons indicate the correctness of the later tradition, which asserts that the apostle Peter made a stay in Rome, this alone, as we have noted, is still insufficient to furnish a foundation for the papal claim.

It is fortunate, therefore, that with the passage of time those confessional and polemic considerations have largely disappeared from scholarly discussion. In recent years it has actually been Protestant or confessionally independent scholars who have carried on the debate among themselves; in this debate some answer affirmatively the question whether Peter made a stay in Rome, while others deny it.[3] In the following pages we shall first sketch briefly the history of the problem, and then investigate whether it is possible to derive from the archaeological and literary witnesses to which appeal is made at least indirect indications of a Roman stay of our apostle.

2. *History of the Debate Whether Peter Resided in Rome*

The question was first raised in the Middle Ages by Christians for whom the Bible was the sole norm, the Waldensians. We can understand why it was they who did so. As we have seen, the New Testament nowhere tells us that Peter came to the chief city of the

---

[1] We may add that more or less cautious doubts have been expressed from time to time even by Roman Catholic scholars. Ellendorf goes the furthest in this sense, in *Ist Petrus in Rom und Bischof der römischen Kirche gewesen?*, 1941 (cited by F. Chr. Baur, *Paulus*, 2nd ed., 1867, Vol. II, p. 322; Eng. Tr., *Paul*, Vol. II, 1875, p. 296).

[2] See below, p. 232.

[3] For the earlier history of the problem I refer to K. Heussi, *War Petrus in Rom?*, 1936, pp. 8 ff., and F. Chr. Baur, *Paulus*, 1845, pp. 671 ff.; 2nd ed., 1867, Vol. II, pp. 316 ff. (Eng. Tr., *Paul*, Vol. II, 1875, pp. 291 ff.)

Empire and stayed there. For the Waldensians, the silence of the
Bible was quite decisive.[4] Later, in the year 1326, Marsilius of Padua,
in his *Defensor Pacis*, expresses cautious doubts as to whether Peter
was ever in Rome. He, too, appeals to the fact that from the sacred
Scriptures nothing can be proved concerning this. Perhaps—but
only perhaps— he did come to Rome and was bishop there; that
he held such a position can be asserted with certainty only for
Antioch.

For the next two hundred years we hear nothing of a real attack
upon the tradition. Not until 1519–1520 does an anonymous author
write an essay contending "that the apostle Peter was never in
Rome."[5] For him, too, as for the Waldensians, the chief argument
is the silence of the sacred Scripture. He is not content to express
doubts; like them, he goes on to direct denial. Sebastian Franck
echoes his thesis and his line of argument.[6] It might seem striking,
on the contrary, that the Reformers took no special interest in this
problem. In their fight against the Pope they did not build upon this
comfortable argument. This is the more noteworthy since they
plainly had at least a trace of doubt concerning the stay of Peter at
Rome.[7] Thus Luther writes: "There are some scholars who say that
Peter never came to Rome. And it is said to be difficult for the Pope
to defend himself against such scholars. I will not here be judge of the
question whether Peter was there or not. St. Paul alone was certainly
there, as Luke writes in The Book of Acts and Paul himself in his
letters; he can very well have instituted the Church and the bishops
at Rome."[8] He further reports that in Rome he saw and heard that
one did not know the graves of Peter and Paul.[9] But he adds: "And
the apostles St. Peter and St. Paul may then lie in Rome or not; that

---

[4] Concerning the opposition by the Waldensians see P. Moneta of Cremona
O. P., *Adversus Catharos et Waldenses*, V, 2, Rome, 1743, p. 411.

[5] His pseudonym is Ulricus Venelus Minhoniensis. See Melchior Goldast,
Monarchia S. Romani Imperii, Vol. III, 1613, where the tract is printed on
pp. 1–16.

[6] See H. Oncken, "Sebastian Franck als Historiker" (*Historische Zeitschrift*, 1899,
p. 412).

[7] In any case it is incorrect when J. Zeiller, *L'Eglise primitive* (*Histoire de l'Eglise*,
Vol. I, 1946 ed., p. 227; Eng. Tr., *History of the Primitive Church*, Vol. I, 1942,
p. 233) writes that the denial of the Roman residence of Peter arose in the
time of the Reformation, as a part of the Protestant polemic against the papal
primacy.

[8] M. Luther, *Wider das Papsttum vom Teufel gestiftet*, 1545 (Weimar edition, 54),
cited from E. Mülhaupt, *Luthers Evangelien-Auslegung*, 1947, Vol. II, p. 551.

[9] See below, p. 132.

makes no difference."[10] The Protestant church historian from the
second half of the sixteenth century, Flacius Illyricus, writes somewhat cautiously in 1554 that it is "not absolutely certain" that Peter
was in Rome,[11] while later in his great work, the Magdeburg
Centuries, he speaks of the martyrdom of Peter and Paul in Rome.[12]
A scientifically grounded challenge to the Roman tradition about
Peter is offered only at the end of the seventeenth century, by the
Reformed scholar Friedrich Spanheim.[13] His arguments are in part
worthy of note even today. In spite of his critical spirit, however, the
eighteenth century took no great interest in this problem. Gibbon,
in his great History of the Decline and Fall of the Roman Empire,[14] does
indeed question whether any or the disciples of Jesus became a martyr
outside of Palestine. In the year 1804 the Göttingen scholar in ancient
philology, J. G. Eichhorn, champions the view that the stay and
martyrdom of Peter at Rome were not historical events, but were
erroneously deduced from 1 Peter 5:13.[15] F. Schleiermacher, in his
lectures concerning church history, numbers himself among those
who "doubt the entire account of Peter's stay in Rome."[16] Likewise,
W. M. de Wette, in his Introduction to the New Testament,[17] declares
that the alleged fact, already improbable in itself, is a "saga." The
majority of the Protestant theologians at the beginning of the nineteenth century, however, affirm the tradition of the Roman stay of
Peter. Chief among them are the two great church historians A.
Neander and J. Gieseler. The former describes the denial of the
tradition as "hyper-criticism,"[18] the latter as an expression of
"partisan polemic."[19] So much the more impressive was the attack

[10] He further writes in the same passage (Mülhaupt, p. 552): "They lie and invent
hundreds and thousands of things about St. Peter himself, so that the idea has
occurred to me that neither St. Peter nor St. Paul laid the first stone of the Church
of Rome. Perhaps a disciple of the apostles came from Jerusalem or Antioch to
Rome . . ."

[11] Historia certaminum inter Romanos Episcopos etc., de primatu seu potestate papae bona
fide ex authenticis monumentis collata, p. 267.

[12] Centuries, I, Book II, pp. 28 and 527.

[13] Dissertatio de ficta profectione Petri apostoli in urbem Romam deque non una traditionis
origine. See Works, II, 1703, Col. 331 ff.

[14] History of the Decline and Fall of the Roman Empire, 1776 ff.

[15] Einleitung in das neue Testament, Vol. I, 1804, pp. 554 f. See also Vol. III, 1812,
pp. 603 f.

[16] Complete Works, Section One, Vol. XI, edited by E. Bonnell, 1840, p. 69.

[17] Einleitung in das N. T., p. 314.

[18] Geschichte der christlichen Religion und Kirche, Vol. I, 1826, p. 317.

[19] Lehrbuch der Kirchengeschichte, Vol. I, 2nd ed., 1827, p. 189.

which the Tübingen theologian F. Chr. Baur undertook against the tradition in 1831, in connection with his Hegel-inspired view of Primitive Christianity.[20] The ensuing discussion, however, was burdened by debate over this exaggeration of the opposition between Jewish Christianity and Gentile Christianity. The thesis of Baur, therefore, was almost universally rejected.

In the following period the denial of the Roman tradition about Peter was almost universally abandoned. A man like Ernest Renan assumed as a fact Peter's stay in Rome, and in the year 1897 it was the critical Protestant theologian and historian A. Harnack who wrote the notable sentence that the denial of the Roman stay of Peter is "an error which today is clear to every scholar who is not blind." So one had the impression that the tradition was finally confirmed. Harnack was of the opinion that "the martyr death of Peter at Rome was once contested by reason of tendentious Protestant prejudices, and then by reason of tendentious critical prejudices."[21] Although for most persons the question appeared settled, it was raised anew by the confessionally independent historian Ch. Guignebert in 1909, in his book on "The Primacy of Peter and the Coming of Peter to Rome."[22] He answered the question in the negative. In Germany C. Erbes and in Switzerland P. W. Schmiedel likewise opposed Harnack's conclusion.[23]

However, it seemed again that the last word had been spoken on the side of Harnack and the Roman Catholic tradition when Harnack's successor, the Protestant theologian H. Lietzmann, published in 1915 his important book, *Petrus und Paulus in Rom* (second ed., 1927). Lietzmann uses his archaeological and especially his wide liturgical knowledge to illuminate the question. He comes to the conclusion that the testimony from the year 170 concerning the graves

[20] "Die Christuspartei in der Korinthischen Gemeinde, der Gegensatz des petrinischen und paulinischen Christentums in der ältesten Kirche, der Apostel Petrus in Rom" (*Tübinger Zeitschrift für Theologie*, 1831, pp. 137 ff.). See also*Paulus, der Apostel Jesu Christi*, 1845, pp. 212 ff.

[21] *Die Chronologie der altchristlichen Literatur bis Eusebius*, Vol. I, 1897, p. 244, note 2.

[22] *La Primauté de Pierre et la venue de Pierre à Rome.*

[23] C. Erbes, "Petrus nicht in Rom, sondern in Jerusalem gestorben" (*Zeitschrift für Kirchengeschichte*, 1901, pp. 1 ff., 161 ff.). In his publications concerning the date of the death of the apostles Paul and Peter (*Texte und Untersuchungen*, 1899) and concerning the graves of the Apostles in Rome (*Zeitschrift für Kirchengeschichte*, 1924, pp. 38 ff.), Erbes is much more reserved in his judgment concerning the question of the Roman stay of Peter. P. W. Schmiedel's view is found in "War der Apostel Petrus in Rom?" (*Protestantische Monatshefte*, 1909, pp. 270 ff.); also in Th. K. Cheyne's *Encyclopaedia Biblica*, IV, pp. 459 ff.

of the two apostles at Rome must be correct. That is, the two apostles were actually buried in the two places in Rome which today are reverenced as their graves, Peter at the Vatican, Paul on the road to Ostia.

Nevertheless, this did not put an end to the dispute. It has been continued, chiefly among Protestant theologians, in connection with Lietzmann's book. In the year 1930 appeared my own essay concerning First Clement, ch. 5.[24] In it I conclude, from what we derive by inference from this text concerning the circumstances of the two martyrdoms of Peter and Paul, that Rome was the place of their martyrdom. E. Molland agreed with me,[25] and with the addition of some supplementary points A. Fridrichsen also accepted my interpretation.[26]

Lietzmann's conclusion, however, was opposed by Adolf Bauer, in the series of "Vienna Studies,"[27] by Ch. Guignebert,[28] and further by H. Dannenbauer.[29] The latter actually formulated the result of his investigation in these words: "Every little village in Palestine can claim with greater justification than can the imperial capital to be the place of Peter's death." To the opponents of the Lietzmann thesis belong further J. Haller[30] and E. T. Merrill,[31] while G. Krüger[32] championed the traditional thesis, chiefly on the basis of First Clement.

The chief arguments of the opponents of the tradition were gathered up in 1936 by Karl Heussi in the brochure he directed against Lietzmann, *War Petrus in Rom?* ("Was Peter Ever in Rome?"). This writing, which announced as its reliable result that "Peter never set foot in the city on the Tiber," aroused great interest. It called Lietzmann himself to the field of battle with a reply, "Peter:

---

[24] O. Cullmann, "Les causes de la mort de Pierre et de Paul d'après le témoignage de Clément Romain" (*Revue d'Histoire et de Philosophie Religieuses*, 1930, pp. 294 ff.).

[25] *Theologische Literaturzeitung*, 1937, columns 439 ff. There is also given here a good discussion of the controversy between Lietzmann and Heussi.

[26] "Propter invidiam. Note sur I. Clém. V" (*Eranos Rudbergianus*, 1946, pp. 161 ff.).

[27] "Die Legende von dem Martyrium des Petrus und Paulus in Rom" (*Zeitschrift für klassische Philologie*, 1916, pp. 270 ff.).

[28] "La sépulture de Pierre" (*Revue historique*, 1931, pp. 225 ff.).

[29] "Die römische Petruslegende" (*Historische Zeitschrift*, 1932, pp. 239 ff.); "Nochmals die römische Petruslegende" (*Historische Zeitschrift*, 1931, pp. 81 ff.).

[30] *Das Papsttum*, Vol. I, 2nd ed., 1950, pp. 1 ff., 472 ff. (polemic in a disagreeable and irritated tone).

[31] *Essays in Early Christian History*, 1924, pp. 267 ff.

[32] "Petrus in Rom" (*ZNW*, 1932, pp. 301 ff.).

Roman Martyr" (1936).[33] In the following years Heussi attempted again to defend his thesis that the assertion of the martyrdom of Peter at Rome is nothing but a legend.[34]

The war did not completely stop the discussion. Lietzmann, who died in 1942, took no further part. K. Heussi, however, has continued even into recent years to publish a series of articles which defend his position with vigour and with partly new arguments.[35] In 1942 M. Dibelius published an essay concerning "Rome and the Christians in the first century."[36] In it he too concerns himself chiefly with the most important indirect witness for the martyrdom of Peter, First Clement, ch. 5. He sides with Lietzmann, but seeks to explain the brevity of the notice chiefly by the literary character of the author.

In addition we should mention particularly the various studies which the Old Catholic scholar Katzenmayer published, during and after the war, in the *Internationale Kirchliche Zeitschrift*. In them he seeks in his own peculiar way to establish that both the Roman stay, which he assumes, and the death of Peter occurred long before the Neronian persecution, in the year 55.[37]

Since the end of the war the chief interest has focused on the excavations under the Church of St. Peter in Rome. Since, as we shall see, the results were kept an official secret much too long, while it

[33] "Petrus römischer Märtyrer" (*Sitzungsbericht der Berliner Akademie der Wissenschaften*, 1936, pp. 392 ff.).

[34] "War Petrus wirklich römischer Märtyrer?" (*Christliche Welt*, 1937, columns 161 ff.); *Neues zur Petrusfrage*, 1939. On the whole controversy between Heussi and Lietzmann, see also R. Draguet, *Revue d'Histoire ecclésiastique*, 1938, pp. 88 ff.

[35] *Deutsches Pfarrerblatt*, 1949, p. 82: "Das Grab des Petrus;" *ib.*, p. 301: " 'Papst' Anenkletus I. und die Memoria Petri auf dem Vatikan;" *ib.*, p. 420: "Die Nachfolge des Petrus;" *ib.*, p. 501: "Der Stand der Frage nach dem römischen Aufenthalt des Petrus"; *Theologische Literaturzeitung*, 1952, pp. 67 ff.: "Gal. 2 und der Lebensausgang der jerusalemischen Urapostel."

[36] "Rom und die Christen im 1. Jahrhundert" (*Sitzungsbericht der Heidelberger Akademie der Wissenschaften, Philologisch-historische Klasse*, 1942.

[37] There appeared even before the war: "Zur Frage, ob Petrus in Rom war," 1938, pp. 129 ff.; "Das Todesjahr des Petrus," 1939, pp. 85 ff. We have already mentioned, p. 54, note 55, the essay, "War Petrus in Korinth?" (1943, pp. 20 ff.). See also "Die Schicksale des Petrus von seinem Aufenthalt in Korinth bis zu seinem Märtyrertod", 1944, pp. 145 ff.; "Die Beziehungen des Petrus zur Urkirche von Jerusalem und zu Antiochien," 1945, pp. 116 ff. In further articles in the same journal the author seeks to prove that a primacy of Rome or of its bishop is lacking until the end of the third century. Unfortunately, in the essays that are of interest to us in our study, the argument is often somewhat forced, and at times is built on arguments from silence.

was officially announced by the Pope that the grave of Peter had been found, the study of the literary sources has become somewhat hesitant in recent years. Scholars obviously desired to await the publication of the results of the excavations.[38]

The general tendency, even with regard to the literary witnesses, seems indeed to be moving in the direction of accepting the Roman stay of Peter. C. T. Craig expresses himself in favour of it in his presentation of Primitive Christianity.[39] So do H. von Campenhausen[40] and C. King.[41] M. Goguel, in his great book on the rise of Christianity,[42] reaches no decision, but rather inclines to strong scepticism toward the traditional theory.[43] As the latest study we mention the investigation by the Danish scholar, J. Munck, *Petrus und Paulus in der Offenbarung Johannis* ("Peter and Paul in the Book of Revelation," 1950); he makes the interesting attempt to find in Revelation 11:3-13 the earliest testimony to the martyr death of the two apostles at Rome.

3. The Literary Sources

What *sources* are to be considered in our study of the question of the Roman residence and martyrdom of Peter? The earliest Christian writings, the *letters of Paul*, contain no direct or indirect data whatever concerning a stay of Peter in Rome or concerning his death. At the time when Paul writes I Corinthians, Peter is making missionary journeys in company with his wife (I Cor. 9:5). That is all we hear in the letters of Paul concerning this period of Peter's life.

---

[38] On the Roman Catholic side, however, interest in I Clement, ch. 5, has continued: M. Schuler, "Klemens von Rom und Petrus in Rom" (*Trierer Theologische Studien*, I, 1941, pp. 94 ff.); L. Sanders, *L'hellénisme de S. Clément de Rome et le paulinisme*, 1943 (see below, pp. 98 f.); O. Perler, "Ignatius von Antiochien und die römische Christusgemeinde" (*Divus Thomas*, 1944, pp. 442 ff.); St. Schmutz, "Petrus war dennoch in Rom" (*Benediktinische Monatsschrift*, 1946, pp. 122 ff.); B. Altaner, "Neues zum Verständnis von I Clem. 5, 1-6, 2" (*Historisches Jahrbuch*, 1949, pp. 25 ff.).

[39] *The Beginning of Christianity*, 1943, p. 266.

[40] *Verkündigung und Forschung*, 1946-47, p. 230.

[41] "The Outlines of New Testament Chronology" (*Church Quarterly Review*, 1945, p. 149).

[42] *L'Eglise primitive*, 1947, pp. 203 ff. (a good presentation of the problem).

[43] A similar scepticism, although in its final result rather favourable to the acceptance of a late arrival of Peter in Rome and his martyrdom there, is represented by G. Miegge in his popularly written but quite instructive little writing, *Pietro a Roma* (n. d.).

From the mere fact of this silence we cannot infer that a Roman stay by Peter or his martyrdom there is excluded. The failure of the letters of Paul to report his *death* is no cause for wonder; we scarcely can assume that Peter died so long before Paul[44] that the latter could have spoken of it explicitly or by implication in a letter, even had he had occasion to do so. The situation is different with regard to the *stay* of Peter in Rome. There is, to be sure, no *a priori* necessity to claim that Paul must have spoken of this fact. Nevertheless, we possess from him a letter addressed to the Roman church itself, and although we must be cautious in using so-called arguments from silence, yet it must be said that if Peter were actually sojourning at the time in the church of the capital city, it would be astonishing for Paul not to refer to him at all in this letter, which greets by name numerous Roman Christians.[45]

The assertion that he purposely refrained from speaking of Peter, because the latter by his Judaizing preaching had worked in Rome in a way contrary to the teaching that Paul set forth in his letter to the Romans, shatters on the already established fact that Peter cannot be called a mere Judaizer; in reality, he stood much closer to the theology of Paul than to that of James.[46] The opposition that Romans expresses to Judaizing teachings no more presupposes a stay of Peter in Rome than does the anti-Judaizing polemic of the letters to Corinth or Galatia become intelligible only on the supposition of a personal stay of Peter in Corinth or in Galatia—although as far as

[44] K. Heussi, indeed, thinks that Peter died as early as the year 55. He holds that when Paul wrote Galatians, Peter was no longer alive (Gal. 2:6: "whoever they *were*"); *Theologische Literaturzeitung*, 1952, pp. 67 ff. H. Katzenmayer (see above, p. 76) also accepts the early date of 55 as the year of Peter's death.

[45] Even if ch. 16 should not belong to Romans, the silence concerning Peter in the other chapters would still be amazing. (T. W. Manson gives noteworthy new arguments—especially in the light of papyrus manuscript P[46], known since 1935—in favour of the old hypothesis that ch. 16 went to Ephesus; see his essay, "St. Paul's Letter to the Romans—and Others," in *Bulletin of the John Rylands Library*, 1948, pp. 3 ff.). Nor can this silence be explained by the hypothesis of Graber (see above, p. 38).

[46] H. Lietzmann, "Zwei Notizen zu Paulus" (*Sitzungsbericht der Berliner Akademie der Wissenschaften*, 1930, No. 8), has proposed the probably untenable thesis that Paul wrote Romans to oppose the Jewish Christian propaganda carried to Rome by Peter, and so to avert the danger that his gospel might find closed doors at the outset. E. Hirsch, "Petrus und Paulus" (*ZNW*, 1930, p. 63), makes extensive concessions to this thesis, but nevertheless reacts against Lietzmann's presentation, which would make of Peter a full-fledged Judaizer. In so doing Hirsch opposes at the same time Ed. Meyer's hypothesis, which sees Peter behind the false teachers in Galatia.

Corinth and Galatia are concerned we have not excluded the possibility that Peter at an earlier time made a stay in these regions.[47] In any case, we are forced to deny that Peter was present in the Roman church *at the time when Paul wrote Romans to them*; otherwise he could not possibly have been omitted from the list of the persons addressed in this letter.

It still does not follow, be it noted, that the tradition concerning the stay and martyrdom of Peter at Rome is therefore to be entirely rejected; the conclusion applies only to the time of writing of Paul's letter to Rome. Theoretically, Peter could have been in Rome prior to the sending of Paul's letter; he could then have left the capital city, and only later have returned there and suffered martyrdom. Nevertheless, this is not probable.[48] In any case, Paul's writing forces us in our study to the following conclusion: *at the time when Paul wrote his letter to Rome, Peter was not there*; if he came there at all, this can only have happened either before or, more likely, after that time.

For any stay of Peter in Rome, however, Romans 15:20 comes indirectly into consideration. We have already seen[49] that Paul here excuses himself for coming to a church which he has not founded. Such a step he previously has avoided; he probably regarded this, in keeping with the spirit of the Jerusalem agreement, as irreconcilable with his apostolic honour. In view of this fact, and in connection with what we have concluded from Galatians 2:9, we probably are justified in concluding that the parallel Jewish Christian mission of the Jerusalem group regarded the Roman church as their field, since this church, which probably arose apart from the missionary programme, had an original membership of Jewish Christians.[50] Since the Jewish population of Rome was then large—it is estimated at 30,000 to 40,000[51]—such an original membership may certainly be assumed. This is especially convincing when we consider that when Paul writes his letter to Rome, the Jewish Christians are quite strongly represented in the Roman church along with the Gentile

---

[47] See above, p. 55.

[48] C. Cecchelli, *Gli apostoli a Roma*, 1938, p. 64, also declares this impossible.

[49] See above, p. 45.

[50] If the Jews from Rome who, according to Acts 2:10, were present at Pentecost in Jerusalem, brought the gospel to the capital city, this too points to Jewish Christian origin. So F. J. Foakes-Jackson, *Peter: Prince of Apostles*, 1927, p. 196.

[51] J. Juster, *Les Juifs dans l'empire romain*, 1914, pp. 209 f., actually speaks of 50,000 to 60,000.

Christians.[52] Of course, we dare not conclude with finality from this fact that Peter came to Rome or even founded that church. But we must ask whether in this case it is not probable that in his capacity as leader of the Jewish Christian Jerusalem-based mission, Peter himself did not at some time come to this church, founded as it was by Jewish Christians and still containing a strong Jewish Christian membership. Such a visit is especially likely since it was the capital city which was in question. If there was a Jewish Christian mission and if Peter was entrusted with it, then his coming to Rome, while not proved by these facts, is an assumption strongly suggested, especially if at a certain time traces of internal difficulties appear.[53]

Nothing more can be derived from the letters of Paul in either a positive or a negative sense.

*　*　*

If anywhere in our ancient sources, we should expect a report concerning the end of Peter's life in *The Book of Acts*. As a matter of fact, however, it does not contain even the slightest indirect allusion to a stay of this apostle in Rome. For as we have seen, it is arbitrary to understand the notice in ch. 12:17 as such an allusion.[54] It must be conceded at the outset that the silence of The Book of Acts constitutes a minus for the traditional view, inasmuch as thereby one of the earliest sources that could attest the tradition fails us. Nothing more, however, may be concluded from this silence; it is not permissible to go further and see in it any support for the attempt to prove impossible the fact that tradition asserts. To be sure, those whom we mentioned, in our survey of the history of the problem, as challengers of the stay of Peter at Rome take particular pleasure in citing this silence to establish their thesis.[55]

It is indeed striking that a "history of the apostles," in whose first part Peter plays so large a role, contains no word about the *end of his life*. Doubtless *this* notable fact calls for some explanation. As to the question, however, whether or not Peter was in Rome we can

---

52 M. J. Lagrange, *Epître aux Romains*, pp. xxix f., even considers it the chief tendency of the letter to instruct the Gentile Christians concerning the role of Judaism in redemptive history and to warn them against any contempt for the Jewish Christians.

53 See below, pp. 106 f.　　　　　54 See above, pp. 37 ff.

55 K. Heussi, to be sure, does not belong in this group. For he rightly admits (*War Petrus in Rom?*, pp. 17 ff.) that from the evidence in The Acts one cannot reach a certain conclusion.

draw no conclusion of any kind from this silence. For The Acts not only says nothing concerning the *Roman* stay of Peter we now are discussing; it is silent concerning his entire missionary activity, which by the evidence of I Corinthians 9:5 is an established fact, and also concerning his death.

There is the additional fact that nothing is reported concerning the martyr death of Paul, which nevertheless is not disputed. The Book of Acts ends abruptly with the mention of Paul's arrival at Rome and the remark that he remained there two years. In view of the detail with which the journeys of Paul are described in the closing chapters, this is much stranger than the silence concerning Peter. It calls even more urgently for an explanation. However, no matter what solutions have previously been given for the riddle of the abrupt ending of The Book of Acts, the different answers leave open the question as to whether or not Peter was in Rome.

These answers assume either that the author *knew nothing* concerning the unreported end of Paul's life—and probably also of Peter's—or that *he did not want to tell of it.* In the former case one must presuppose that he completed his book immediately after the close of the two years that followed Paul's arrival in Rome. In that case there would be the possibility—but only the possibility—that Peter reached Rome later and, like Paul, suffered martyrdom there.

The assumption, however, that the author completed his work exactly two years after the arrival of Paul in Rome is not probable. A long series of reasons that need not here be cited favour the view that the book was written only later, after the Neronian persecution and after the death of Peter and Paul. In this case we probably must assume that the author was as well informed concerning the end of Peter's life as concerning that of Paul. That he possessed no information about it is scarcely possible. There remains then only the explanation that he *chose* not to tell anything about it. The reason for this could be literary in character. Often, indeed, it actually is assumed that he chose to extend this book only to this point; he stopped with the arrival of Paul at Rome, whether he planned a third book[56] or not.[57] Or the reason was of theological character; on

[56] So Th. Zahn, *Einleitung in das Neue Testament*, 4th ed., 1924, pp. 16 ff., 861 f. (see Eng. Tr., *Introduction to the New Testament*, 2nd ed., 1917, Vol. III, pp. 57 ff.), and M. Goguel, *Introduction au Nouveau Testament*, Vol. III, 1922, *Le livre des Actes*, p. 340.

[57] W. Michaelis, *Einleitung in das Neue Testament*, 1946, p. 133, considers the possibility that the author could so limit his goal because his readers had been informed concerning the further course of events.

this view, to have told of these unreported events would in some way have been out of keeping with the theological aim of the book. These cases also permit no *a priori* conclusions either for or against the stay and martyrdom of Peter in Rome. For in principle both possibilities remain open: either that Peter after those two years (or possibly even earlier[58]) died in Rome as a martyr, or that after this time (possibly even earlier) he ended his life elsewhere.

Only if the further course of this investigation should prove that the very occurrence of the event in Rome gave the author a special theological reason for not mentioning the end of Peter's life—only then could his silence possibly be considered as indirect confirmation of the assumption that Peter suffered martyrdom in Rome. As a matter of fact, I shall at least propose such a hypothesis.[59] But this will be possible only by drawing upon other texts. For the time being we must say that The Book of Acts deserves mention in our study only to establish the fact that in its case one of our oldest sources fails to help us in the question as to Peter the Martyr.

Can we learn something positive from the letters that appear in the New Testament as *letters of Peter*? Whether they bear his name rightly or wrongly is of no importance for our present purpose; even if an unknown author put them under the authority of Peter, it is important to learn whether he knew that Peter was in Rome and whether accordingly he carried through the fiction of representing himself as present in Rome.

The Second Epistle of Peter contains no reference of any kind to Rome. It only refers to the martyrdom of Peter in ch. 1:14: "I know that the striking of my tent will come soon, as our Lord Jesus Christ has revealed to me." This writing, however, like the later apocryphal Petrine literature, does not require consideration here. This is primarily because, in the judgment of the great majority of scholars, it is the latest document included in the New Testament. It thus comes from a later period—at the earliest from the middle of the second century—when the tradition concerning the Roman stay of Peter begins to appear elsewhere as well. We arc seeking here only the early witnesses.

Among them The First Epistle of Peter calls for mention. At the end of its final chapter stands a greeting. Concerning this greeting it

[58] *A priori*, indeed, it is not absolutely necessary to assume with regard to Peter the same reasons for silence that one does with reference to the death of Paul.
[59] See below, pp. 89 ff., 103 f.

is usually assumed that whether the writing is genuine or not, it presupposes the stay of Peter in Rome: "The fellow-elect (Church) in Babylon greets you, and so does Mark my son" (I Pet. 5:13).

Even this statement, to be sure, yields no absolute certainty. It seems to me far the most probable explanation that Babylon is a cryptic name for Rome. For if the author writes from Rome, his reason for substituting Babylon for Rome may very well have been similar to that which the author of the Apocalypse of John had. Either he wishes to avoid it out of fear of the Roman authorities, or more probably, he used the term Babylon because in his day that city, which with all that it meant for the people of Israel had been so important in Old Testament prophecy, had become a theological concept which could be applied especially well to Rome.[60]

We know indeed from ancient Christian literature how popular this typological use of geographical names was. We may think, for example, of Galatians 4:26, where the Church is called the "Jerusalem that is above," or of Hebrews 12:22, which speaks of the "heavenly Jerusalem." So for the author of I Peter "Babylon," in connection with the theological ideas that he held, may be a term meaning "exile," just as in ch. 2:11 (see also ch. 1:1) he has called the readers "aliens and sojourners." At the same time, however, it is also an expression of the capital city's power-linked corruption; this meaning connects with the Old Testament prophetic tradition, for example, Isaiah 43:14 and Jeremiah, chs. 50 and 51.[61] Since the greeting must have a definite city in mind, there could have been in the time of the writer no other place but Rome to which this figurative meaning of the ancient Babylon was applied.

The presupposition for this conclusion, of course, is that we do have here a figurative use of the word. This conclusion is rendered

[60] K. Heussi, *War Petrus in Rom?*, p. 38, does not see the reason for such a hide-and-seek game. But for the author of the Apocalypse of John it is clear that he was *unwilling* to name Rome. Moreover, the chapter that Heussi devotes to our passage is unsatisfactory; he discusses it only on the presupposition that I Clement, ch. 5, already proves with finality that Peter was not in Rome. It will not do, however, to interpret I Peter 5:13 on the basis of this conclusion, which we shall see is not at all assured, instead of considering the source in itself. On I Pet. 5:13, see further H. Windisch, *Die katholischen Briefe*, 3rd ed., 1951, revised by Herbert Preisker, p. 82; further, A. Schlatter, *Geschichte der ersten Christenheit*, 1926, pp. 299 ff., and B. W. Bacon, *Is Mark a Roman Gospel?*, 1919, pp. 23 ff. See also the article by G. Kuhn on "Babylon" in *Theologisches Wörterbuch zum Neuen Testament*, Vol. I, pp. 512 ff.

[61] This has been pointed out especially by E. G. Selwyn, *The First Epistle of St. Peter*, 1949, pp. 303 ff.

likely by the fact that such a use, with reference to Rome itself, is certainly attested in other writings. It occurs above all in the Apocalypse of John, where there can be no doubt that in chs. 14:8; 16:19; 17:5 ff.; 18:2 ff. Rome is meant by "Babylon." Perhaps the expression "Sodom and Egypt" in Revelation 11:8 is likewise a cryptic name for Rome.[62] We further find "Babylon" as a figurative designation for Rome in the pseudepigraphic late Jewish literature. It appears, for example in the Sibylline Oracles V, 159, where it is said: "The deep sea will burn, and so will Babylon itself and the land of Italy"; in the Apocalypse of Baruch 11:1; and in Fourth Esdras 3:1 ff., 28, 31.[63] Both in the Apocalypse of John and in the late Jewish texts, of course, we are dealing with writings which can hardly be earlier than our First Episle of Peter.[64] Nevertheless, they belong to approximately the same period.[65] In addition, the word "mystery," which in Revelation 17:5 refers to the saying concerning Babylon-Rome, appears to indicate that this covert manner of expression was already known to Christians.[66] For all these reasons, the interpretation that the word "Babylon" in I Peter 5:13 refers to Rome is doubtless the most natural, if we approach the passage without prejudice and without first taking into account the controversy concerning Peter's stay in Rome. Papias already explained the verse in this way.[67]

It must be said, however, that it is not completely certain that the

[62] So J. Munck, *Petrus und Paulus in der Offenbarung Johannis*, 1950, pp. 30 ff., in opposition to the majority of interpreters, who think they find in the expression a reference to Jerusalem.

[63] See on this point H. Fuchs, *Der geistige Widerstand gegen Rom*, 1938. The rabbinic passages are given in Strack-Billerbeck, *Kommentar zum Neuen Testament*, Vol. III, p. 816.

[64] E. G. Selwyn, *op. cit.*, pp. 243 and 303, believes that our passage contains the first witness to this usage of the word Babylon = Rome; he finds that usage in this passage.

[65] In the Church Fathers this use of the word Babylon is common; it occurs in Tertullian, *Adversus Judaeos*, 9; *Adversus Marcionem*, 3, 13, and is especially favoured by Origen and Augustine. See on this point H. Fuchs, *Der geistige Widerstand gegen Rom*, 1938, pp. 74 f., and B. Altaner, Article on "Babylon" in *Reallexikon für Antike und Christentum*, columns 1131 ff. It should also be mentioned that two minuscule manuscripts have replaced the word Babylon by Rome in their text. (See Th. Zahn, *Einleitung ins Neue Testament*, 3rd ed., Vol. II, pp. 17 ff.; cf. Eng. Tr., *Introduction to the New Testament*, 2nd ed., Vol. II, pp. 158 ff.).

[66] So E. G. Selwyn, *op. cit.*, p. 243.

[67] Eusebius, *Ecclesiastical History*, II, 15, 2. The explanation is frequently found in later times. See Jerome, *De viris illustribus*, 8.

expression *must* here be understood in a figurative way. We cannot fully exclude the possibility that the long famous ancient *Mesopotamian* city of Babylon was really meant. We know from Josephus[68] and from Philo[69] that this place was still inhabited in the New Testament period, although it had lost all importance, and according to another notice of Josephus that refers to the middle of the first century, the Jews had left the place to settle in the city Seleucia,[70] which in the meantime had come to outrank the ancient Babylon. So it has actually been assumed that on one of his missionary journeys Peter came to Babylon in Mesopotamia, or if not into the city itself, at least into the region of Babylonia, and wrote our letter[71] from there. One cannot exclude this possibility. Nevertheless, it is not probable, and it is not supported by the later Christian tradition, which knows nothing of a missionary work of Peter in these regions. To them it brings only the apostle Thomas. To this we must add the fact that the Babylonian Talmud attests the presence of Christians in this region only from the third century on.

The assumption that the author who ascribed the letter to Peter knew nothing definite concerning the places where the apostle worked, and therefore chose the nebulous distant Babylon,[72] finds no support in fact. It is improbable also because of the explicit mention of Mark.

Theoretically still another Babylon might be considered. This is the military camp in *Egypt*, near the modern Cairo. It is mentioned by Strabo[73] and Josephus.[74] One can scarcely accept, however, the misguided idea that I Peter 5:13 refers to this rather obscure Babylon. The only possible support for this view is the fact that the apocryphal Gospel of Peter and the Apocalypse of Peter are of Egyptian origin.

The other cities which have been proposed, Jerusalem[75] or even Joppa,[76] have still less claim to serious consideration. It is impossible

[68] *Antiquities*, XV, 2, 2.   [69] *Legatio ad Caium*, 282, p. 587.

[70] Josephus, *Antiquities*, XVIII, 9, 8. See on this point Th. Zahn, *Einleitung ins N. T.*, Vol. II, 2nd ed., 1900, pp. 17 ff. (Eng. Tr. of 3rd ed., see note 65 above); and H. Windisch, *Die katholischen Briefe (Handbuch zum Neuen Testament*, herausgegeben von G. Bornkamm), 3rd ed., revised by H. Preisker, 1951, p. 82.

[71] A. Schlatter, *Geschichte der ersten Christenheit*, 1926, p. 299, and others; in earlier times, Erasmus. It is often argued that the rather friendly attitude of the letter towards the State speaks against the identification of Rome and Babylon. (See J. Haller, *Das Papsttum*, Vol. I, 1951, p. 477.)

[72] K. Heussi, *op. cit.*, p. 38, note 6.

[73] XVII, 30, p. 807.   [74] II, 15, 1.

[75] A. Harnack, *Chronologie der altchristlichen Literatur bis Eusebius*, 1897, p. 459.

[76] Syncellus ad a. m. 5540 (ed. Bonn 627), probably in view of Acts 9:36 ff.

to explain how they could have been designated by the name "Babylon." The passage in Revelation 11:8, concerning the city which "spiritually is called Sodom and Egypt," has been cited as an analogy at least for Jerusalem. But as we have already mentioned, this verse cannot be taken as a certain reference to Jerusalem; it possibly refers to Rome.[77] It is pure fantasy to assume, on the basis that Clement of Alexandria declares The Second Epistle of John to have been addressed to a certain Babylonia, that the reference here is to a highly esteemed lady named Babylonia, who belonged to a church in Asia Minor.[78]

We thus reach the conclusion that First Peter, whether genuine or not, quite probably means by its place reference "Babylon" the city of Rome. It thereby presupposes a stay of Peter in Rome, although another interpretation of this reference is not entirely excluded.

Another passage from the same First Epistle of Peter (ch. 5:1) is still to be mentioned. However, it deals only with the other question, whether Peter died as a martyr. The author here speaks of himself as a "witness of the sufferings of Christ and a partaker of the glory soon to be revealed." This expression also is not unequivocal. Yet it probably justifies us in assuming that the author, whether Peter or someone else, refers to a sharing in Christ's sufferings, including his death. For the witness here mentioned probably refers not only to something once seen and now proclaimed, but in keeping with the demonstrably early usage of the Greek word, refers to a witness in act.[79]

In the same connection we still must mention, of the New Testament books that should be considered in our study, *The Gospel of John*. Of especial importance is ch. 21:18 ff.: "As long as you were

---

[77] See J. Munck, *op. cit.*, pp. 30 ff.

[78] This proposal comes from K. Heussi, *op. cit.*, p. 39, note 6, but he himself puts a question mark after it.

[79] So also R. Knopf, *Die Briefe Petri und Judä*, 1912, p. 188; H. Windisch—H. Preisker, *Die katholischen Briefe*, 3rd ed., 1951, p. 79; also K. Heussi himself: *War Petrus in Rom?*, p. 31, note 21; likewise H. Lietzmann, "Petrus römischer Märtyrer" (*Sitzungsbericht der Berliner Akademie der Wissenschaften*, 1936, p. 399). The expression is referred only to the apostolic office, on the contrary, by F. Hauck, *Das Neue Testament Deutsch*, Vol. III, 1930, p. 203, and C. Bigg, *The Epistles of St. Peter and St. Jude*, 2nd ed., 1910, p. 186. H. Strathmann, in G. Kittel's *Theologisches Wörterbuch zum N. T.*, Vol. IV, p. 499, admits a "sharing in Christ's sufferings," but rejects here the technical martyrological meaning. On the entire question see O. Michel, *Prophet und Märtyrer*, 1932; H. v. Campenhausen, *Die Idee des Martyriums in der alten Kirche*, 1936; H. W. Surkau, *Martyrien in judischer und frühchristlicher Zeit*, 1938; E. Günther, *Martys*, 1941.

young, you girded yourself and went wherever you chose; but when you have become old, you will stretch out your hands, and another will gird you and carry you where you do not want to go." It is almost universally recognized that these words are intended as a prediction of the martyrdom of Peter, even if there should lie behind them a proverb which simply says: The young go where they choose, the old must permit themselves to be carried.[80] When the following verse says that these words indicate by what kind of death Peter "is to glorify God," it is beyond doubt that this "glorifying" can only mean his martyrdom. Perhaps John 13:36 ff. also belongs here.

It is not entirely certain whether the "stretching out of the hands" in John 21:18 is intended to indicate a special manner of execution, by crucifixion.[81] The Greek expression makes this quite likely.[82] Concerning the place of martyrdom the prediction contains no precise information. Even if ch. 21 was only added later to the Gospel of John, we still are dealing with a text that is relatively early. We thus have two rather early witnesses to the essential fact of the martyrdom of Peter: certainly John 21:18, and possibly I Peter 5:1, to which about the middle of the second century II Peter 1:14 is added. This evidence, it is true, does not prove the "historicity" of this manner of Peter's death, but it renders it probable.[83] For the question whether Peter was in Rome this preliminary question, whether he died as a martyr at all, is not unimportant. For in ancient

---

[80] So R. Bultmann, *Das Evangelium des Johannes*, 2nd ed., 1950, p. 552.

[81] This is rejected by R. Bultmann, *op. cit.*, p. 552. See on the contrary already in Tertullian, *Scorpiace* 15: "Peter is girded by another when he is fastened to the cross."

[82] ἐκτείνειν ("stretch out"). See on this point W. Bauer, *Das Johannesevangelium* (*Handbuch zum Neuen Testament*), 3rd ed., 1933, p. 238. He points out that in assuming this the order of stretching out the hands and being girded is not reversed (as R. Bultmann says, *op. cit.*, *ad loc.*), since "the criminal had to carry the cross to the place of execution with arms spread out and chained to it."

[83] K. Heussi raises the question whether Peter died as a martyr at all. The manner, however, in which he seeks to minimize the testimony of John 21:18 ff. is not convincing; he claims that this tradition, which he concedes the author must have found already in existence, deals with the transfer of Paul's martyr death to his rival Peter (*War Petrus in Rom?*, p. 30, note 21; *Neues zur Petrusfrage*, 1939, p. 24; see on this point more recently, "Der Stand der Frage nach dem römischen Aufenthalt des Petrus," in *Deutsches Pfarrerblatt*, 1949, p. 503). R. Bultmann, *op. cit.*, p. 553, writes in opposition to this view that if, on the one side, one cannot establish by this prediction the historicity of the martyrdom, yet on the other side one cannot prove that verses 18 f. have the aim of establishing the legend.

times it was hardly customary to hand down accounts of the martyr-doms with no indication of place.[84] Thus we must at least assume that those who, in the texts mentioned, show that they know the tradition of Peter's martyrdom knew also the place, even though in this passage they had no occasion to name it. This fact will call for consideration in forming a judgment concerning First Clement, ch. 5.

As the last New Testament text which we need to discuss in con-nection with our problem we now may add *Revelation* 11:3 ff. The hypothesis has recently been proposed that the Apostles Peter and Paul are meant here by the "two witnesses," who, after they have given their witness, are attacked, overcome, and killed by the "beast from the abyss." In the same passage it is said that the corpses of the two witnesses continue to lie upon the street of the "great city," where earlier their Lord had been crucified. For "three and a half days" men of all peoples see them lying there and refuse to permit their burial. These two witnesses have so troubled the inhabitants of the earth that the latter, out of joy over their death, now send presents to one another. The spirit of life from God re-enters the two dead men; a voice resounds from heaven: "Come up here," and they ascend to heaven in a cloud.

These witnesses, who previously were always interpreted to be Moses and Elijah, could in fact be Peter and Paul.[85] If this hypo-thesis is correct, we probably would have here the oldest tradition concerning the two martyrdoms. The "great city" in this case would have to be Rome.[86] We would have to assume that the two apostles,

---

[84] This is rightly stressed by H. Lietzmann, *Petrus und Paulus in Rom*, 2nd ed., 1927, pp. 235 f.

[85] This hypothesis, first expressed by the Jesuit, Juan de Mariana, *Scholia in Vetus et Novum Testamentum*, Madrid, 1619, pp. 1100 f., has now been given a scholarly foundation by Johannes Munck in his recently published monograph, *Petrus und Paulus in der Offenbarung Johannis*, 1950. This thesis is also presented, inde-pendently of J. Munck, by the Roman Catholic exegete, R. P. Boismard, *L'Apocalypse* (*La Sainte Bible*, Jérusalem), 1950, pp. 21 f., 53 f.; in doing so, however, he tries to find in the resurrection and ascension of the two witnesses a symbol of their "triumph with God" or even of their "resurrection in the person of their successors."

[86] See above, p. 84, on "Sodom and Egypt." In that case the words "where earlier their Lord was crucified" are hard to interpret. J. Munck, *op. cit.*, pp. 34 ff., knows no other escape here except either to consider the words as an interpola-tion or to understand them not in a geographical but in a figurative sense, which then might possibly be applied to Rome. R. B. Boismard, *op. cit.* above in note 85, considers the words an interpolation inspired by Matt. 23:37. The manuscript evidence, however, does not justify striking out the words concerned.

even if they did not do missionary work at the same time, did suffer martyrdom there *simultaneously*, and that contrary to later accounts, they were not buried, but their corpses continued to lie on the public street in Rome. In addition this tradition would tell of the ascension of these two martyrs, such as possibly is attested for Paul in The Acts of Paul.

The only possible time for these events would be the Neronian persecution. This is especially true since other features of the Apocalypse of John continue to find their best explanation as references to Nero.

Although much favours the correctness of this new hypothesis concerning this passage, we nevertheless cannot regard it as a *certain* basis for assuming that Peter was martyred at Rome. The cryptic manner of speech of the Apocalypse inevitably makes uncertain every interpretation in terms of contemporary history. In our passage, for one thing, the names of the "two witnesses" are not given; moreover, the designation "apostle" is lacking, although it is correct that elsewhere in the New Testament the apostles are called "witnesses" in crucial passages;[87] furthermore, the name of the "great city" where the Lord was crucified is not given, and the explanation that it means Rome does not appear immediately convincing, but actually offers difficulties. The passage permits other interpretations. Thus here also only a *possibility* remains. If, however, we could identify more clearly, on the basis of another text, an early tradition of the stay and martyrdom of Peter in Rome, then this interpretation also, which in itself is possible, would acquire greater value as a testimony.

Up to this point, however, we have nowhere found a solid foundation. The New Testament attests only the fact of the martyrdom of Peter. As far as the place is concerned, even the interpretation of I Peter 5:13 has offered us thus far only a great probability, and the silence of Romans permitted us to conclude only that at a specific time Peter certainly was not in Rome.

* * *

We still have two texts which contain brief references to Peter and Paul and *in point of time* at least still belong in the New Testament sphere: the First Epistle of Clement, which probably dates from the end of the first century, and the Letter of Ignatius of Antioch to the

[87] See J. Munck, *op. cit.*, pp. 17 f.

Romans, from the beginning of the second century. Of these two *First Clement* is by far the more important for our question; it is rightly regarded as the decisive literary witness, by both the defenders and the opponents of the tradition concerning the Roman stay of Peter. We therefore shall make a more detailed study of it. For if a relatively great probability is anywhere attainable for one view or the other, it must be in the fifth chapter of this writing.

The Epistle quite probably dates as early as the end of the first century. It has even been said that it is the document of ancient Christianity which can be dated with the greatest certainty; and it is usual to give the year 96 as the date of its composition.[88]

I too consider this important text the most solid basis for a solution of our question. As we approach the study of it, we must emphasize at the outset a twofold necessity. On the one hand, we must read the decisive section without any prejudice; on the other hand—and this seems to me of crucial importance—we must not tear it out of the context in which it stands, as is continually done, but must explain it strictly in that setting. Hence before we speak of the section which directly interests us, I first of all sum up the content of the immediately preceding chapters.

Ch. 5, which we must study in greater detail, stands in a larger context which embraces chs. 3 to 6. Over the entire section we could place as a heading: *Concerning the Results of Jealousy*. The theme is formulated at the end of the third chapter, where, with a citation from Wisdom 2:24, the author defines jealousy as follows: "*The unrighteous and godless jealousy through which death entered into the world.*" Ch. 9:1 speaks again of strife and of the jealousy "which leads to death."

The writing undertakes to prove by examples that jealousy among brothers brings harmful results. The examples cited form two groups of seven.[89] The former contains examples from earlier times, and

---

[88] A. Harnack, *Chronologie*, Vol. I, p. 255: "between 93 and 95." Recently Ch. Eggenberger, *Die Quellen der politischen Ethik des 1. Klemensbriefes*, 1951, has thought it necessary to bring the date down into the beginning of the reign of Hadrian. This dating is connected with the much too one-sided perspective in which he regards the entire writing as an "apology for the court." Everything that is said concerning conditions in Corinth, he says, is fiction! With other reasons A. Loisy, *La Naissance du Christianisme*, 1933, p. 33, also transfers the writing to the years 130–135.

[89] See R. Knopf, *Die Lehre der Zwölf Apostel; die zwei Klemensbriefe (Handbuch zum Neuen Testament, Ergänzungsband)*, 1923, pp. 48 ff.

stands in ch. 4. They are taken from the Old Testament: 1. Cain and Abel. 2. Jacob and Esau. 3. Joseph and his brothers. 4. Moses and the Jew who reproaches him for having killed the Egyptian. 5. Moses and Aaron and Miriam. 6. Moses and Dathan and Abiram. 7. David (the Philistines) and Saul.

The second group comprises the examples from the *immediate* past. It too contains seven members, and it stands in chs. 5 and 6. Here, then, we come to the much-disputed passage which, on account of its importance, I give in full in translation:

Chapter 5: "But now, to leave the examples from ancient times, let us come to the contestants of the most recent past. Let us take the noble examples of our own generation. On account of jealousy and envy the greatest and most righteous *pillars* were persecuted and contended unto death. Let us set before our eyes our excellent apostles:[90] *Peter*, who because of unrighteous jealousy had to bear not one or two but many torments, and so, after he had given his witness, went to the place of glory which was due him. On account of jealousy and strife *Paul* displayed the prize of endurance. Seven times he was chained; he was exiled; he was stoned; he became a herald both in the east and in the west; and so he received for his faith glorious fame. After he had taught the whole world righteousness, had reached the furthest boundary of the west, and had given witness before the authorities, he thus was freed from the world and went to the holy place, as the greatest example of endurance."—Chapter 6: "To these men, who have lived a holy life, was joined a great *multitude of elect ones*, who on account of jealousy suffered many kinds of outrage and tortures and so became most glorious examples *among us*. On account of jealousy *women* were persecuted; as Danaids and Dircae they suffered fearful and horrible ill-treatment, and so they reached the goal of their steadfast course of faith and received a glorious prize—

[90] The literal translation here, depending on whether one refers "our" to "apostles" or to "eyes," would be either "let us set before *our* eyes the excellent apostles" or "let us set before *the* eyes *our* excellent apostles." P. Monceaux, "L'apostolat de Saint Pierre à Rome, à propos d'un livre récent (*Revue d'Histoire et de Littérature religieuses*, 1910, pp. 225 f.), holds that only the translation "our excellent apostles" is possible; and he thinks that this expression should be understood in the sense of "the apostles who have preached in Rome and Corinth." But in ch. 44:1 the expression "our apostles" designates the apostles in general. M. Dibelius, "Rom und die Christen im ersten Jahrhundert" (*Sitzungsbericht der Heidelberger Akademie der Wissenschaften*, 1942, p. 20), interprets ἀγαθοί ("good," "excellent") in the sense of *fortes*, "valiant." See examples for this in B. Altaner, "Neues zum Verästndnis von 1. Klem. 5, 1–6, 2" (*Historisches Jahrbuch*, 1949, p. 25).

they, the physically weak ones. Jealousy has estranged *wives* from their husbands and perverted the saying of our father Adam: 'This is now bone of my bone and flesh of my flesh.' Jealousy and strife have destroyed *great cities* and uprooted great peoples."

This is thus the only early text that speaks explicitly of the death of Peter, and it should be said at the outset that we do not learn much from it. We therefore must see whether and how far it is permitted to derive more from the context.

Here again seven victims of jealousy are assembled:[91] 1. The pillars. 2. Peter. 3. Paul. 4. The great multitude of the elect. 5. The martyred women. 6. The separated spouses. 7. The destroyed cities. Of these seven examples the first, sixth, and seventh are described in quite general terms; they do not permit us to think of particular concrete events. The last two evidently are intended only to complete the number of seven. In our interpretation we must take into account the deliberately artificial arrangement of this section,[92] and we must note the difficulty which Clement inevitably encountered in finding for the relatively short period of the most recent (that is, the Christian) past the number of examples that would correspond with the group taken from the Old Testament. So perhaps in the first example also we should not think of particular names when—probably in dependence on Galatians 2:9—the passage speaks of the "pillars." The author seems to think here in a general way of apostles and leading men of the Primitive Church who have suffered martyrdom. In

[91] So rightly R. Knopf, *Handbuch zum Neuen Testament, Ergänzungsband,* 1923, p. 49.

[92] Even for this reason we must reject the new thesis which K. Heussi strangely continues to advance in his second reply to II. Lietzmann, *Neues zur Petrusfrage,* 1939. His thesis is that the passage concerning Peter, in paragraphs 3 and 4, can be a later *insertion.* But in this way the entire carefully constructed pattern of Clement would be destroyed. Apart from that fact, this thesis, which he proposed to supplement his original view, witnesses that he feels some uncertainty concerning his own arguments as presented in his earlier writing, *War Petrus in Rom?,* 1936. In the main chapter of that book he actually sought to show that in this passage Clement reports the vague and empty generalities that he knows about Peter, and that μαρτυρήσας ("having borne witness") does not refer to the martyr death. In his writing of 1939 he writes astonishingly that if the paragraph concerning Peter is an insertion, then μαρτυρήσας, in correspondence with the μαρτυρήσας that refers to Paul, would still be understood in the sense of a martyr death! But he further explains: Anyone who cannot accept the thesis of interpolation should hold to those other results which his earlier study of the passage brought to light! Here one gets the painful impression that *at any price* it *must* be proved that the letter of Clement cannot be used as a proof of the martyr death of Peter in Rome.

any case the "conflict unto death" means martyrdom.[93] Probably the author includes Peter and Paul among these men, but in order to obtain the number seven he probably first, before he speaks of each of them separately, names them together with the others who are collectively described as pillars. These two cases, especially that of Paul, seemed to him particularly fitted to prove the thesis he seeks to establish, that envy and jealousy lead to ruin. For we wish to establish without delay this fact: we owe the mention of Peter and Paul entirely to the circumstance that the author, in order to give greater emphasis to his warning to the Corinthian church against envy and strife, used examples from the history of the Primitive Church, and chose exactly seven for the sake of symmetry.

Unfortunately he expresses himself very briefly in the lines that deal with Peter. The thing particularly regrettable from our standpoint is that the point in which we are especially interested, the place where Peter suffered the many torments, is not named at all. Thus even this single early text which finally gives us a certain reference to the death of Peter seems to fail us. Indeed, it is not even clearly said that the apostle died as a martyr. The text in its actual form only says that sometime and somewhere Peter had to endure many torments, that he "bore witness," and that he then attained to the place of glory.

If one reads these statements apart from the context in which they occur, then indeed, in company with those who contest the Roman stay of Peter, one must deny that the passage gives any information of any kind concerning a Roman martyrdom or even concerning any martyrdom whatever. The sentences regarding Peter theoretically permit the interpretation that in his life he had to suffer manifold trials, that (through preaching) he bore witness, and that then, somewhere and at some time, he died a natural death and finally, as the reward of his endurance, was taken up to the place of glory.

---

[93] The remark of K. Heussi, in *War Petrus in Rom?*, p. 25, is indeed correct: in ch. 4:9 it is said of Joseph that he was persecuted "unto death" ($\mu\acute{\epsilon}\chi\rho\iota\ \theta\alpha\nu\acute{\alpha}\tau\sigma\upsilon$), and yet he escaped with his life. Consequently, according to Heussi, neither is the "struggle unto death" in ch. 5:2 to be interpreted of the martyr death. But in connection with $\dot{\alpha}\theta\lambda\acute{\epsilon}\omega$ ("struggle," "contend") the words $\ddot{\epsilon}\omega\varsigma\ \theta\alpha\nu\acute{\alpha}\tau\sigma\upsilon$ ("unto death") are probably not merely rhetorical emotion as they are in the example of Joseph. In the latter example, moreover, the author makes clear that a real death is not in mind. For he expressly adds, "unto slavery." The preceding emotional "unto death" he put here only in view of the main thesis expressed in ch. 3:4 (9:1).

It has been correctly pointed out that the author cites the series of Old Testament examples, beginning with Cain and Abel, in chronological order. Hence it has been considered necessary to conclude from this fact that Peter died before Paul suffered martyrdom. The fact that the author reports so little concerning Peter, while he says much more about Paul, is said to be explained by the fact that he knows nothing more about Peter than the very vague facts mentioned above.[94]

With reference to the martyr death itself (apart from the question of where it occurred), we must first of all recall that this death, as we have seen, is attested about the time of the writing of First Clement, at least in John 21:18, and perhaps also in I Peter 5:1. Could it be then that Clement knew nothing of such a death? This is indeed improbable.

Furthermore, the context shows that the two items concerning Peter and Paul are constructed in a quite similar way, even if it is true that the one concerning Peter is much shorter. Now it is universally conceded that in any event the notice concerning Paul speaks of his martyr death.[95] But if in that account the expression "bear witness" is, to say the least, closely connected with the words, "and so he went to the holy place," then it cannot properly be understood otherwise when it is similarly said of Peter: "and so, after he bore witness, he

---

94 This is *grosso modo* the thesis developed by K. Heussi, *War Petrus in Rom?* H. Dannenbauer, "Die römische Petruslegende" (*Historische Zeitschrift*, 1932, pp. 246 f.), also asserts that I Clement is completely ignorant concerning the fate of Peter. He explains this ignorance by the fact that the Neronian persecution completely destroyed the Roman church and broke the chain of all living Christian tradition. For the contrary view, see G. Krüger, "Petrus in Rom" (*ZNW*, 1932, pp. 303 f.). That Clement had no definite knowledge at all concerning Peter is asserted also by Ch. Guignebert, *op. cit.*, p. 275, and K. Holl, *Gesammelte Aufsätze*, Vol. II, 1928, p. 65, note 1. The latter, however, assumes that Peter came to Rome, though only after the death of Paul, and then was there but a short time; he explains in this way the fact that precisely in Rome the church had as few memories of Peter as I Clement, ch. 5, shows us they did (*Gesammelte Aufsätze*, Vol. II, 1928, p. 67). Accordingly, it is quite remarkable when one reads the following in J. Haller, *Das Papsttum*, Vol. I, p. 476: " . . . who knows how many have protested in silence (against the acceptance by modern scholarship of a Roman stay of Peter), without raising their voice! I know concerning the most learned and acute church historian of the last fifty years, Karl Holl, that he did not share the 'prevailing view.' "

95 K. Heussi also assumes this, though here too he still does not understand μαρτυρήσας ("having borne witness") as a reference to martyrdom (*War Petrus in Rom?*, p. 25).

went to the place of glory that was due him."[96] In addition, we must also take into account the elsewhere attested usage in stories of martyrdom, in which the Greek word *doxa* refers to glory. The word *martyrein* for "bear witness" is at least already on the way to becoming the technical term for witness by martyrdom.[97]

Not as proof but as confirmation we may also recall that according to the theme stated at the end of ch. 3, it is death that is portrayed as the result of jealousy.[98] To be sure, in most examples of the first group the trial does not lead to death, but doubtless the writer's special concern is with the cases which ended in this way. That is why the first example of the entire section, the story of Cain and Abel, is treated with disproportionately large detail.[99]

If we thus must assume with the greatest probability that Clement here refers to the martyr death of Peter, then—we must repeat—he himself at least knew also the place of the martyrdom, since it is not customary to hand down narratives of martyrdoms without any indication of place.[1] In our passage Clement does not need to mention it, since he can assume that it is known; moreover, he is not giving a report about martyrs but an example of the results of envy and strife.[2]

[96] This testimony probably does not resume the preceding "suffering of manifold torments," but cites the μαρτυρεῖν ("bear witness") as a further point; for οὕτω ("so," "thus") is best referred to ἐπορεύθη ("went"), just as οὕτως in the notice concerning Paul belongs to ἀπηλλάγη ("was freed"). So H. von Campenhausen, *Die Idee des Martyriums in der alten Kirche*, 1936, p. 54, who shows that what is involved is a "martyrological" way of speaking, which here is applied to Peter and to Paul, and in Eusebius, *Ecclesiastical History*, II, 23, is used of James. So also H. Lietzmann, *Petrus römischer Martyrer*, 1936. This is in opposition to Heussi, *op. cit.*, p. 24, note 12.

[97] So J. B. Lightfoot, *The Apostolic Fathers*, I, 1–2, 2nd ed., 1890, *ad loc.* R. Knopf, *Handbuch zum Neuen Testament*, Ergänzungsband, 1923, p. 51, also interprets μαρτυρήσας ("having borne witness") in the sense of martyr death. So do H. Delehaye, *Sanctus, Essai sur le culte des Saints dans l'antiquité*, 1927, p. 79, and H. v. Campenhausen, *op. cit.*, p. 54. On the contrary, E. Günther, *Martys, Geschichte eines Wortes*, 1941, pp. 117 ff., rejects the meaning "be a martyr," and H. Strathmann, in G. Kittel's *Theologisches Wörterbuch zum N. T.*, Vol. IV, p. 511, is very hesitant. L. Sanders, *L'hellénisme de S. Clément de Rome et le paulinisme*, 1943, pp. 21 f., wishes to give the word the same meaning it has in Epictetus.

[98] See above, p. 90.

[99] This is rightly emphasized by R. Knopf, *Handbuch zum Neuen Testament*, Ergänzungsband, 1923, p. 49.

[1] So H. Lietzmann, *Petrus und Paulus in Rom*, 2nd ed., 1927, pp. 235 f. See above, pp. 87 f.

[2] B. Altaner, "Neues zum Verständnis von 1. Klem. 5, 1–6, 2" (*Historisches Jahrbuch*, 1941, p. 25), shows that ch. 9 of the Epistle of Polycarp uses I Clem.,

There is the further fact that examples one, three, and four, and probably also the disputed fifth one,[3] speak of Christians who have suffered death as martyrs. The fourth example is reasonably clear in this respect; the great multitude of the elect here mentioned are, as is *universally recognized*, the Christians who suffered the martyr death under Nero, for we know nothing of any other persecution of a "great multitude"[4] in this period apart from that which Nero instigated. Concerning it, the narrative of Tacitus, *Annals*, XV, 44, speaks exactly as does Clement of a *multitudo ingens*, a "great multitude."

But the notice concerning this fourth example contains still another item that is very important for our study: "they became a glorious example *among us*."[5] Since Clement writes from Rome, we thus possess, at least for this group of martyrs, the information concerning the place. It is Rome. This confirms the conclusion that we are here dealing with the martyrs of the Neronian persecution.[6] However, the champions of the Roman tradition about Peter are often much too hasty in drawing from this place reference of the fourth example a conclusion concerning the preceding examples, in which, as we have seen, nothing is said concerning the place. If the examples of the second group are actually to be separated from one another and placed, like those of the first group, in a strictly chronological series, then we have so much the less right to say without further evidence that the words "among us" refer also to Peter and Paul. This is particularly true if the "pillars" of the first example likewise did not all "suffer persecution and contend unto death" in Rome.

---

ch. 5, almost word for word, and he seeks to show that Polycarp understood the passage to mean that Paul, Ignatius, Zosimus, and "other apostles" suffered martyrdom in Rome.

[3] One usually thinks of cruelties, especially executions, in the form of mythological presentations (Tertullian, *Apology*, 15). That would correspond also to the *ludibria* attested for the Neronian persecution in Tacitus, *Annals*, XV, 44. Another explanation: L. van Liempt, Handelingen van het veertiende nederlandsche Philologen-Congres te Amsterdam, 1931, pp. 37 f., whom M. Dibelius follows (*op. cit.*, p. 24), says that the martyr women are here only *named* after the mythical heroines, to express the greatness of their sufferings, not the manner of their punishment: "They are true Dircae and Danaids." The most recent, interesting conjecture is by A. Dain, in *Recherches de Science religieuse*, 1951–52, pp. 353 ff.: there is here a scribal error for *neanides paidiskai* ("slave maidens").

[4] πολὺ πλῆθος.   [5] ἐν ἡμῖν.

[6] This is recognized also by K. Heussi, *op. cit.*, although on p. 21, note 9, he does not intend to exclude the possibility that ἐν ἡμῖν means "in the midst of us Christians."

We dare not be too hasty in adding the words "in Rome" to the verb in the statement, "they (the great multitude) were joined[7] to these men (Peter and Paul)," as though there were any necessity to ask at what place they were joined to them. The assembling here mentioned is not necessarily meant in a geographical sense. Nor is it meant in the sense in which the challengers of the Roman tradition are accustomed to interpret it: "at the place of glory." Rather, the question as to the "where" should not be asked at all.[8] The intent of the verb "they were joined to them" is probably to add to the other examples as a simple *fact* the example of the great multitude; it is a further illustration, from the quite recent past, of Christian martyrdoms suffered as a result of jealousy.

Precisely on the basis of this factual connection, however, we must ask whether in examples two to five we are not dealing with the same outward circumstances. If so, the division into four particular cases could again be connected with the fact that the author was determined to attain the number of seven for this second group also. Indeed, we have seen that he added examples six and seven only for this reason. But if that is true, we must consider the possibility that the sequence of examples two to five need not be understood as a chronological succession.[9]

The possibility thus exists of assigning all four examples to the Neronian persecution in Rome. It is indeed correct that the expression "nearest to us" in ch. 5:1[10] is given a temporal sense only to distinguish the second group from the first; this conclusion is also indicated by the phrase "our generation," which stands in the following sentence. But the fact that, at least in the fourth example, Clement uses the words "among us" proves that he is concerned to give in the second group examples that are particularly close to him also in place.

We have no right, however, to extend the words "among us" to the notice concerning Peter, unless it can be proved that other really

---

[7] συνηθροίσθη.

[8] Against K. Heussi, *op. cit.*, p. 22; but also against M. Dibelius, *Rom und die Christen im ersten Jahrhundert*, 1942, p. 23. The latter in connection with his thesis that Clement here follows the pattern that popular philosophy draws from athletic contests and wishes to give examples of Christian "endurance" and Christian "athletic prowess," writes: "the place where the two groups meet is rather the imaginary arena in which the contests of the Christian 'athletes' occur."

[9] In that case the argument mentioned above on p. 96 collapses.

[10] ἔγγιστα.

important features connect examples two to four (and perhaps also five) so closely together that we must assume that all three or four occurred at the same time and at the same place.

Here again we must recall the aim that this entire enumeration serves. What is common to all these examples of both groups, the Old Testament as well as the Christian ones? Each of them, with deliberate monotony, is introduced by the words "on account of jealousy," or "on account of jealousy and envy," or "on account of jealousy and strife." The citation of each example contains at least one of these words. The connecting link between all these very different cases is therefore this: jealousy, envy, and strife have always caused disaster. At times it is suffered by the righteous, that is, by the victims; at times by the guilty, that is, the authors of envy, jealousy and strife—as is the case in examples five and six of the first group.

This context should be given more careful attention not only in the general interpretation, but also in the explanation of details. Special emphasis has recently been laid on the idea that Clement is strongly influenced by *Hellenism* and is concerned to apply to the Bible and to the history of the beginnings of the Church the literary artistry and concepts of the Cynic-Stoic philosophy.[11] This is undoubtedly correct. But it will not do to see in this attempt, so to speak, the main aim of the discussions in our section, as though Clement intended to offer here a moralistic and philosophical discussion concerning endurance, and clothed it in the favourite Cynic and Stoic illustration of the contest in athletic games. No doubt Clement borrows illustrations from this pattern to describe the afflictions of the apostles. But it constitutes a misunderstanding of his purpose when it is said that he here desires to show the exemplary character of the endurance of the apostles. The central theme of the section is not endurance but envy, jealousy, strife.

Thus the brevity of the statement concerning Peter, as compared with the much more detailed report concerning Paul, could be con-

---

[11] M. Dibelius, "Rom und die Christen im ersten Jahrhundert" (*Sitzungsbericht der Heidelberger Akademie der Wissenschaften, Philologisch-historische Klasse*, 1942), has shown this in a thorough study. See above, p. 76, note 36, and p. 97, note 8 (even before him E. Dubowy, *Klemens von Rom . . .* 1914). Still more comprehensive is the work written independently of M. Dibelius by the Roman Catholic theologian L. Sanders, *L'héllenisme de S. Clément de Rome et le paulinisme*, 1943. On the illustration of the contest, much used in popular philosophy, see also P. Wendland, *Die urchristlichen Literaturformen*, 1912, p. 357, note.

nected with the fact that *in this respect* the example of Peter had less to offer than that of Paul.[12]

Perhaps, however, the above mentioned central theme may actually permit us to draw indirect conclusions as to the unnamed place of the events. Clement is characterizing the vice which is causing such devastating results in the previously so exemplary church of Corinth that he is addressing. It is the vice which has caused such bad results in the earlier Biblical period as well as in the quite recent Christian past. The word or rather the words that he uses to describe it do not mean simply in a general way, "hate of the world for the children of God."[13] This is the meaning some have given, in an attempt to escape the only possible conclusion that results from our text when it says that Peter and Paul suffered on account of jealousy and strife. The three synonymous Greek words mean jealousy, envy, strife. The word that we have translated jealousy[14] appears sixteen times in our section; the one that we have translated envy,[15] four times; the one that we have translated strife,[16] three times.

It is of course correct that the first-named word, that is, the one most often used here, means primarily "zeal" in a good sense, and

---

[12] M. Dibelius, *op. cit.*, p. 28, explains this brevity from the fact that Clement did not wish to speak more in detail of the martyr death of the two for political reasons; he did not wish to present the Roman state as the opponent of the Christian athlete. Rather, in connection with his philosophical scheme of Christian athletic activity, he preferred to limit himself to the πόνοι ("torments," "troubles") and ἔργα ("works"). Concerning that subject, there was much more to tell of Paul than of Peter, who probably came to Rome only for execution, perhaps, like Ignatius, as a prisoner.

[13] So L. Sanders, *op. cit.*, p. 5, note 1, and J. Munck, *op. cit.*, pp. 58 ff., both of whom think they must therefore oppose the thesis that I defended in "Les causes de la mort de Pierre et de Paul d'après le témoignage de Clément Romain (*Revue d'Histoire et de Philosophie religieuses*, 1930, pp. 294 ff.). R. Knopf, *Handbuch zum Neuen Testament, Ergänzungsband*, p. 47, in his comment on ch. 3:2, quite correctly defines ζῆλος as "jealousy of the esteem, position, advantages of the other." With this, however, does not agree the fact that on p. 50 he writes of "*hate*, envy, and jealousy of the world against the children of God." P. Meinhold, "Geschehen und Deutung im 1. Clemensbrief" (*Zeitschrift für Kirchengeschichte*, 1939, p. 90) correctly states that "ζῆλος ('jealousy') and ἔρις ('strife') are used by Clement in a sense similar to that in which they are used by Paul in Rom. 13:13; I Cor. 3:3; II Cor. 12:20; Gal. 5:20. For Clement as well as for Paul they signify those moral weaknesses of *ill will* and *envy* which proceed from the dominance of the passions over the man who is no longer led by the Spirit." Meinhold, however, does not draw from this the consequences for the explanation of I Clement, ch. 5.

[14] ζῆλος.   [15] φθόνος.   [16] ἔρις.

so understood it actually appears as a divine quality.[17] But the very
change of meaning from the good to the bad quality shows that the
vice which finally is characterized by this word is primarily not
simply hate in a general sense, but rather jealousy that has sprung
from zeal (*aus Eifer entstandene Eifer-Sucht*).[18] To be sure, the word can
also take on the more general meaning of "hate." But the fact that
the three words are here grouped together shows that what is here to
be thrown into the foreground is precisely that which is common to all
three, and this is not simply hate but specifically envy and jealousy.[19]

I cannot understand how one can even suggest that the word here
means hate in the general sense; this entire section is introduced by
Clement only because it is this particular vice of jealousy that
threatens to corrupt the whole church to which he writes. He says
this quite plainly in the introduction of the Letter, in the three opening chapters which immediately precede our section. In them he does
not speak of "hate in general," but of jealousy, envy, and strife,
which have arisen among the members of the Christian church at
Corinth (ch. 3 :2, 4). It is for this reason, and only for this reason, that
Clement speaks in the following chapters of this vice "through which
death entered into the world," as he says with an allusion to the envy
of the devil at the very beginning of the world (chs. 3 :4 and 9:1).[20]

---

[17] See A. Stumpff in Kittel's *Theologisches Wörterbuch*, Vol. II, pp. 879 f.

[18] Chr. Eggenberger, *Die Quellen der politischen Ethik des 1. Clem.*, 1951, p. 36, thinks
here of "Zealots." Similarly, but with better arguments, Bo Reicke, *Diakonie,
Festfreude und Zelos in Verbindung mit der altchristlichen Agapenfeier*, 1951, pp. 373 ff.

[19] The example that J. Munck, *op. cit.*, pp. 60 f. cites from I Clem. 45:4 would be
no counterproof sufficient to outweigh the weighty majority of clear examples
where ζῆλος means "jealousy" in chs. 3 and 4, even if ch. 45:4 were an exception
that had in mind only the hate of the world. But, as he himself concedes, jealousy
is certainly present in one of the two examples cited in ch. 45:4 ff.; also in the
case of the three men in the fiery furnace it is not to be forgotten that the starting
point is a denunciation by some Chaldeans against certain Jews who had been
entrusted by Nebuchadnezzar with the administration of the province Babylon
(Dan. 3 : 12).

[20] J. Munck, *op. cit.*, p. 60, note 84, concedes that in this quotation from Wisdom
2 : 24 the devil is intended; in doing so, he refers to B. Noack, *Satanas und Soteria*,
1948, pp. 43 f. But that which is involved in this passage is *envy*, and *death* as its
result; it is not the fact of the hate of the "powers hostile to God." There at the
beginning envy appears in its clear original form as the power of the devil hostile
to God. But it is the special characteristic of this devilish vice that since its
entrance into the world it has been at work *among brothers*. This belongs to the
very nature of "jealousy," "envy," and "strife." This is seen in the Corinthian
church, and this is what Clement wishes to prove by his examples, at the head
of which he puts in detailed form the one of Cain and Abel.

It is further clear that in the Old Testament examples the author, following his explicit aim, deals with envy and jealousy among *brothers*. According to the passage of Wisdom 2:24 cited in ch. 3:4, it is admittedly the power hostile to God, the death-dealing devil, who is here at work. But among brothers! It is for this reason that the classic example of Cain and Abel, with which the entire series is introduced, takes so disproportionate an amount of space. It is the example that is especially typical. Only one among the Old Testament examples could be considered an exception; it is that of David and the Philistines. But it is connected with the example of David and Saul; it is only mentioned with reference to that example, and for the very purpose of emphasizing that Saul belongs to the same people that David does. Hence Clement writes, "On account of jealousy David not only had to endure envy from foreigners, but he also was persecuted by Saul, the King of Israel." The emphasis rests upon the latter fact.

The other examples are quite clear in this respect: the jealousy of Cain for his *brother* Abel; of Esau for his *brother* Jacob; of the sons of Jacob for their younger *brother*. The fourth example is particularly interesting. Here the author explicitly stresses the fact that Moses had to flee from Pharaoh on account of the jealousy of one of *his own people*.[21] The two remaining examples from the earlier period also have this point in common with the others.

The examples of the second group, with the exception of that of Paul, are not known from other sources, or are too little known to serve to support or undermine this result. Only the quite generally stated example of the married partners readily confirms the previous conclusion. But even with regard to the others, we must assume from the start that Clement chose these particular Christian examples so that they not only harmonize with the Old Testament ones but are convincing for the readers in view of the *aim of the writer*. What meaning would it have in this letter simply to adduce in so general a way examples that illustrate persecutions of Christians and show their endurance? The thing needed here is rather to prove to the Corinthian Christians, divided by jealousy and envy, where these vices lead. We therefore must expect that in this second group also the author is speaking of jealousy among members of *one and the same fellowship*.

From this fact, however, there results an important conclusion for the examples which are here of particular interest to us. When

21 ὁμόφυλος.

Clement, in this very passage, writes that Peter had to suffer "on account of unrighteous jealousy," and Paul "on account of jealousy and strife," and the great multitude of the elect "on account of jealousy," this in the context of our letter can only mean that they were victims of jealousy from persons who counted themselves members of the Christian Church. In saying this we naturally do not mean that they were martyred or perhaps murdered by other Christians, but that the magistrates were encouraged by the attitude of some members of the Christian Church, and perhaps by the fact that they turned informers, to take action against others. In just the same way Moses, in one example of the first group, had to flee from the Egyptian King because of the jealousy of a fellow-countryman.

We are, of course, unable to say anything more definite concerning the nature of this jealousy. It should be remembered, however, that even the examples of the first group would be in part *quite unintelligible if we did not have the Old Testament*. In any case, however, the discussion must deal with the jealousy and envy of other Christians and not, for example, with that of the magistrates. The latter really had no reason at that time to be envious or jealous of the Christians, but they might well have had reasons for taking action against Christians.[22]

We have seen that statements are made concerning the life and the death of Peter as well as Paul. It has indeed been asserted that the mention of jealousy refers only to the life and not to the death of the two apostles.[23] In the notice concerning Peter, however, the words "on account of jealousy," which stand at the beginning of the relative clause, must be connected grammatically not only with the first part, "he endured many torments," but also with the second part, " he went to the place of glory." Since this second part of the sentence marks so to speak the climax, we must assume that the words "on account of jealousy" are to be connected also and particularly with this second part, and we have seen that the "entrance into the place of glory" obviously presupposes his death. But in that case Peter attained martyrdom "on account of jealousy." Moreover, in the statement concerning Paul, the words "on account of jealousy and strife" are so placed that they clearly have in view the end. They look to the time when Paul receives the victor's prize, even if the subsequently mentioned sufferings, troubles, and glorious deeds

---

22 The Jews cannot be meant here as authors of jealousy, for in the time of Clement they were no longer regarded as belonging to the same fellowship.
23 J. Munck, *op. cit.*, pp. 61 ff.

which precede his death are connected with the crowning with the victor's prize and form its presupposition. Grammatically, no doubt, this description is no longer dependent on the words "on account of jealousy and strife," and since the characterization of Paul's activity here has a greater rhetorical and factual detail, it is possible that we should not ask how far each individual event is conditioned by jealousy. However, it should certainly be emphasized that in II Corinthians 11:26, in the enumeration of his afflictions, Paul names in particular the "dangers among false brothers!"[24] Apart from this fact, it should also be recalled that Clement, in keeping with the theme announced for the section in ch. 3:4, must necessarily be interested particularly in those cases that have "led to *death*" (ch. 9:1).

We find a confirmation of this interpretation of our passage in ch. 47, which refers directly to the aim of the writing. Here are mentioned the quarrels which have broken out in the Corinthian church and threaten not only its unity but its very existence. The author reminds the disunited church members that in their own church at Corinth there had once been dissension. He recalls that Paul at that time warned them against divisions, when some had declared that they belonged to the party that used his own name, others that they belonged to that of Cephas, and others that they belonged to that of Apollos. Clement ends this exhortation with the following decisive words, which are really a commentary on ch. 5 and prove that one cannot possibly interpret it in any other way than we have done: "The news (of your present quarrels) has reached not only us but also *persons of different faith*, so that your folly causes the name of the Lord to be blasphemed and *brings you yourselves into danger*" (that is, at the hands of those of different faith).

We now understand still better why Clement, the Roman Bishop, reminds the divided Corinthians how, not long before, jealousy and strife among Christians had led to the suffering of martyrdom by the greatest apostles and by a great multitude of elect ones. The situation is the same, in so far as the danger of death threatens from *those outside the Church*, while the occasion for their intervention is given by the jealousy of *Christian brothers*. That, according to ch. 4:10, was exactly the situation of Moses and his fellow countryman in relation to the king of Egypt.

In all of these cases Clement is content to mention, without giving detailed circumstances, the mere fact of the jealousy; it is the thing

24 κίνδυνοι ἐν ψευδαδέλφοις.

with which he is concerned. He could omit details because he could assume that the facts were known. The death of the two apostles, indeed, cannot be dated much more than thirty years before the writing of First Clement. So he can limit himself to references, just as in giving the Old Testament examples he could assume that the detailed circumstances were known in part from the Bible.

It is of course probable that not much was said of the particularly painful circumstances that contributed to those martyrdoms. The Christians who had caused the death of other Christians did not offer an edifying example for others. Moreover, it is possible that the abrupt ending of The Book of Acts may be explained in this way.[25] Did the author, who wishes to show the working of the Holy Spirit in the Church of Christ, perhaps have scruples about speaking of this grievous and momentous jealousy? However that may be, Clement on the contrary had every reason for mentioning it in *his* writing, in order to show what danger threatens the most valuable members of a church at the hands of pagan persecutors, if the church is divided by jealousy.

I find a further confirmation of the correctness of this explanation of our text by comparing the statement of Clement concerning jealousy with what we read on the same subject in the letters of Paul. This comparison will then lead us straight back to our main problem, the question as to the place. Thus far we have learned from the letter of Clement only that Peter, like Paul and others, fell victim to non-Christian persecutors as a result of disunity caused by jealousy. We now ask: *in what place*, according to the sources at our disposal, could *such events* have occurred? Where, in the time of Peter and Paul, did there exist in a local church jealousy which could lead to persecution and the death of martyrs?

We possess a letter of Paul in which the apostle explicitly writes that envy and strife reign in the church where he is at the time of writing; he further says that he is there as a prisoner. This is found in Philippians 1:15–17: "There are some people here who preach Christ out of *envy and strife*. Others do it out of good will. Some proclaim Christ out of love, for they know that I lie here (in prison) for the defence of the Gospel. Others, however, do it because of *a quarrelsome spirit*, not out of pure motives; they wish to *bring affliction upon me in my imprisonment*." It is startling that we find here in a letter of Paul, written from a place where the apostle is held prisoner, almost the same words that occur in I Clement, ch. 5: envy, strife.[26]

[25] See above, pp. 80 ff.   [26] φθόνος, ἔρις, ἐριθεία.

The place of writing of Philippians is of course uncertain, since it is not definitely named in the letter. Independently of our problem I, like many scholars, have long assumed that it must refer to the imprisonment in Rome.[27] We have seen that the great multitude of elect ones who are mentioned in I Clement 6:1 as having suffered martyrdom on account of jealousy must *certainly* be sought in Rome; "among us" proves that. Furthermore, we shall see in particular that *Romans* contains features which point to friction between the Jewish Christian and Gentile Christian sections of the Roman church. Without reasoning in a "vicious circle," we thus may combine these data and conclude that only concerning the *Roman* church do we know (1) that jealousy ruled in it (I Clem. 6:1); (2) that Paul seems to have feared difficulties in it due to the fact that its membership included both Jewish and Gentile Christians (Rom. 15:20); (3) that Paul spent a time in it as a prisoner of the Roman Empire and during his imprisonment had to expect "affliction"[28] from other members of the church (Phil. 1:15 f.).

We here should recall the vigorous tone which Paul uses in this same Epistle to the Philippians against the Jewish Christians, who are probably to be sought in the circles of those whom he designates in Galatians 2:4 as "false brothers." In Philippians 3:2 he actually goes so far as to call them "dogs." These people, who have caused him difficulties everywhere on his journeys, he accordingly encountered also in Rome. *Peter* certainly did not belong to their number. We have seen that he, on the contrary, always stood closer to Paul, and it would be an error to believe that after the episode in Antioch a break occurred between Peter and Paul.[29] According to I Clement, ch. 5, it is rather to be assumed that Peter himself had to suffer at the hands of those people.

[27] So among others A. Jülicher—E. Fascher, *Einleitung ins N.T.*, 7th ed., 1931, pp. 120 f.; K. Holl, *Gesammelte Aufsätze*, Vol. II, p. 67. The necessity of assigning the letter to the doubtful imprisonment at Ephesus, as do P. Feine—Behm, *Einleitung in das N. T.*, 1936, pp. 174 ff., W. Michaelis, *Einleitung ins N. T.*, 1946, pp. 205 ff., and recently also P. Benoit, *La S. Bible* (Jerusalem), *Les Epîtres de S. Paul. Aux Philippiens*, 1949, pp. 11 f., and others, I have never really seen, even if it is true that the mention of the "praetorium" and of the people "of the house of Caesar" does not *necessarily* refer to Rome. The distance between Rome and Philippi I do not feel to be a difficulty. In content the letter fits much better at the end of the life of Paul.

[28] θλίψιν (Phil. 1:17).

[29] This is rightly challenged also by M. Dibelius—W. G. Kümmel, *Paulus* (Göschen), 1951, p. 124.

We recall that in the preceding chapter[30] we concluded on other grounds that Peter, as a delegated representative of the Jerusalem church, found himself by reason of his free attitude toward the Law *in an even more difficult situation than Paul* (Gal. 2:11 ff.). In view of this fact, one could very well say that the *"varied* troubles" caused by jealousy (I Clem. 5:4) refer to such difficulties with the Jerusalem leaders who commissioned him and with their over-zealous helpers.[31]

That such conflicts already existed in Rome before Paul arrived there is indicated above all by Paul's *letter to Rome.* Paul must have heard of such things. Only so can we explain the way he opposes Judaism in this letter, which he addresses to a church he has not yet visited. We mentioned above [32] how concerned he is in ch. 15:20 ff. to excuse himself for making an exception this time and coming to a church that he has not founded. We have seen further the reason why this troubles his conscience so much; he thereby is untrue to a principle whose observance he has considered a "point of honour," because it seems to him to correspond to the spirit of the Jerusalem agreement (Gal. 2:9). The emphasis with which he speaks of this in ch. 15 proves that he does not go without some anxiety to this church which probably was founded and then cared for by the Jewish Christian group. If he already had to contend, in the churches which he had brought into being, against the opposition of the Jerusalem mission, how much more in this church, where he may be treated from the outset as an intruder. That entire section in ch. 15 clearly betrays anxiety. It is possible that this anxiety presupposes in Paul special knowledge of the situation in Rome, which plainly is controlled by the Jewish Christians. This explains the unusually long and careful description of himself in the opening verses, and also the special content of the letter.[33]

The events in Rome show only too well how justified was Paul's fear.[34] The conflicts there became acute. Even Peter, who as the

---

[30] See above, p. 51.
[31] That these difficulties had already begun for Peter at an earlier time is rightly emphasized by W. Grundmann, "Die Apostel zwischen Jerusalem und Antiochien" (*ZNW*, 1940, p. 128).
[32] See above, p. 45.
[33] We have seen above that one cannot conclude from this fact with H. Lietzmann, *Sitzungsbericht der Berliner Akademie der Wissenschaften*, 1930, that Peter came to Rome and agitated against Paul. See p. 78. On this subject see E. Hirsch, "Petrus und Paulus" (*ZNW*, 1930, pp. 63 ff.).
[34] C. Cecchelli, *Gli Apostoli a Roma*, 1938, p. 101, has actually proposed the hypothesis that Paul, on account of conditions in Rome, asked Peter to come

responsible organizer of the Jewish Christian mission had come at this time to the capital city, perhaps for the very purpose of removing internal difficulties, was apparently singled out for attack and was deserted by some of his own group. This was doubtless the result of the very conciliatory standpoint that he took. As the official leader of the Jerusalem mission he no doubt had everywhere, as we have mentioned, a difficult position. But now he was made the object of unusually strong hostility by the extremists of the Jewish Christian party.

After the writing of Philippians, therefore, the conflicts, which seem to have become more acute after Paul's arrival at Rome, may finally have degenerated into open attacks, and things may even have gone so far that during the time of persecution those people did not shrink from pointing out to the magistrates the leading men, when summoned to do so. This furthermore may find a confirmation in the pagan source which tells of Nero's action against the Christians; in Tacitus, *Annals*, XV, 44, we read: "The (Christians) first seized who made a confession were convicted, and then upon their evidence a great multitude . . ."[35] It has been said that such informing during a persecution, when the hearing is accompanied by torture, is nothing abnormal.[36] Nevertheless, Tacitus makes it a special point to mention this fact. Naturally we cannot prove, but can only suppose, that the zealous ones were really to be sought among those "first seized." In any case, this would correspond completely with the saying of Jesus preserved in Matthew 24:10: "They will deliver up one another."

It could also be that the attention of the Empire was turned to the apostles by some other way than by direct report. This much, however, is certain: *according to the opinion of Clement* it happened as a

to the capital city. The fact that Peter was so to speak responsible for the Jewish Christian part of the Church could indeed argue for this hypothesis. Moreover, C. Cecchelli also assumes a betrayal of the two apostles by a "new Judas." See *op. cit.*, p. 96.

[35] *Igitur primo conrepti qui fatebantur, deinde, indicio eorum, multitudo ingens . . .* On recent interpretation of this text see H. Fuchs, "Tacitus über die Christen," (*Vigiliae christianae*, 1950, pp. 65 ff.), and A. Kurfess, "Tacitus über die Christen" (*Vigiliae christianae*, 1951, pp. 148 f.). According to Chr. Eggenberger, *Die Quellen der politischen Ethik des 1. Klem.*, 1951, pp. 127 f., Clement would be dependent on Tacitus at this point.

[36] J. Munck, *op. cit.*, p. 63.—He further writes that from this passage it follows that the persecution was already going on. That is correct. But I do not understand how this is supposed to argue against my interpretation. After all, it is not necessary to assume that Peter and Paul had been seized at the very beginning.

result of the jealousy which separated the members of a church from
one another; and since such an assertion, which runs contrary to all
later tendencies, could not possibly have been invented, the opinion
that Clement here expresses must have corresponded with the
reality.

Theoretically, of course, the possibility remains open that what
took place in Rome could also happen elsewhere, that therefore disputes in the Church could become the external occasion for executions of other Christians by the Empire, so that we would not
have to assume as a certainty that the martyrdom of Peter occurred
in the same place as did that of Paul and the great multitude. But
this is improbable, and in any case the fact remains that the existence
of such jealousy is attested only for Rome, where it is attested by
I Clement 6:1, almost certainly by Paul's letter to Philippi, and indirectly also by the letter to the Romans. Therefore the indication
of place in ch. 6:1, "among us," that is, in the church of Bishop
Clement of Rome, quite probably refers to all the Christian martyrdoms mentioned by the author and caused by jealousy.

It is likely, moreover, that by way of warning for the disunited
Corinthians Clement recalled, in addition to the parties which at an
earlier time had split their church (ch. 47), precisely such Christian
examples of jealousy and division as he could report from his own
Roman church.

Furthermore, it has been suggested that in Mark 15:10 the Evangelist added the remark, "Pilate knew that the high priests had delivered
Jesus up *out of envy*,"[37] under the special influence of the events in
Rome; Mark indeed wrote his Gospel in Rome, and so was a witness of those events.[38]

Finally, a further trace of these unhappy events appears to have
been preserved in the *later legends* of the Acts of Peter. When we
there hear that Peter was executed because he induced prominent
Roman ladies to leave their husbands, the element of jealousy may
constitute at least the historical kernel of this legend.[39]

Still more striking, however, are two passages of the Acts of
Paul.[40] They reproduce legends in which Paul expressly appears as

[37] διὰ φθόνον.
[38] This thesis has been defended, in conjunction with my article (see above, p. 75),
by A. Fridrichsen, "Propter invidiam, Note sur 1. Clém. Rom. V" (*Eranos
Rudbergianus*, 1946, pp. 161 ff.).
[39] *Actus Vercellenses*, 33 ff.
[40] I owe this reference to my colleague Erik Peterson. See ΠΡΑΞΕΙΣ ΠΑΥΛΟΥ.
Acta Pauli nach dem Papyrus der Hamburger Bibliothek, edited by C. Schmidt, 1936.

the victim of jealousy. First, in Ephesus, it is said that a certain Diophantos, whose wife was a disciple of Paul and was with him day and night, became jealous and occasioned his battle with wild beasts.[41] It is further told[42] that in Corinth a Spirit-filled man predicted to Paul that he would depart from this world in Rome as a victim of jealousy.[43] Here, no doubt, statements of Paul (I Cor. 15:32) are combined with I Clement, ch. 5. In any case both the Acts of Peter and the Acts of Paul have correctly preserved from I Clement, ch. 5, the fact that the death of the two apostles had been occasioned by jealousy, although they could only conceive this jealousy in the primitive form of the jealousy of a pagan husband with regard to his Christian wife. The idea of jealousy among church members, of a "danger among false brethren" (II Cor. 11:26), was far from their minds; such a thought contradicted their entire outlook.

We reach the following conclusion. From the investigation of I Clement we conclude, not with absolute certainty but yet with the highest probability, that Peter suffered martyrdom at Rome about the time of the Neronian persecution, while divisions existed in the church there. Peter and Paul, therefore, became martyrs at about the same time, not necessarily on the same day, but probably in the same period of persecution, which may have covered a more or less extended period.[44] Concerning Peter, First Clement does not permit us to say whether he also carried on a real activity in Rome as a missionary or church leader. Just as little can we learn from this text when he came to Rome.[45] The quarrels of which we hear render likely the assumption that this happened shortly before the persecution, and specifically in connection with his responsibility for the Jewish Christian part of the Church.

We now come to the last of the early literary witnesses, the *Letter of Ignatius of Antioch to the Romans*. At the beginning of the second

---

[41] Page 2, line 8 of the Papyrus.   [42] Page 6, line 27 of the Papyrus.

[43] ζηλωθέντα ἐξελθεῖν.

[44] A greater separation in time, such as K. Holl, for example, assumes in *Gesammelte Aufsätze*, Vol. II, 1928, p. 67, note, is naturally not excluded.

[45] J. Munck, *op. cit.*, assumes that they both came thither as condemned men. That both suffered martyrdom *together* he believes it necessary to conclude from the fact that only the common death can have caused the *ancient* tradition to name the two apostles together, although they had worked quite separately; indeed, all the later apocryphal Acts, apart from the Acts of Peter and Paul, which dates only from the fifth century, also tell of them separately. He finds the common martyrdom confirmed also in Rev. 11:3.

century this martyr, a prisoner condemned to execution in the Circus at Rome, writes while en route to the Christian church of that city, which soon will witness his martyrdom.

In ch. 4:3 of this writing we read: "Not like Peter and Paul do I give you commands.[46] They (were) apostles, I am a condemned man; they were free, I am even till now a slave; but when I suffer, I shall become Jesus Christ's freeman, and I shall arise in him as a free man." This is what Ignatius writes to the Roman church. It is to be noted that he recalls to the mind of this particular church the examples of Peter and Paul.

To be sure, not a word is said to indicate that the two apostles were in Rome. The sentence could be taken simply to mean that Ignatius wished to say: "I do not command you *as if* I were Peter and Paul." The parallel passages in the letter of Ignatius to the Ephesians (ch. 3:1) and to the Trallians (ch. 3:3) could support such an interpretation. There Ignatius actually does write in very general terms: "I do not command you as though I were somebody," "not as an apostle."[47] Nevertheless, it is noteworthy that precisely in his letter to the *Romans* he is not content with such a general way of expressing himself, but refers to Peter and Paul *by name*. In no case can it be said that the combined mention of Peter and Paul would *necessarily* force itself upon a writer as soon as he sought for apostles to name. This might be true in a later time, but not in the time of Ignatius. One cannot evade the question: How could it happen at that time that Ignatius named the two together? After all, these two apostles, apart from their meetings in Jerusalem and their conflict in Antioch, nowhere worked together. Indeed, according to the Jerusalem agreement of Galatians 2:9, they headed two separate missionary organizations.[48]

The most plausible answer seems to me to be the reference to their common martyrdom in Rome, especially since it can be shown that in another passage (ch. 3:1) Ignatius refers to First Clement.[49] Thus the combined mention of the two in our writing is also best explained by saying that Ignatius cites by name to the Romans those

[46] οὐχ ὡς Πέτρος καὶ Παῦλος διατάσσομαι ὑμῖν.

[47] K. Heussi rightly points to these parallels in *War Petrus in Rom?*, pp. 40 ff.

[48] J. Munck, following W. Bauer, *Rechtgläubigkeit und Ketzerei*, 1934, p. 116, rightly puts this question. In any case, the answer of H. Dannenbauer, "Die Römische Petruslegende" (*Historische Zeitschrift*, 1932, p. 258), that the two apostles had been together in Antioch, is insufficient.

[49] O. Perler, "Ignatius von Antiochien und die römische Christengemeinde" (*Divus Thomas*, 1944, pp. 442 f.), has demonstrated this.

apostles who were with them as martyrs, just as he himself is now coming to them as a martyr. Even if he here emphasizes the difference between them and himself, yet this negative comparison has meaning only if the writer is conscious that he nevertheless has something in common with them. This is not the apostolic office, but probably the martyrdom in Rome. In the parallel passage in the Letter to the Trallians (ch. 3:3) Ignatius gives no names of apostles, precisely because in relation to this church, which no apostle has visited, there is no occasion to do so. In his letter, on the other hand, to the Ephesians, whom *Paul* had visited, he mentions the name of this apostle, even if in a quite different context (ch. 12:2).

It must be admitted, of course, that even these texts of Ignatius do not give us absolute certainty. However, we again must conclude that Ignatius in all probability knew of a Roman martyrdom of Peter and Paul.

Does this passage also permit the conclusion that the two apostles were active in Rome prior to their martyrdom? The expression "give commands"[50] appears to make this likely. It has, indeed, been said that this word simply refers to the instructions of Paul's letter to Rome. In that case, however, Peter would then be wrongly linked with Paul. It therefore could be that Ignatius here refers to a missionary and ecclesiastical activity of the two apostles. The connection, however, in which Ignatius here speaks of "giving commands" makes this unlikely. The chapter at whose end stands the sentence that interests us contains in its first part the famous summons to the Roman Christians not to intervene with the imperial authorities on behalf of Ignatius, since he does not want to be deprived of martyrdom. The mention of the commands of Peter and Paul, therefore, stands in a context in which Ignatius is speaking of his martyrdom and of the attitude of the Roman church towards this martyrdom. Ignatius himself is compelled at the beginning of this chapter to "give a command" regarding this.[51] So the most natural explanation probably is that the giving of commands by Peter and Paul also was connected with their own martyrdoms. If so, this mention contains no indication concerning a longer preaching activity of the two apostles, although on the other hand it does not exclude such preaching. It is sufficient, then, to assume that before their death the two apostles had an opportunity to give instructions to the Roman church with reference to their martyrdom.

[50] διατάσσεσθαι.
[51] Ch. 4:1: ἐντέλλομαι; this means that he gives a command "to all churches."

With some reservations we can add as a further indirect witness from the first century a passage from the apocryphal writing, the *Ascension of Isaiah*,[52] of which it has been said that it is the first and earliest document that attests the martyrdom of Peter in Rome. The passage in question is ch. 4:2 f., where we read the following prediction: ". . . then will arise Beliar, the great prince, the king of this world, who has ruled it since its origin; and he will descend from his firmament in human form, king of wickedness, murderer of his mother, who himself is king of this world; and he will persecute the plant which the twelve apostles of the Beloved shall have planted; one of the Twelve will be delivered into his hands." It seems beyond doubt that Nero is here meant by Beliar, who descends in human form and murders his mother. Less clear is the mention of the "one of the Twelve" who is delivered into his hands. As apostles who were victims of Nero, Peter and Paul are to be considered.[53] Paul, however, cannot be meant here, for according to ch. 3:17 the author uses the phrase "the Twelve" in the narrower sense.[54] In that case this passage probably refers to Peter. The statement is of course vague, and the mention of the "delivering up" stands in need of further definition.[55] Above all, the indication of the place is also lacking. Nevertheless, the passage speaks of an apostle who fell into Nero's hands, and so we probably can think only of Rome. The difficulty, however, lies in the dating of the Christian apocalypse, chs. 3:13 to 4:19, to which this passage belongs. While some think it was written in the lifetime of Nero,[56] others wish to put it later, in the third century.[57] Even if the decision for a date about 100 is the most probable,[58] we cannot reach a certain conclusion. Nevertheless, this witness should not be simply ignored, as has often happened in recent discussions.

*   *   *

[52] See R. H. Charles, *The Ascension of Isaiah*, 1900; E. Tisserant, *Ascension d'Isaïe*, 1909; J. Flemming—H. Duensing, *Die Himmelfahrt des Jesaja*, in E. Hennecke, *Neutestamentliche Apokryphen*, 2nd ed., 1924, pp. 303 ff.

[53] According to E. Zeller, *Zeitschrift für wissenschaftliche Theologie*, 1896, pp. 558 ff., what is involved is the exile of the apostle John.

[54] E. Tisserant, *op. cit.*, p. 117, rightly points to this fact.

[55] For this reason A. Harnack, *Geschichte der altchristlichen Literatur, Die Chronologie*, Vol. I, 1897, p. 715, denies that this passage speaks of the martyrdom of Peter.

[56] C. Clemen, "Die Himmelfahrt des Jesaja, ein ältestes Zeugnis für das römische Martyrium des Petrus" (*Zeitschrift für wissenschaftliche Theologie*, 1896, pp. 388 ff.).

[57] A. Harnack, *op. cit.*, pp. 578 f.

[58] So R. H. Charles, *op. cit.*, and E. Tisserant, *op. cit.*, p. 60.

We have reached the end of our study of the early literary documents[59] and can now sum up the results:

Prior to the second half of the second century no document asserts explicitly the stay and martyrdom of Peter in Rome. Nevertheless, we have established: 1. As far as the *fact of the martyr death* of Peter is concerned, we possess an ancient tradition concerning it, John 21:18 ff., and this seems presupposed also in other texts. 2. As far as the *stay of Peter in Rome* is concerned, this is excluded for the time at which Paul writes his letter to the Romans. The founding of the Roman church by Peter can neither be proved nor regarded as probable. Since, however, according to Romans 15:20, it was the work of Jewish Christians, there exists a cogent reason for saying that he came to the capital city as the responsible leader of the Jewish Christian mission. The First Epistle of Peter probably presupposes in ch. 5:13 that at some time Peter was in Rome. As far as his *activity* in the Roman church is concerned, no early text compels us to contest it. But on the other hand, neither is it explicitly mentioned by a single text of the ancient period, and in any case it is difficult, for reasons of chronology, to include a very long activity. Of an episcopal office of Peter nothing is ever said. In the form in which this office is first asserted in the fourth century,[60] it is historically impossible. From everything that we know concerning the situation within the Roman church from Paul's letters to Rome and Philippi and from First Clement, his activity, like that of Paul, may be connected with the relations between the Jewish Christian and Gentile Christian parts of the Church. 3. As far as the *martyr death of Peter in Rome* is concerned, we have concerning it two texts that must be regarded as indirect witnesses: I Clement, ch. 5, and Ignatius, Romans 4:3. Neither of them says explicitly that Peter had been in Rome. In both cases,

---

[59] J. Zeiller, *L'Eglise primitive* (*Histoire de l'Eglise*, 1946 ed., p. 229; Eng. Tr., *History of the Primitive Church*, Vol. I, 1942, p. 235), adds as a further witness from the first half of the second century that of Papias; as reported by Eusebius, *Ecclesiastical History*, III, 39, 15, he tells that Mark wrote his Gospel in accord with the sermons of Peter. But that the Gospel was written in Rome ("composé à Rome") and that the sermons of Peter were preached in that city ("en cette ville"), as J. Zeiller asserts, this text of Papias does not say at all!

[60] *Catalogus Liberianus* (year 354): "After the resurrection of Christ the blessed Peter received the episcopal office . . . for twenty-five years, one month, and eight days he was (bishop) in the time of Tiberius Caesar, Gaius, Claudius, and Nero, from the consulate of Minucius and Longinus to that of Nerinus and Verus."—That would be from 30 to 55. All these statements stand in such flagrant contradiction to The Acts and the letters of Paul that it is unnecessary even to discuss them.

however, and particularly in First Clement, which presupposes in the Church definite circumstances that fit only Rome, we can establish a great probability. It is sufficient to let us *include the martyrdom of Peter in Rome in our final historical picture of the early Church, as a fact which is relatively though not absolutely assured.* We accept it, however, with the self-evident caution that we have to use concerning many other facts of antiquity that are universally accepted as historical. Were we to demand for all facts of ancient history a greater degree of probability, we should have to strike from our history books a large proportion of their contents.

The argument from silence cannot be used as a counterproof against the martyr death of Peter at Rome, especially since the reason for that silence can be explained from the special circumstances of the martyrdom, as we can deduce them from I Clement, ch. 5. Furthermore, from the later silence of the Roman Bishop Anicetus, in the first Passover debate about the middle of the second century, we cannot conclude that at that time nothing was known as yet of a stay of Peter in Rome. In that controversy Polycarp, the Bishop of Smyrna, appeals to John and other apostles with whom he has associated to support the way of celebrating the Passover festival which he defends, while Anicetus only recalls the usage of those who were "the most ancient ones before him," and says not a word concerning Peter.[61] This, however, could at the most be cited as evidence that Anicetus knew nothing of a leading activity of Peter in Rome; in no case can it be cited to show lack of knowledge concerning his martyrdom.[62]

If it were not imperative to handle with caution all arguments from silence, one could reverse the argument. To support the indications we possess of a martyrdom in Rome one could cite the fact that the entire early Christian literature is *completely* silent concerning the death of Peter. We do not have even the slightest trace that points to any *other* place which could be considered as the scene of his death. In favour of Rome there are at least important even if indirect hints, which there are good grounds for so interpreting. Their value as proof, moreover, is increased precisely by their indirect and merely

---

[61] Eusebius, *Ecclesiastical History*, V, 24, 16.
[62] Apart from that fact, Anicetus also could not boast, as Polycarp could, of direct relations with the apostles. M. Goguel, *L'Eglise primitive*, 1947, p. 213, explains the failure of Anicetus to appeal to the apostles by the consciousness of the Roman church that the Easter festival had been introduced only a short time before, and so did not reach back into the apostolic age.

allusive character. It is a further important point that in the second and third centuries, when certain churches were in rivalry with the one in Rome, it never occurred to a single one of them to contest the claim of Rome that it was the scene of the martyrdom of Peter. Indeed, even more can be said; precisely in the east, as is clear from the Pseudo-Clementine writings and the Petrine legends, above all those that deal with Peter's conflict with Simon the magician, the tradition of the Roman residence of Peter had a particularly strong hold.

In the second half of the second century the Roman tradition about Peter begins to be explicitly attested. It can scarcely be proved that this is to be explained as a defence against Marcion, who recognized only Paul as a true apostle.[63] It is sufficient rather to take account of the universal effort, which appears in this period, to prove the apostolic origin of the churches. It will not do, however, to ascribe to such tendencies the *invention* of Peter's stay and martyrdom at Rome; their function can be limited to the emphasizing and development of traditions that already existed independently of them.

On the other hand, the chief value for historical study of these *late* texts, which now in increasing number assert that Peter was in Rome and became a martyr there, concerns only the history of dogma; they attest the *development* of the tradition. In theory the possibility cannot be excluded that perhaps here and there the basis of the tradition is a good earlier source which we no longer possess. Yet even if this is so, we must be fundamentally sceptical toward these later texts, when we see how in this very period the development of Christian legend flourishes and how it seeks to fill out the gaps in the New Testament narrative. Where in addition contradictions between these texts and the early sources appear, their trustworthiness must be challenged from the start. With this reserve, however, it is interesting to get acquainted with at least the earliest of these witnesses, those of the second and third centuries.

* * *

First of all, however, we must note the silence of a Christian writer who lived in Rome. This is *Justin Martyr*, from whom we possess extensive writings that date from the middle of the second century.

---

[63] So K. Heussi, *op. cit.*, p. 56, according to whom Peter's stay and death in Rome were first invented to meet the necessities of this anti-Marcionite struggle.

Neither in his Apologies nor in the Dialogue with Trypho is Peter's Roman residence mentioned. This is the more striking in view of the fact that he speaks three times of Simon the magician, who in this period was regarded as the great opponent of Peter.

Among the later texts the chief one is the letter, already mentioned, from the Corinthian Bishop *Dionysius* to the Romans. Its date is about the year 170. Eusebius has preserved some fragments of it for us.[64] We have already spoken of it in connection with the question concerning the stay of Peter in Corinth.[65] Dionysius takes pains to prove the common bond between the two churches of Rome and Corinth. He recalls first the letter of Clement, which, he says, was regularly read in Corinth, and which bound the two churches together. For example, Peter and Paul had "planted" the church of Corinth and had taught there; in like manner, both had taught together in Italy as well, and had borne witness at the same time. We have already seen[66] that at least *one* historical error occurs here: the assertion that Peter together with Paul *founded* the church of Corinth. This is excluded by I Corinthians 3:6 and 4:15. In addition, Dionysius here asserts that they had taught *together* [67] in Italy, which certainly refers to Rome. This *joint* preaching activity is not indeed impossible in view of the early texts, but the statement scarcely goes back to early tradition.

Toward the end of the second century *Irenaeus* writes,[68] chiefly in connection with a description of gospel origins that goes back to Papias, that Peter and Paul had preached in Rome and founded the church, and he repeats this assertion when he speaks of the Roman church as the "very ancient and universally known church founded and organized by Peter and Paul." Here, too, occurs at least *one* error: the Roman church in any case was not *founded* by Paul. That is entirely clear from his letter to the Romans. This at once calls in question the historical trustworthiness of the statement. Concerning the martyr death of Peter in Rome, be it noted, nothing is said here. But from this fact no negative conclusion can be drawn,

---

[64] Eusebius, *Ecclesiastical History*, II, 25, 8.
[65] See above, p. 54.   [66] See above, p. 54.
[67] It is impossible to defend the assertion that ὁμόσε ("to the same place," "together") only indicates that they went to the same place, Italy, but not at the same time. For ὁμόσε here as often stands for ὁμοῦ ("together"). See Blass-Debrunner, *Grammatik des neutestamentlichen Griechisch*, 7th ed., 1943, Part II, Supplement, Par. 103, p. 19. See also W. Bauer, *Griechisch-deutsches, Wörterbuch*, ὁμόσε.
[68] *Adversus Haereses*, III, 1–3.

for neither is anything said here concerning the martyr death of Paul.[69]

In contrast to this, *Tertullian*[70] at about the same time congratulates the Roman church because the apostles "have spread their teaching" in it "with their shed blood," because in it Peter has suffered a martyrdom "like the death of the Lord," and Paul in the manner of John the Baptist has attained the "palm of martyrdom." When, however, he adds at the same time the legend that the apostle John was dipped in boiling oil at Rome and yet survived uninjured, the value of his statements concerning Peter and Paul is thereby lessened. We must speak later of a further text of Tertullian[71] which probably refers to the *grave* of Peter.

Clement of Alexandria reports[72] that Peter wrote his first letter in Rome and "used a cryptic word in designating the city of Rome by the name Babylon." This is a notice which at the most need be considered in the history of the interpretation of I Peter 5:13.

The statement of *Origen*[73] that Peter was crucified in Rome with his head downward scarcely has historical value, even if the crucifixion as such appears to be attested in John 21:18 f.[74]

The statement of the Roman Presbyter *Gaius*, however, deserves greater respect. Not as though the fact of the stay and martyrdom of Peter in Rome could be based upon it. It dates only from the beginning of the third century. The importance of this account, which comes from Rome itself, consists rather in the fact that here the Roman tradition about Peter is given a definite topographical support, which can serve as a clue in the archaeological search for Peter's grave.

Gaius is here opposing the Montanist Proclus, who in his polemic had appealed to the fact that the church of Hierapolis in Asia Minor possesses the graves of Philip and his daughters.[75] Gaius writes the following words:[76] "But I can show the trophies[77] of the apostles,

---

[69] This is rightly stressed by M. Goguel, *L'Eglise primitive*, 1947, p. 216, in opposition to Ch. Guignebert, "La sépulture de Pierre" (*Revue historique*, 1931, pp. 225 ff.).

[70] *De praescriptione haereticorum*, 36; *Scorpiace*, 15; *Adversus Marcionem*, IV, 5.

[71] See below, p. 121. [72] Eusebius, *Ecclesiastical History*, II, 15, 2.

[73] *Idem*, III, 1, 2.

[74] In Christian typology the phrase ἔκτασις τῶν χειρῶν ("stretching out of the hands") refers to the crucifixion. Tertullian, *Scorpiace*, 15, already refers the ζώσει ("he will gird") of John 21:18 to the binding to the cross.

[75] Eusebius, *Ecclesiastical History*, III, 31, 4.

[76] *Idem*, II, 25, 7. [77] τρόπαια.

for if you go to the Vatican Hill or to the highway to Ostia, you will find the trophies of those who have founded this church."

We need not stop to consider the statement concerning the joint *founding* of the Roman church by the two apostles; this statement, in spite of its historical inaccuracy, had become by this time a fixed tradition. It is important, however, to know that in the time of Gaius the places which were connected with the martyrdoms of Peter and Paul were definitely located.

Whether the word "trophies" here means graves is disputed. The Greek word can also mean simply "victory memorials" and need not always designate a definite object. It can be meant quite generally as a place which recalls a victory or an event interpreted as a victory,[78] and in the ancient Christian view martyrdom belongs to this category. The narrower meaning of "burial place," however, is also clearly attested.[79] Thus there are two possibilities. The two places designated as "trophies" were regarded either as the burial places of the apostles[80] or as the places where they had been executed.[81]

It is clear in any case that Eusebius understood the word in the sense of "burial places." For he introduces the quotation from Gaius with the remark that Gaius, who is speaking against Proclus, speaks of the places "in which were buried the sacred bodies of the apostles named (Peter and Paul)."[82] Furthermore, the mention of the places by Gaius is probably to be considered parallel to the appeal that his Montanist opponent Proclus makes to the graves of Philip and his daughters in Asia Minor, although Eusebius reports this latter point in another part of his book.[83] If the two are parallel, the assumption is still more likely that in the opinion of Gaius the "trophies" of Peter and Paul meant their graves.

[78] See F. Lammert, Article on τρόπαιον in Pauly-Wissowa, *Reallexikon der klassischen Altertumswissenschaft*.

[79] See P. Monceaux, "Enquête sur l'épigraphie chrétienne d'Afrique" (*Mémoires présentés à l'Academie des Inscriptions et Belles-Lettres*, Vol. 88, 1910, p. 260.

[80] So H. Lietzmann, *Petrus und Paulus in Rom*, p. 210, and also K. Heussi, *War Petrus in Rom?*, p. 64. Likewise, H. Delehaye, *Les origines du cult des martyrs*, 1933, p. 264.

[81] So C. Erbes, "Das Alter der Gräber und Kirchen des Paulus und Petrus in Rom" (*Zeitschrift für Kirchengeschichte*, 1885, pp. 1 ff.); *Die Todestage der Apostel Paulus und Petrus und ihre römischen Denkmäler*, 1899; "Die geschichtlichen Verhältnisse der Apostelgräber in Rom" (*ZKG*, 1924, pp. 38 ff.). Likewise Ch. Guignebert, *La primauté de Pierre et la venue de Pierre à Rome*, 1919, pp. 305 ff. See also Th. Klausner, *Jahrbuch für Liturgiewissenschaft*, 1924, p. 296.

[82] Eusebius, *Ecclesiastical History*, II, 25, 6.

[83] Ch. Guignebert, *op. cit.*, believes for this reason that this reference must be denied.

Thus the only certain fact is that about the year 200 there were shown in Rome the places with which was connected the memory of the martyrdoms of Peter and Paul. For it is inconceivable that Gaius only invented these locations to serve the needs of his anti-Montanist polemic. The tradition which designated these two places *must therefore have existed before he wrote.*

This still does not prove, however, that the tradition is true as far as the *graves* are concerned. For in any event almost a century and a half lies between the death of the apostles and this earliest testimony as to the place where it occurred. In favour of its correctness it has been argued, as we shall see, that if the tradition were only a later invention, these places would not have been invented in such great geographical distance from one another as are the Vatican Hill and the highway to Ostia. It has further been argued that in this case the burials would have been located not in pagan cemeteries but rather, in accordance with a later tendency, in Christian catacombs.[84] This argument certainly deserves serious consideration. On the other hand, it still is not completely decisive, for as has already been remarked, the tendency to join the two apostles is not common in the ancient apocryphal literature.[85]

Should the word "trophies" refer to *graves*, the following argument can be made against the correctness of the tradition that Gaius attests concerning their location. It is hard to conceive that the surviving Roman Christians could have recognized the bodies of the apostles among the many corpses, largely charred as they probably were by fire, and could then have taken them away and have honoured Peter with a grave in the very garden of Nero. This is hardly conceivable if we are dealing with the Neronian persecution, in which we must assume that the remains were thrown into the Tiber.[86] We should also emphasize that in the first century *not the slightest trace of a cult of martyr relics* can be found. The first testimony to that we find only about A.D. 150, in the Martyrdom of Polycarp.[87] In view of the *expectation of the end of the world* in the immediate future, a concern for relics clearly constitutes an anachronism in thinking of the sixth decade of the first century, especially in those terrible days of persecution under Nero. We shall return to this point

---

[84] So H. Lietzmann, *Petrus und Paulus in Rom*, pp. 246 ff.

[85] See above, p. 109, note 45; p. 110.

[86] See K. Holl, *Gesammelte Aufsätze*, Vol. II, p. 65, note 1.

[87] According to H. Grégoire's latest thesis (see below, p. 150, note 70), the year is 177

when we speak of the archaeological results. Finally, should the most recent hypothesis be correct, according to which "the two witnesses" of Revelation 11:3 ff. are to be identified with the two apostles Peter and Paul, then their bodies were not buried at first and the rise of the tradition of their direct rapture to Heaven would exclude any know-ledge of the place of their burial.[88]

In case the "trophies" mentioned by Gaius, however, are not the ancient burial places, there still remains the possibility that the two places were the *places of execution*, which then without further evi-dence were later regarded, perhaps even by the time of Gaius, as the burial places. On the other hand, it can be assumed that the executed persons, if buried at all, were buried at the place of their execution, or at any rate in the immediate neighbourhood. This being so, the graves would then be at least approximately located, though not precisely identified—this was not possible or even attempted in the earliest period.

We must return to this text of Gaius when we speak of the results of the excavations under the Church of St. Peter. At present our chief task is to evaluate the significance of this literary witness as such. Although it dates only from the beginning of the third century, yet greater importance attaches to it than to the previously discussed witnesses of equal antiquity. It is true that a purely topographical tradition is not free from the influence of partisan interests. This is especially clear since, as we know also from the Letter of Polycrates,[89] the possession of graves was regarded at this time as a guarantee of the genuineness of a tradition, and so led also to the making of "de-position lists." Yet such a tradition naturally offers a greater guarantee of correctness than does a tradition concerning the events themselves.

The attempt has been made to explain this locating of the graves as a later deduction from the narrative of Tacitus. It locates the place of martyrdom of the persecuted Christians[90] in the gardens and the Circus of Nero, which according to the latest excavations were located not, as one had believed, under the present Cathedral of Peter, but probably quite close to it.[91] It is doubtful, however, whether that sort of scholarly reflection, resting upon the study of pagan sources, could conceivably have been at work at that time in the origin of a Christian tradition about where things happened. Apart from this fact, this assumption in any case does not apply to the "trophy" of

[88] See above, pp. 88 f.   [89] Eusebius, *Ecclesiastical History*, V, 24, 2 ff.
[90] See below, p. 142.
[91] So K. Heussi, *War Petrus in Rom?*, p. 66, and M. Goguel, *L'Eglise primitive*, p. 214.

Paul on the highway to Ostia, and if one does not come to our text with the *a priori* presupposition that Peter was not in Rome, it is hard to see why the traditional statement that Gaius attests concerning the place of execution or the grave of Peter deserves less credence than does the tradition concerning that of Paul.

Nevertheless, the only certain conclusion that we can retain from the text of Gaius is that about the year 200 not only was it universally accepted in Rome that the martyrdom of Peter and Paul occurred in this city, but Christians also *pointed out there the places which were regarded as the places of their execution or perhaps even as their graves.*

In this connection should be mentioned the well-known text of *Tertullian,* which according to the most probable assumption was directed against the Roman Bishop *Callistus,* and specifically against the edict he had issued. According to this edict, and contrary to the early practice of the Church, penance should be granted also for sins of unchastity.[92] On this occasion Tertullian turns against what seems to him the arrogant presumption of this Bishop, who refers to himself, and so to "every church that is near Peter" (*ad omnem ecclesiam Petri propinquam*), the saying of Jesus to Peter concerning binding and loosing, when in fact this saying was directed to Peter alone. In recent study these quoted words have been explained, and probably correctly, in the sense of a purely local nearness, that is, "at the grave of Peter." [93] According to this interpretation, Tertullian reproaches Callistus because he refers Matthew 16:18 to himself, with the argument that he is Bishop of a church that has the grave of Peter near it. In this case we find the view attested here that from the grave of Peter, so to speak, the power to loose and bind which had been given to Peter actually streams forth in physical manner and passes over to the Bishop of the church in whose district the grave is located.

[92] *De Pudicitia,* 21. The passage of interest to us is as follows: "I now inquire into your opinion, (to see) from what source you usurp this right to 'the Church.' If, because the Lord has said to Peter, 'Upon this rock I will build my Church,' 'To thee have I given the keys of the Kingdom of Heaven,' or 'Whatsoever thou shalt have bound or loosed in earth, shall be bound or loosed in heaven,' you therefore presume that the power of binding and loosing has derived to you, that is, to every church near to Peter, what sort of man are you, subverting and wholly changing the manifest intention of the Lord, conferring (as that intention did) this (gift) personally upon Peter?" (See *The Ante-Nicene Fathers,* Vol. IV, 1890, p. 99.)

[93] W. Köhler, "Omnis ecclesia Petri propinqua" (*Sitzungsbericht der Heidelberger Akademie der Wissenschaften, Philosophisch-historische Klasse,* 1938). H. Koch. *Cathedra Petri,* 1930, pp. 5 ff., takes a different view.

If this explanation is correct, it is here presupposed at the beginning of the third century that Peter was buried at the place of execution or near it. This does not necessarily mean that one possessed relics or that the "trophy" was connected with an actual grave. But the tradition concerning the place of execution also included a statement concerning the place of burial, in so far as it was the custom for executed persons to be buried in the neighbourhood. Whether one knew the *exact* place of burial thus remains doubtful, even if we accept the above interpretation.

Among the later literary witnesses we should mention further the statement of *Macarius Magnus* (III, 22), since it goes back to *Porphyrius*, the Neo-Platonic foe of the Christians. In this passage, evidently with the malicious purpose of setting the great promises to Peter in contrast with his actual insignificant work, it is reported that Peter was "crucified after he had shepherded the sheep for only a few months." Although this information dates no earlier than the end of the third century, it still has greater value than the witnesses from the second century, since it goes back to an enemy of the Christians and contradicts the Christian tendencies that aim rather to glorify Peter and so seek to extend as much as possible his Roman activity.[94]

In this text Porphyrius, the foe of the Christians, alludes to the command of the Risen One in John 21:16 f. and wishes to show that the "feeding of the sheep" there promised was not very extensive, since it only lasted so short a time. To be sure, he does not mention Rome. But in this passage no other place need be considered. This results at once from the simple consideration that Porphyrius, in speaking of the brief "feeding of the sheep," can only have thought of the same place at which occurred the crucifixion mentioned in the same sentence; the "few months" would not cover the entire preceding missionary activity of Peter in the rest of the Empire. But we know, on the other hand, that in the time of Porphyrius the tradition concerning the martyrdom of Peter in Rome was already so widespread that he certainly must have said so if he had thought of any other place but Rome.[95] Thus we probably can conclude from this

---

[94] A. Harnack, "Porphyrius gegen die Christen" (*Abhandlungen der Berliner Akademie der Wissenschaften*, 1916); *Mission und Ausbreitung des Christentums in den ersten drei Jahrhunderten*, 1924, Vol. I, p. 63, note 2, rightly ascribes to this notice the highest value as a source. The older assumption of Carl Schmidt, *Die alten Petrusakten*, 1903, pp. 167 ff., that it was taken only from the *Acts of Peter*, would indeed if correct lessen this value, but his theory is incapable of proof.

[95] I should like to argue this against H. Dannenbauer, "Die römische Petruslegende" (*Historische Zeitschrift*, 1932, p. 243), and K. Heussi, *War Petrus, in Rom?*, p. 61.

text that Peter came to Rome only a short time before his martyr death.

Thus of the later witnesses discussed in this section which assert, beginning with the second half of the second century, the Roman stay and martyrdom of Peter, at least the statement of Gaius, the text of Tertullian against the edict of Callistus, and also the declaration of Porphyrius, must be considered as sources for our study in spite of their later date. They deserve attention in so far as two of them reproduce for the period about the year 200 an exact topographical tradition concerning the places of execution or the graves of the apostles in Rome, while the other one is evidence that Peter worked in Rome but a very short period before he suffered martyrdom.

4. The Liturgical Sources

We still have to study the *liturgical sources* and then examine the results of the excavations. The two are closely connected with one another. The liturgical texts, on the one hand, contain statements concerning the date and place of the martyrdoms or of the martyr festivals, and so can serve as a clue for archaeological investigation; the excavations, on the other hand, can confirm these statements or even show their lack of historical value.

It might be expected that our study could finally gain from such a comparison of liturgical history and archaeology the fully certain result to which none of the previously discussed sources has led us. So one has always approached these studies with great hopes.[96]

The most relevant liturgical texts we find in the calendar prepared for Rome. Furius Dionysius Filocalus, the later secretary of Pope Damasus, issued it in the year 354, probably making use of the episcopal archives.[97] He here unites three collections: 1. the *Depositio Episcoporum*, which contains the days of death and burial of the Roman Bishops from Lucius (†254) to Sylvester (†335). 2. The *Depositio Martyrum*, a list of the festivals for the martyrs and of the

---

[96] H. Lietzmann built his epoch-making work, *Petrus und Paulus in Rom*, entirely upon the connection between the history of liturgy and the study of archaeology.

[97] See Th. Mommsen, *Monumenta Germaniae historica. Auctores antiquissimi* 9, 1892, pp. 15 ff. L. Duchesne, *Le liber Pontificalis I*, 1886, pp. 10 f. C. Kirch, *Encheiridion fontium historiae ecclesiasticae antiquae*, 1923, p. 331. See also H. Lietzmann, *Die drei ältesten Martyrologien* (*Kleine Texte*), 3rd ed., 1921, pp. 2 ff. H. Achelis, "Die Martyrologien, ihre Geschichte und ihr Wert" (*Abhandlungen der Gesellschaft der Wissenschaften in Göttingen, Philologisch-historische Klasse*, New Series, III, 3, 1900, pp. 6 ff.).

fixed festivals of the church year. 3. The *Catalogus Liberianus*, a detailed list of popes from Peter to Liberius (352–366), with notes concerning the duration and the special events of their pontificate; from this list there then arose later, in the sixth century, the *Liber Pontificalis*.

Two statements of the *Depositio Martyrum* concern us here. (The already mentioned statement[98] which the *Catalogus Liberianus* contains concerning his twenty-five-year ministry as bishop is completely worthless.)

One of the statements refers to February 22 and is as follows:

VIII cal. Martias natale Petri de cathedra.

The other refers to June 29 and is as follows:

III cal. Jul. Petri in catacumbas et Pauli
Ostense, Tusco et Basso consulibus (= 258).

We need not pause very long on the former statement. In its present form it is a charge to observe the "anniversary of Peter's entrance upon office," for that is probably what we should understand by *natale de cathedra*. The hypothesis according to which a pagan festival of *cara cognitio* or also *caristia*, in which the Romans held meals at the graves of their dead, is here simply transferred to Peter, is probably correct. Since this festival was also designated by the Greek word *cathedra* ("chair," "seat"), either on account of the custom of sitting at table or of reserving a seat for the deceased, it thus is explained how it was connected particularly with the supposed "episcopal see" of Peter.[99]

It could also be that before June 29 was regarded as the day of the death of the two apostles, February 22 was originally considered, in view of the meaning of the ancient *caristia* celebration, as the *day of their death*.[1]

We need not concern ourselves with the fact that in the so-called Jerome *Martyrologium*, in addition to February 22, there further

---

[98] See above, p. 113.

[99] H. Usener, *Das Weihnachtsfest*, 1911, p. 274; Fedor Schneider, "Ueber Calendae Januariae und Martiae im Mittelalter" (*Archiv für Religionswissenschaft*, 1920–21, pp. 386 ff.); H. Lietzmann, *op. cit.*, pp. 19 ff.; L. Duchesne, *Origines du culte*, 5th ed., 1925, p. 294; Ch. Guignebert, "La sépulture de Pierre" (*Revue historique*, 1931, pp. 225 ff.). Against the connection with the pagan *Caristia* see especially P. Batiffol, *Cathedra Petri*, 1938, pp. 123 ff.

[1] So C. Erbes, *Die Todestage der Apostel Paulus und Petrus*, 1899, p. 44, and M. Goguel, *L'Eglise primitive*, p. 225.

appears as *cathedra Petri* January 18, which corresponds to an ancient Celtic festival. Indeed, February 22 appears as the festival of Peter's episcopal office in Antioch, January 18 of that in Rome. What we have here is a later harmonization of two competing dates for the same festival.[2]

From the statements concerning the festival of Peter's entrance upon office we thus obtain neither directly nor indirectly any addition to our knowledge concerning the activity of Peter.

More important is the already cited notice of the *Depositio Martyrum* for June 29: "Peter in the catacombs, Paul on the Highway to Ostia, in the consulship of Tuscus and Bassus." Its content stands in direct connection with the archaeological work and discussions, for it mentions the catacombs and the highway to Ostia. According to it, the celebration for Peter was held only in the catacombs (not on the Vatican Hill), and that for Paul on the highway to Ostia. The fixing of the date by naming the consulate of Tuscus and Bassus, however, is at first sight obscure. This consulate falls in the year 258, and what we expect is the indication of the year that the apostles died. To identify one of the two consuls, Bassus, with the consul of the same name under Nero is purely hypothetical.[3] But the notice cited from the *Depositio Martyrum* has been compared with a similar one for the same day, June 29, which stands in the late Bern manuscript (eight century) of the *Jerome Martyrologium*. For this day it runs as follows:

> *III. cal. Jul. Romae, via Aurelia, natale sanctorum Petri et Pauli apostolorum, Petri in Vaticano, Pauli vero in via Ostensi, utrumque in Catacumbas, passi sub Nerone, Basso et Tusco consulibus.*
>
> That is, "June 29, on the Aurelian Way, martyr festival of the holy apostles Peter and Paul, of Peter on the Vatican Hill, of Paul on the Highway to Ostia, both in the catacombs, suffered under Nero, in the consulate of Bassus and Tuscus" = 258.

---

[2] By rigorous reasoning H. Lietzmann, *op. cit.*, pp. 29 ff., reached this conclusion.

[3] So P. Monceaux, "L'apostolat de S. Pierre à Rome à propos d'un livre récent" (*Revue d'Histoire et de Littérature religieuses*, 1910, pp. 216 ff.), who expands the text as follows: *passi sub Nerone Basso (et Crasso consulibus; translati in Catacumbas Basso) et Tusco consulibus*, that is, "suffered under Nero in the consulship of Bassus (and Crassus; transferred to the catacombs in the consulship of Bassus) and Tuscus." Dom H. Quentin also, in "Tusco et Basso consulibus" (*Resi conti della Pontificia Accademia de archeologia*, 1926–27, pp. 145–147), traces the mention of the two consuls back to a copyist's error.

Thus here the burial place of Peter on the Vatican Hill is also mentioned.

This notice, which thus connects the martyrdom of Peter with the Vatican Hill and that of Paul with the Highway to Ostia, but then mentions also the catacombs, appears more complete than the one cited above from the *Depositio Martyrum*, whose statement connects Peter and the catacombs on the one hand, and on the other hand Paul and the Highway to Ostia. However, as it stands it too yields no clear meaning. For on the one hand it says that the apostles suffered martyrdom under Nero, while on the other hand the consuls Bassus and Tuscus are named. The consulate of these two, however, is dated, as we have said in the year 258. Therefore it has been proposed to alter the text by striking out the words *via Aurelia* and *passi sub Nerone* and changing *utrumque* into *utriusque*.[4] The following text then results:

> "June 29th: Martyr festival of the holy apostles Peter and Paul, of Peter on the Vatican Hill, of Paul on the Highway to Ostia; of both together in the catacombs. In the consulate of Bassus and Tuscus."[5]

This text presupposes that in the year 258 the memory of *both* apostles was celebrated in the catacombs, and it is now customary to interpret this in the sense that the relics were later *transferred to the catacombs*, and *to this transfer the date of 258 would refer*. The place in question would be the so-called Saint Sebastian Catacomb on the Appian Way, where, as we shall see, the excavations have brought to light a cult room in which, according to the inscriptions it contains, memorial meals, so-called *refrigeria*, were held in the fourth century. In this way it would be explained how the remembrance of Peter was celebrated at two places at the same time, that is, on the Vatican Hill and in the catacombs: His bones were first buried on the Vatican Hill, then in the year 258 were transferred to the catacombs, and finally in the fourth century were brought back to the Basilica that Constantine built on the Vatican Hill at the original place of burial.

Since the persecution of the Christians under Valerian took place in the year 258, the transfer would be explained either by the fear of the Christians that the relics of the apostles might be dishonoured,

---

[4] So L. Duchesne, *Liber Pontificalis* I, pp. civ ff., and H. Lietzmann, *op. cit.*, pp. 110 ff.

[5] Similarly J. P. Kirsch, *Der stadtrömische christliche Festkalendar*, 1924.

or—on account of an imperial ban—by the impossibility of assembling for the memorial festivals at the graves located in pagan cemeteries.[6]

Such a transfer, furthermore, could be supported by a whole series of more or less legendary later traditions concerning the graves. In themselves they have scarcely any historical value; nevertheless, they are to be considered in so far as almost all of them, though indeed in different ways, reckon with a removal of the graves occasioned by definite events.[7] Apart from Prudentius (fifth century), who transfers the two graves together into the "marshland of the Tiber," and the *Acts* of Pseudo-Linus (sixth century),[8] who names as the place the Naumachia, the material in question is chiefly the *Martyrdom of Peter and Paul* (fifth century). It speaks of the attempt—frustrated by an earthquake—which pious eastern Christians made to steal the sacred relics of the two apostles and take them back to the east. This had as its result that the bodies were buried where the Orientals, when they fled, had left them lying; there they remained until a year and seven months later, when they were transferred back to their original place.[9] According to the *Life* of Pope Cornelius (251–253), which stands in the *Liber Pontificalis*, a certain Lucina, with the consent of the Pope, brought the bodies out of the catacombs and buried Paul near the place of his execution, while Peter was

[6] See H. Lietzmann, "The Tomb of the Apostles ad Catacumbas" (*Harvard Theological Review*, 1923, p. 157). As a result of his book on *Petrus und Paulus in Rom* the theory of the *Translatio* (the transfer of the bodies) has been widely accepted. It had already been defended by L. Duchesne, *Liber Pontificalis*, 1886, pp. civ ff., and "La memoria apostolorum de la Via Appia" (*Atti della Pontificia Accademia Romana di Archeologia*, I, 1, 1923, pp. 1 ff.). It is also supported by J. P. Kirsch, "Die neu entdeckte memoria Apostolorum an der Via Appia bei Rom" (*Jahresbericht der Görresgesellschaft*, 1921, p. 27; "Die 'memoria Apostolorum' an der Appischen Strasse zu Rom und die liturgische Festfeier des 29. Juni" (*Jahrbuch für Liturgiewissenschaft*, 1923, pp. 33 ff. See below, p. 129, note 15, for the names of those who oppose this theory.

[7] See Ch. Guignebert, *La sépulture de Pierre*, and M. Goguel, *L'Eglise primitive*, pp. 222 ff.

[8] A. Lipsius, *Die apokryphen Apostelgeschichten und Apostellegenden*, 1883–1890, Vol. II, p. 113.

[9] This story is found in another form in the *Passio* (the story of the suffering) of the Syrian martyr Sharbil (W. Cureton, *Ancient Syriac Documents*, 1864, pp. 61 ff.). Lipsius, *op. cit.*, Vol. II, p. 312, and C. Erbes, "Die Gräber und Kirchen Pauli und Petri in Rom" (*Zeitschrift für Kirchengeschichte*, 1885, pp. 31 ff.), have proved that the origin of this story is to be sought in a misunderstanding of the Damasus inscription in the Saint Sebastian Catacomb, where it is said that the Orient *sent* the apostles. See below, p. 134.

buried by Cornelius on the Vatican Hill in the Temple of Apollo.[10]

Possibly the sole historical kernel in these late traditions is just the memory of a transfer. However, we cannot simply accept this transfer as an assured fact, for in its generally accepted form there is no ancient text that actually mentions it for the year 258. Rather, we are dealing here only with a *hypothesis*; moreover, it rests upon the correction of the text of the Jerome *Martyrologium*, and this correction has not been thoroughly substantiated.[11]

The only solid fact is that the memory of Peter was celebrated on the Appian Way, and as we shall find confirmed by the result of excavations, so was that of Paul. In earlier times the opinion attested by the *Liber Pontificalis*, I, 67, was widely held, that the apostles were buried together here *from the beginning* and only later were transferred to separate graves. In more recent times this view still found occasional defence;[12] it was then almost universally abandoned, but seems again to be receiving at least some consideration in connection with the completely unsolved riddles which the latest excavations under the Cathedral of St. Peter present.[13] The date 258 proves, however, that the entire notice in the *Depositio* and the *Martyrologium* refers to the time not of burial but of another event, which must be connected with the memory of Peter (and Paul).

Nevertheless, this event need not be the transfer of the bones from their original graves to the Appian Way. Due to the authority of Lietzmann, this assumption has become almost a dogma among scholars today, and in St. Sebastian it is presented as fact by the monks who lead conducted tours. But apart from the fact that it is

---

10 Duchesne, *Liber Pontificalis*, I, p. 150. C. Erbes, "Die geschichtlichen Verhältnisse der Apostelgräber" (*ZKG*, 1924, pp. 72 f.), believes that he finds a historical nucleus in the notice regarding Paul.

11 The later Bern text of the Jerome *Martyrologium* from the eighth century perhaps does not deserve unqualified trust, since we could have here a subsequent attempt at explanation by a copyist, who did not know what to make of the date of the *Depositio Martyrum* (June 29, 258). In any case, the year 258 is not necessarily to be connected with the catacombs.

12 P. Styger, *Die römischen Katakomben*, 1933, p. 350 f.; *Römische Märtyrergrüfte*, 1935, I, pp. 15 ff. F. Tolotti, "Ricerche intorno alla Memoria Apostolorum" (*Rivista Archeologia Cristiana*, 1946, pp. 7 ff.).

13 See the report by A. Ferrua concerning the latest excavations: "A la recherche du tombeau de S. Pierre" (*Etudes*, 1952, pp. 35 ff.). A. Ferrua here recalls this ancient tradition in a very involved sentence; in an article that appeared at about the same time, "La Storia del sepolcro di san Pietro" (*La civiltà cattolica*, 1952, pp. 15 ff.), he merely explains that this theory has been given up by scholars.

not really supported by a single text, there is the added fact that other considerations make the assumption of a transfer very difficult *if not impossible*. According to the Roman legislation for the protection of graves, it was a crime punishable by death to remove from the grave the remains of a deceased person. Any infraction of this law by the Christians, moreover, would have been extremely dangerous at the time of Valerian's persecution of the Christians, since Christian meetings at cemeteries were then forbidden and these places therefore were probably closely watched to enforce the ban. Furthermore, it recently has been correctly pointed out that the transfer to the Appian Way in particular is quite improbable; it was one of the busiest streets, and a few hundred yards away, at the tomb of Caecilia Metella, there was an imperial police station.[14] In addition, it is impossible to see how the Christians could have feared injury to the graves, since such a thing was contrary to Roman feelings, and moreover the cult of relics was not yet so developed at that time that the Christians would need to reckon with imperial action against the graves of martyrs. In reality that persecution was directed against the leaders of the church. For these reasons a line of scholars for many years back have completely refused to believe in a transfer of the remains of the two apostles.[15]

[14] I owe this reference to the article by Alfons Maria Schneider, "Die Memoria Apostolorum an der Via Appia" (*Nachrichten der Akademie der Wissenschaften in Göttingen, Philologisch-Historische Klasse*, 1951, p. 5). I was able to see this article while it was still in process of publication.

[15] So J. Wilpert, "Domus Petri" (*Römische Quartalschrift*, 1912, p. 121); G. La Piana, "The Tombs of Peter and Paul ad Catacumbas" (*Harvard Theological Review*, 1921, pp. 81 ff.); C. Erbes in *Zeitschrift für Kirchengeschichte*, 1924, p. 38; especially H. Delehaye, "Hagiographie et archéologie romaines, II, Le Sanctuaire des apôtres sur la voie Appienne" (*Analecta Bollandiana*, 1927, pp. 297 ff.), and *Les origines du culte des martyrs*, 2nd ed., 1933, pp. 264 ff. A. von Gerkan, in the report he adds to the second edition of H. Lietzmann's *Petrus und Paulus in Rom*, pp. 248 ff., also takes a sceptical attitude towards the acceptance of the *Translatio*. Recently E. Schäfer, "Das Petrusgrab" (*Evangelische Theologie*, 1951, pp. 477 f.), has spoken definitely against it. He argues chiefly that no reason existed for a transfer, since Valerian's prohibition against entering Christian cemeteries dates not from the year 258 but from 257. Moreover, the grave of Peter was located not in a Christian cemetery at all, but in a pagan once; fear that the grave would be violated would have been groundless, since indeed nothing is known of violations of Christian graves in times of persecution. Most recently, A. M. Schneider, *op. cit.*; see the preceding note. For further orientation on this entire question see also: H. Leclercq, Article on "St. Pierre" in *Dictionnaire d'archéologie chrétienne et de liturgie*, 1939, columns 822 ff., and L. Hertling—E. Kirschbaum, *Die römischen Katakomben und ihre Märtyrer*, 1950, pp. 102 ff.

This transfer is the more questionable since the excavations under the Basilica of St. Sebastian, of which we still must speak, also prove only that a *cult* of the apostles was practised at that place; they do not prove that the relics were to be found there.

But why, then, was this specific day June 29, 258, connected with this cult? As far as this day is concerned, we should consider first of all the insufficiently noticed fact that June 29 was celebrated as the day of the foundation of Rome by Quirinus Romulus. To the festival for the founder of the city corresponded the festival for the founder of the Church.[16] We may note further that it was also the day on which was deposed the rival pope Novatian, who died about this time. This fact, in connection with other observations, could incite us to propose interesting hypotheses, but we omit them here since there is still much to clarify.[17] For the time being, the following explanation gives the most light. We have seen that the naming of the year 258 cannot refer to the original graves of the apostles, and probably also cannot refer to the more than doubtful transfer of the bones. It is rather concerned only with the rise of a cult dedicated to the apostles. Whether the cult arose at the same time at the three places named—the Vatican Hill, the Highway to Ostia, and the Appian Way—or at first only at the two former places, or only on the Appian Way, cannot be determined from the liturgical sources. Only excavations could throw further light on this point. The need of a cult veneration and of a cult place appeared just at that time, about the middle of the third century, and so at the time when a catacomb for the Roman bishops was laid out, the Callistus Catacomb. So it is intelligible that especially at that time Christians desired to honour the memory of the two apostles who had long been regarded as the founders of the church. In this connection it is very interesting that they still *desired to distinguish clearly the founders from the bishops;*

16 See C. Erbes, *Die Todestage der Apostel Paulus und Petrus und ihre römischen Denkmäler*, 1899, pp. 39 f.: "The festival for the founder of the city of Rome was best suited for the festive celebration of the founder or founders of the Roman Church." Pope Leo the Great, in Sermon 82 on June 29th, points out: "The apostles founded the city better than did those who built the walls and sullied them by fratricide."

17 *Martyrologium Hieronymianum*, in the text on June 29 as contained in the entire textual tradition. See H. Delehaye—H. Quentin, *Acta Sanctorum Novembris*, Vol. I, 1931, p. 342. Concerning the grave of Novatian, found in 1932, and its historical connections, see L. C. Mohlberg, "Osservazioni storico-critiche sulla Iscrizione tombale de Novaziano" (*Ephemerides liturgicae*, 1937, pp. 242 ff.).

they did not choose for the founders simply the Bishop's Vault. Moreover, the same veneration was still paid to Paul that was given to Peter. The theory of the exclusive episcopal office of the Prince of Apostles thus did not yet exist, or at least had not yet fully triumphed.

The two notices cited from the *Depositio Martyrum* concerning June 29 refer to the cult veneration. But if that is true, we can leave as it is the far earlier notice of the two, that is, the brief one; we do not need to change its text.[18] We then understand why Peter is mentioned here only in connection with the catacombs, and why he alone is mentioned. At the time when the Roman calendar originated, that is, in the year 354, the Basilica which Constantine had begun to build for Peter at the place of the Vatican "trophy" was not yet complete.[19] So for a time the only cult site at which Peter was venerated was still the place in the catacombs, while in the case of Paul the Basilica of St. Paul Outside the Walls, which was much smaller and therefore required less time for completion, was already dedicated to the cult.[20]

On the basis of the liturgical sources, therefore, we can only say the following: The remembrance of Peter in Rome was attached to different places, to the Vatican Hill and to the catacombs. June 29 is not the day of the death of the two apostles.[21] It has a connection—probably by association with the memorial day of the founder of the city of Rome—with a Christian celebration of the year 258. This year became decisive for the origin of the cult dedicated to the two apostles. According to the usual thesis, indeed, this was because at that time the transfer of the bones to the Appian Way took place. But according to the more probable view, it was because the memory of the apostles was first venerated without such a transfer, and perhaps without the physical presence of the remains.

The liturgical sources, taken by themselves, thus yield little help in solving our problem. Indeed, in view of the disharmony in the liturgical tradition, which connects the Vatican Hill on the one hand and the catacombs on the other with the memory of Peter, the problem has long since become greatly complicated. This fact has

---

[18] See above, p. 125.   [19] See below, p. 140.

[20] This convincing line of argument is used by E. Kirschbaum, "Petri in Catacumbas" (*Miscellanea liturgica in honorem L. Cuniberti Mohlberg*, 1948, pp. 221 ff.).

[21] So also P. Batiffol, *Cathedra Petri*, 1938, p. 174: "The festival of the two apostles will be celebrated the same day, June 29, not because this date is the anniversary of their martyrdom, but because it is the anniversary of the institution of a joint observance in their honour."

created among scholars as well as among churchmen an embarrassment, which becomes noticeable today as soon as anyone speaks of
this double tradition. This may also explain the fact that even in the
fifteenth and sixteenth centuries there obviously was no certainty
concerning the place of burial of the apostles. This is clear from the
following rarely noted *passage in Luther*:[22] "But this I can cheerfully
say, because I have seen it and heard it at Rome, that at Rome they
do not know where the bodies of St. Peter and St. Paul lie and
whether they lie there. The pope and cardinals know quite well that
they do not know these things."

5. *The Excavations*

Do the results of the excavations carry us further? It corresponds
fully to the statements of the literary and liturgical sources if a burial
took place at two places: on the Vatican Hill, under the present
cathedral of St. Peter, and on the Appian Way, in the catacombs
under the present Basilica of St. Sebastian. A third task still awaits
fulfilment by archaeological investigation; systematic excavations
should also be carried out under the Church of St. Paul Outside the
Walls. It is true that various archaeological observations have already
been made there, following the fire of the year 1823 and in connection with the rebuilding. But a systematic archaeological examination of the place has not been made in recent times.[23]

We speak first of the excavations which were undertaken in 1915
on the Appian Way, in the catacombs under the Basilica of St.
Sebastian.[24] In earlier times this basilica was called the "Basilica of

[22] M. Luther, *Wider das Papsttum vom Teufel gestiftet*, 1545 (Weimar edition, 54),
cited from E. Mülhaupt, *Luthers Evangelien-Auslegung*, Vol. II, p. 551.

[23] Concerning the grave of Paul see C. Cecchelli, "La Tomba de S. Paolo"
(*Capitolium*, 1950, pp. 115 ff.).—Excavations under Saint Paul's would be
especially instructive, inasmuch as less mediaeval plundering would be expected
here than under the Basilica of Peter.

[24] See on that point the already mentioned fifty page report by A. von Gerkan,
published in the second edition of H. Lietzmann, *Petrus und Paulus in Rom*, 1927,
pp. 248 ff. See also J. P. Kirsch, "Das neuentdeckte Denkmal der Apostel Petrus
und Paulus 'in Catacumbas' an der Appischen Strasse in Rom" (*Römische
Quartalschrift*, 1916–1922, pp. 5 ff.); G. Mancini—O. Marucchi, "Scavi sotto la
basilica de S. Sebastiano sulla Appia antica" (*Notizie degli Scavi*, 1923); R.
Chéramy, *Saint-Sébastien-hors-les-murs*, 1925; A. Prandi, "La memoria Apostolorum in Catacumbas" (*Romana sotterranea Cristiana*, 2, 1936); Alfons Maria
Schneider, "Die Memoria Apostolorum an der Via Appia" (*Nachrichten der
Akademie der Wissenschaften in Göttingen, Philologisch-historische Klasse*, 1951,
pp. 1 ff.).

the Apostles"; only later did it serve as the grave of Saint Sebastian, from whom it then received its present name.[25]

According to the *Liber Pontificalis*, Pope Damasus erected a church there, at the place "where the bodies of the holy Apostles Peter and Paul had rested." They had lain there under the *platonia* (*platoma*, marble slab). The excavations, however, have not confirmed this assertion. They have shown, however, that in the first century there was at this place a Roman villa, columbaria, and graves. More important for our question was the discovery of a *triclia*, that is, a cult room; according to the inscriptions, which invoke Peter and Paul,[26] it served for the veneration of the two apostles.

It can be shown that this room can hardly have originated before A.D. 300. Its inner arrangement, with stone benches encircling the room, as well as some of the inscriptions, permit us to see that here were celebrated so-called *refrigeria*, meals for the dead, in honour of Peter and Paul. We read, for example, in one of the graffiti: "For Peter and Paul I, Tomius Caelius, have held a *refrigerium*."[27] The meal eaten in honour of the apostles was naturally considered a meritorious work. This abuse appears to have been especially widespread after the triumph of the Church in the fourth century. It continued the pagan religious meals; since these could not be uprooted, they were given a Christian framework in the Church by being connected with the martyr cult. Augustine later denounced the abuses to which this bad custom gave occasion.[28] In his time such meals had already been banned for several decades, but they continued to be celebrated in secret.

It cannot be disputed that such "meals for the dead" presuppose in theory the presence of the relics of the martyrs venerated. This has been made the chief support for the assertion that the apostles were

---

[25] See on that point F. W. Deichmann, *Frühchristliche Kirchen in Rom*, 1948, pp. 22 f.

[26] 191 graffiti have been discovered, 33 of them in Greek. They are in part written in low Latin and invoke the intercession of the apostles; for example, *Paule et Petre petite pro Victore* ("Paul and Peter, pray for Victor"). We certainly have here a popular cult. It is conceivable that the pilgrims who came to Rome from abroad stopped here on the Appian Way before their entrance into the city. See concerning the graffiti: E. Diehl, *Inscriptiones latinae christianae veteres*, 1924; H. Lietzmann, *op. cit.*, pp. 163 ff. A. M. Schneider, *Refrigeria nach literarischen Quellen und Inschriften*, 1928; P. Styger, *Die römischen Katakomben*, 1933, pp. 341 ff.

[27] *Petro et Paulo Tomius Caelius refrigerium feci XIV kal. Apriles.*

[28] Augustine, Epistle XXIX *ad Aurelium.*

actually buried for a time in the catacombs.[29] But in view of the fact that the Church prohibited these *refrigeria*, it is possible that in exceptional cases *refrigeria* were held in spite of the absence of relics.[30]

That the cult in memory of the apostles could arise here, even if their bones were not present, becomes explicable from an inscription which has been found near the crypt of the Basilica of St. Sebastian. It is a thirteenth century copy of an inscription that goes back to Damasus. Its text is probably to be translated as follows:[31] "Whoever you may be who searches for the names of Peter and Paul, you should know that here the holy ones once dwelt. The Orient has sent us the disciples—that we concede without argument; but on account of the merit of the (shed) blood—for indeed they have followed Christ beyond the stars and have reached the heavenly bosom and the kingdom of the pious—Rome has the greater right to claim them as its citizens. Damasus desires to sing this to your praise, ye new stars."

The statement concerning the "dwelling" of Peter and Paul is usually explained to mean that their remains once rested in St. Sebastian.[32] To be sure, there are other possible interpretations of this word. One could think, for example, of a tradition according to which the apostles had actually lived here during their lifetime. With this would agree the fact that this place was in a Jewish quarter.[33] One could even assume that the inscription had in mind a cult presence of the two apostles. It is of course doubtful whether Damasus, when in the fourth century he used the word "dwelling," thought only of a cult presence. But in any case the most natural

---

[29] For H. Lietzmann this is one of the decisive arguments that favour acceptance of the theory of the transfer of the bones in the year 258 ("The Tomb of the Apostles ad Catacumbas," *Harvard Theological Review*, 1923, pp. 147 ff.).

[30] So G. La Piana, "The Tombs of Peter and Paul ad Catacumbas" (*Harvard Theological Review*, 1921, pp. 81 ff.).

[31] *His habitasse prius sanctos cognoscere debes, nomina quisque Petri pariter Paulique requiris. Discipulos Oriens misit, quod sponte fatemur. Sanguinis ob meritum— Christumque per astra secuti aetherios petiere sinus regnaque piorum—Roma suos potius meruit defendere cives. Haec Damasus vestras referat, nova sidera, laudes.*

[32] See above, p. 133.

[33] According to Juvenal, *Satire* III, 12 ff., the sacred grove of Egeria is leased to the Jews. See G. La Piana, "Foreign Groups in Rome during the First Centuries of the Empire" (*Harvard Theological Review*, 1927, pp. 341 ff.; further, J. B. Frey, "Les communautés juives à Rome aux premiers temps de l'Eglise" (*Recherches de Science religieuse*, pp. 275 ff.). Actual dwelling here was first assumed by J. Wilpert, *Römische Quartalschrift*, 1912, pp. 117 ff.

thing is to explain the origin of the cult on the Appian Way in the third century not by the presence of relics, but by the need of venerating the memory of the two founders of the Roman church at a place where such veneration was possible, even if the bones were not there. This view is the more probable since we can point out in St. Sebastian, though not indeed in the *triclia*, possible traces of a double cenotaph, that is, a fictitious grave, such as one often set up in ancient times when one wished to celebrate the memory of a deceased person at a place other than the site of the actual grave. The choice of the Appian Way as a cult site can be explained by the fact that in the immediate vicinity the Callistus Catacomb had been laid out, from the time of Pontianus (A.D. 235), for the burial of the Roman bishops; Christians wished to assemble in the vicinity of the later bishops for the cult veneration of the founding apostles.

Without the use of hypothesis we cannot hope to explain the fact that there was in the catacombs a common memorial place for the two apostles, which still served this purpose even when Christians definitely fixed the location of the graves not here, but on the Vatican Hill and on the Highway to Ostia. Quite improbable is the supposition that in the catacombs we have the *original* grave of the apostles.[34] Another hypothesis is that in the third century the remains were *transferred* to the catacombs for a limited time. As we have seen, this hypothesis, in spite of its wide popularity, which it owes chiefly to Lietzmann's book, offers so many difficulties that the current tendency to give it up is doubtless justified.[35] It is theoretically possible to assume that in the third century Christians sought out relics of the apostles that up to then they had not possessed, and so in the year 258 there occurred the so-called discovery, *inventio*, of the (genuine or spurious) remains, objects such as we find were held to be martyr relics in the fourth and fifth centuries.[36] This, however, is nothing more than an unproved and unprovable possibility.

Thus concerning the place at the Sebastian catacombs we conclude that even if one did not have the bones at this place, there arose here in the third century a cult in honour of the two apostles.[37] Did this

---

[34] See above, p. 128.   [35] See above, p. 129.

[36] See H. Achelis, *Die Martyrologien, ihre Geschichte und ihr Wert*, 1900, pp. 74 ff.; E. Schäfer, *Die Epigramme des Papstes Damasus I. als Quelle für die Geschichte der Heiligenverehrung*, 1932, pp. 101 ff.; also "Das Petrusgrab" (*Evangelische Theologie*, 1950, pp. 474 f.).

[37] Alfons Maria Schneider, *op. cit.* (see p. 129, note 14), pp. 1 ff., does not believe that this happened as early as the year 258; rather, in this year arose the cult on the Vatican Hill and the Highway to Ostia.

happen because at the site of the "trophies" of Peter and Paul on the Vatican Hill and on the Highway to Ostia, which *as places* certainly had been venerated in earlier times, assemblies for worship became difficult since they were located in pagan cemeteries? Or was it, on the contrary, one of the schismatic churches of the third century which first of all created the cult site on the Appian Way, before the great Church took it over at the beginning of the fourth century? In favour of the second possibility weighty reasons have recently been presented.[38]

*   *   *

Even before the rise of a *cult* of the apostles the *memorial places* for the apostles already existed on the Vatican Hill and on the Highway to Ostia. For even before the year 258, probably for more than half a century before, efforts were being made to possess the relics or at least the burial places of the apostles. In the east, this need had made itself felt much earlier than in Rome, where, as we shall see, there was no interest at all in relics or burial places, not even in those of the great martyrs of Rome, prior to the end of the second century.[39] In the Martyrdom of Polycarp we hear for the first time of a cult of relics, devoted to the memory of the great Bishop of Smyrna. Towards the end of the second century Polycrates, the Bishop of Ephesus, writes to the Roman Bishop Victor concerning the Easter celebration. In this connection he appeals explicitly to the fact that "in Asia great stars, who will arise on the last day when Christ returns, have found their resting place,"[40] and he enumerates them. The more the time receded when Christians could still see on the basis of living tradition the connection of a church with apostles, so much the greater need did the east feel of proving apostolicity in another way, namely by the possession of apostolic burial places. We have every reason to assume that this tendency arose in the east, where, in the debates over the claims of Rome, which were presented with ever increasing vigour, this argument was not overlooked.

In order not to leave this claim to fame to the eastern churches alone, there arose in Rome at the very end of the second century the effort to make a similar appeal to the possession of apostolic "trophies." To this effort we owe that statement of Gaius concerning

---

[38] See A. M. Schneider, *op. cit.*   [39] See below, pp. 150 f.
[40] Eusebius, *Ecclesiastical History*, III, 31, 3.

the "trophies" on the Vatican Hill and on the Highway to Ostia; it
comes from precisely this time. With this also agrees quite well the
view that we have found attested for this same period, according to a
likely interpretation, in the text of Tertullian.[41] It declares that from
the grave of the apostle Peter the power committed to Peter streams
forth upon the Roman Bishop. Hence there was created—again
about that same time—a burial place for the Roman bishops.

We thus establish the fact that the church in Rome, in the decades
that immediately precede the origin of the cult of the apostles in the
year 258, also became interested in possessing apostolic "trophies."
But just for this reason it is improbable that Christians would have
transferred these trophies away from the Vatican Hill and the Highway to Ostia, after having appealed to them, as the Gaius reference
proves, for a period of limited duration. Those places remained un-
molested. If an additional cult centre was also created on the Appian
Way, those ancient "victory sites" retained their power to attest and
prove the apostolicity of the church. But what now is the situation
with reference to these "trophies," in particular the "trophy" of
Peter on the Vatican Hill?

*   *   *

We thus come to the actual question concerning the *excavations*
under the Church of St. Peter. Quite recently, in the year 1939, work
highly important for archaeology was here undertaken. In an unusually clear manner it gives us information concerning the nature
of the terrain lying under the present Church of St. Peter and the use
made of it in ancient Christian times. If archaeology is in any position
to throw light upon the question concerning Peter, it could be expected that it would do so here, and many probably cherished the
hope that here, at one stroke, a final solution would be found for
the much debated historical question whether Peter died in Rome
as a martyr.

It was not the first time that excavations had been made there. As
early as the year 1615, when the present *Confessio* of the Cathedral
of St. Peter was built, and especially in 1626, when the foundations were laid under the dome for the four spiral bronze pillars of
the Bernini Canopy, discoveries were made concerning the secrets
concealed underneath. It was discovered that the place at which one
locates the grave of Peter contains exclusively pagan graves and

41 See above, pp. 121 f.

burial chambers. They date from the years 150 to 300, and are at
different depths, of which several more were later found. The
seventeenth century reports of these first diggings have been carefully
studied in recent times.[42] But only the systematic work of 1939
has finally clarified the topography under the Church of St. Peter.
They also have put an end to erroneous earlier assumptions that
rested on false reports. Although they were undertaken in a way that
excluded broad participation by scholars, their results, thanks to a
series of articles by competent writers, were made known as early as
the years 1941–1950,[43] except for the archaeological details concerning a simple ancient monument located under the present altar, and
three ancient graves found close by, which probably date from the
first century. In a radio broadcast in the year 1942 Pope Pius XII
referred quite briefly to this monument, and identified it with that
"trophy" of Peter which Gaius mentioned.

In his Christmas message on December 23, 1950, he definitely
asserted that "the grave of the Prince of Apostles has been found."
At the same time he conceded in all honesty that the remains of
human bones found in the region of the grave cannot be identified
with certainty as the mortal remains of the apostle.

Now at last the categorical assertion that the grave itself has been
found can be tested by the archaeologists. A year later, at the Christmas season of 1951, appeared the long announced official publication
concerning this part of the excavation. It had been impatiently
awaited by the scholarly world, and appeared after a remarkable
delay.[44] The impatience was the more intelligible since, except for
the excavation leaders appointed by the Vatican, almost no archaeo-
logist was permitted to see that place under the altar, while the

[42] See H. Lietzmann, *Petrus und Paulus in Rom*, 1927, pp. 191 ff.

[43] From the unusually numerous and steadily increasing reports we select the
following: C. Respighi, "La tomba apostolica del Vaticano" (*Rivista di Archeologia Cristiana*, 1942, pp. 5 ff.); E. Josi, *Gli scavi nelle sacre Grotte Vaticano: Il
Vaticano nel 1944*, pp. 189 ff.; *Idem*, *Le Sacre Grotte: Vaticano*, edited by G.
Fallani and M. Escobar, 1946; E. Kirschbaum, "Die Ausgrabungen unter der
Petruskirche in Rom" (*Stimmen der Zeit*, 1949, pp. 292 ff.); *Idem*, "Gli scavi sotto
la basilica di S. Pietro" (*Gregorianum*, 1948, pp. 544 ff.); L. Lemerle, "Les fouilles
de St-Pierre de Rome" (*La Nouvelle Clio*, 1950, pp. 393 ff.); E. Schäfer, "Das
Petrusgrab" (*Evangelische Theologie*, 1951, p. 459).

[44] B. M. Apollonj-Ghetti, A. Ferrua, E. Kirschbaum, E. Josi (Foreword by L. Kaas),
Esplorazioni sotto la Confessione de S. Pietro in Vaticano, 2 Vols. (one volume of
text and one of illustrations), 1951 (cited hereafter as *Espl. Vat.*, 1951). As the
title says, this work deals only with the result, kept secret up to this time, of the
excavations under the altar; it does not deal with the rest of the cemetery.

remaining part of the excavations was already accessible, at least to scholars. It is to be expected and hoped that now numerous archaeologists of all faiths will form their independent judgment, not only by means of the elaborately presented publication, splendidly illustrated in a second volume,[45] but on the spot and at the site itself. It is certain that in view of the result of the excavations, which as we shall see permits quite different interpretations, a vigorous discussion will develop.[46] Without anticipating this discussion, which must deal first of all with the technical side of the question, it is already possible, on the basis of the information that the publication contains, for us to take a provisional position; it permits us to decide whether these most recent excavations are capable of solving the question concerning the Roman stay of Peter in one way or another. Even here, however, I note explicitly that even if this question should be answered in the negative, this does not mean at all that Peter was never in Rome. *The question concerning the grave of Peter and the question concerning his stay in Rome are to be kept strictly separate.*

Let us now begin with that part of the new excavations concerning which a rather detailed documentation has already been published. We must first recall that under the present Church of St. Peter was the ancient basilica which Constantine erected in the fourth century in honour of Peter. It was completely torn down at the building of the present Church of St. Peter, which was begun in the year 1506 and completed about 150 years later. Unfortunately there is no ancient text which tells of its origin. However, we possess an early description of its form from Canon Tiberius Alfaranus of the sixteenth century;[47] we also possess ancient engravings. Various extensive studies have been carried on recently to sift this material.[48]

---

45 Unfortunately the plans contained in it do not have a uniform scale, and cross-sections of the strata are lacking; this makes use of the work difficult.

46 Up to the present time (beginning of February, 1952), important statements have appeared only from the Roman Catholic side. Apart from purely journalistic reports, two articles particularly deserve mention here. Both come from one of the leaders, A. Ferrua: "La Storia del sepolcro di san Pietro" (La Civiltà cattolica, 1952, pp. 15 ff.), and "A la recherche du tombeau de S. Pierre" (*Etudes*, 1952, pp. 35 ff.). It is noteworthy that his results diverge *in essentials* from those of the official publication which he shared in issuing (see below, pp. 147 f.). Differences in nuance exist also between the two above-named articles.

47 Tiberius Alfaranus, "De Basilicae Vaticanae antiquissima et nova structura" (*Studi e testi*, 1914).

48 H. Grisar, "Die alte Petruskirche zu Rom und ihre frühesten Ansichten" (*Römische Quartalschrift*, 1895, pp. 237 ff.).

It appears that this building was begun under Constantine about the year 333;[49] it probably was completed under Constantius.[50] It lay about three metres under the level of the present church, and so upon the level of the present grottoes of the Vatican, in which many popes, even in recent times, have been buried.

The excavations undertaken several years ago had at first no scientific purpose whatever. They were intended simply to enlarge these grottoes and at the same time to lower their floor level about eighty centimetres. This had become necessary in connection with the burial of Pope Pius XI, who died in 1939. He had left behind the direction that his remains should rest in the grottoes of the Vatican. During the work Roman walls were laid bare, and this gave occasion for a systematic uncovering of the terrain situated beneath the grottoes.

The chief thing that the workmen encountered was an unusually thick wall of considerable size. It was believed at first that this could be identified with the wall of the Circus of Nero, since, according to

[49] Of the older datings, the most favoured fixed upon the year 324 (Lietzmann, Nicolosi, Marucchi). More recent ones have preferred the year 325 (Th. Klausner, "Vom Heroon zur Märtyrerbasilika," *Kriegsvorträge der Universität Bonn*, 62, p. 22), and Fr. W. Deichmann, *Frühchristliche Kirchen in Rom*, 1948) or the year 326 (H. von Schoenbeck, *Beiträge zur Religionspolitik des Maxentius und Constantin*, Supplementary volume to *Clio*, 1939, p. 89). In opposition to these views, a promising hypothesis has been proposed, in connection with the latest excavations under the Church of St. Peter, by W. Seston, "Hypothèse sur la date de la Basilique constantinienne de Saint-Pierre de Rome" (*Cahiers archéologiques*, 1946, pp. 153 ff.). This theory is that the law which Constans promulgated on March 28, 349, allows us to fix the beginning of the construction under Constantine in the year 333. That law fixes the amount of the punishments for all who have removed parts of tombs, and the act is made retroactive to the year 333. We shall see that Constantine was compelled to dig up an entire necropolis in order to erect the basilica for Peter. It is intelligible that this act, which Constantine was forced to take in his capacity as *Pontifex Maximus*, gave occasion for more and more violations of graves, which were justified by appeal to what Constantine had done. This hypothesis could find confirmation in the fact that precisely in the year 333 paganism quite obviously recedes in Constantine's region. See A. Piganiol, *L'empereur Constantin*, 1932, p. 185. This suggestion is confirmed especially by the latest excavations; the graffiti at the *Tropaion* show the monogram (see below, p. 145).

[50] See the inscription on the apse in Diehl, *Inscriptiones latinae veteres*, No. 1753.— If the assumption is correct (see above, p. 131), according to which at the time of the composition of the *Depositio Martyrum* the basilica for Paul was completed, but that of Peter was not yet dedicated to the cult, the completion of the latter must have taken place after 354. See E. Kirschbaum, "Petri in Catacumbas" (*Miscellanea Liturgica in honorem L. C. Mohlberg*, 1948, pp. 221 ff.).

a misleading report from the beginning of the seventeenth century,[51] the southern walls of the Basilica of Constantine stood upon the northern walls of the Circus of Nero, so that the Church of St. Peter would be situated over the Circus. As early as 1895 a futile effort was made to find traces of the Circus. Now for the first time, however, it has become clear what was the real purpose of this thick Roman wall, which had evidently been seen when the present church was being built in the sixteenth and seventeenth centuries. It did not belong to the Circus of Nero; it simply served to make level the sloping hillside under the present church, in order to serve as a sub-structure for the Basilica of Constantine. The result was that the emperor erected his church directly above this slope. The summit of the hill lies north of the church, approximately where the Vatican buildings stand today. The hill slopes away in two directions: in a gradual slope toward the east, and so in the direction from the altar to the entrance of the church, to the Piazza of St. Peter and on to the Tiber; and in a much steeper abrupt drop to the south, and so on the left side of the present basilica when viewed from the Piazza of St. Peter.

It was on this steep slope that Constantine erected his Basilica of Peter. The terrain was thus extremely unfavourable; in order to level it off, it was necessary to erect, on the south, high walls, which at the deepest point of the valley reach a height of thirteen metres. On the north, the surface of the hill had to be partly removed, and it required great quantities of soil to make a level site. These extensive labours could have been avoided if the church had been built either above on the hill top or below in the valley. We therefore must assume that there was *a special reason* for building it right over the steep slope, and this reason can only be that in the time of Constantine it was not simply the Vatican Hill in general but rather this very slope, and probably a particular spot on this slope, that was regarded as the place where Peter was executed or buried.

This is further confirmed by another difficulty that the builders had to accept and overcome when they built the church at this place. The most important discovery that came to light in the course of these excavations is an entire cemetery, situated on this very slope. It consists of two rows of well preserved mausoleums, separated by a narrow passageway.

[51] Giacomo Grimaldi, *Codex Ambros. A. 178*, edited by Ch. Huelsen (*Miscellanea*, 1910, pp. 257 ff.). *Cod. Barb. lat. 2732, 2733*, Bibl. Vat. H. Lietzmann, *op. cit.*, pp. 311 ff.

Thus while previously one knew only of separate graves under the Church of St. Peter, there has been discovered here an extensive necropolis. The graves date from the second and third centuries after Christ, with the exception of some that are located in the western portion, under the present *Confessio*. They can be dated at the end of the first century, but not before the year 70. The two rows run along the slope, about eight metres under the present church, in the direction of the longitudinal axis of the church; indeed, they are so situated that they run slightly uphill towards the west, and so to the place beneath the altar.

The fact that Constantine had to destroy this entire site, in which actual works of art were found, shows anew that there must have been a special reason for him to build the church right at this point. This is especially clear since destruction of cemeteries was regarded in antiquity as especially serious, and he doubtless could permit himself to do this only in his capacity as *Pontifex Maximus*.[52]

How distant the cemetery was from the famous Via Cornelia, on which the grave of Peter is supposed to have been situated,[53] cannot be said with certainty, since no trace of this street has been found where it has been customary to look for it, on the longitudinal axis of the church. Probably it ran to the north, and so above the northern row of graves; the mausoleums of this row are in most cases provided with steps which lead up the hill, so that in addition to the lower entrance on the south they had also an entrance from the upper slope of the hill. It is possible therefore that the Via Cornelia passed by on that side.

We have already mentioned that the Circus of Nero, contrary to the earlier view, was not situated under the Church of St. Peter. But it doubtless was in the vicinity. For in the mausoleum of a certain C. Popilius Heracla, located on the extreme east, an inscription mentions the wish of this deceased pagan that he may rest on the Vatican Hill at the Circus, *in vaticano ad circum*.[54]

Those buried in the cemetery belonged to the most varied pagan cults. Some few Christians of this period also were buried in these pagan mausoleums with their relatives of other faiths, and a complete Christian mausoleum, adorned with Christian mosaic motifs and

---

[52] See W. Seston, *op. cit.*, p. 156.
[53] H. Lietzmann, *Petrus und Paulus in Rom*, 1927, pp. 178 f.
[54] That the Circus lay on the Vatican Hill is attested by Tacitus, *Annals*, XIV, 4, and *Historia Augusta*, Elagabalus, 23, and further by Pliny, *Natural History*, XXXVI, 11, 74.

dating from the third or the beginning of the fourth century, is found among the pagan graves. It is of the greatest importance for the beginnings of Christian art.[55] For our question, the important thing in this connection is that this room is found in this vicinity, that is, only a few metres east of the *Confessio*. Did the Christian who had this mausoleum built at this place wish to be buried as near as possible to the place which was held to be the place where the apostle Peter was buried or executed? In this period, indeed, the tendency was already widespread to have oneself buried by the graves of the martyrs. It is a striking fact, however, that the Christian inscriptions of the graves of the Vatican cemetery do not mention the name of Peter.[56]

But what is the truth about the grave of Peter itself? Is it really true, as the Pope explicitly announced in his Christmas message of December 23, 1950, that a grave has been found in which Peter had been buried? We have seen that at the time of Constantine there must have existed a fixed tradition that located the site of the "trophy," whatever the latter was, at the place where the altar was erected in the Basilica of Constantine. Otherwise, we could not explain the choice of so unsuitable a terrain and especially of a cemetery.

We take the following information from the official publication that has recently appeared. First of all, those conducting the excavations were forced to conclude that the sixth century statement of the *Liber Pontificalis*, I, 176, according to which Constantine surrounded the entire grave of Peter with huge bronze slabs and erected over it a *Confessio* with a golden cross, belongs in the realm of legend. The excavations, at any rate, failed to bring to light anything of that sort; but above all, no traces were discovered to suggest the possibility that such an adornment was present.

In the area under the altar, on the contrary, traces were found of a columnar monument. It may be reconstructed (see p. 144), although but little of its original form is preserved. Its west wall is formed by the middle part of a strong wall, more than seven metres long and about two and a half metres high; it runs from north to south. To this wall a multiple purpose is ascribed. On the one hand, the so-called *Memoria* is supported by it; on the other hand, it is intended to support a stairway that leads up the hill and is built parallel to it on the back side, that is, on the west. Under these steps ran a small

(see p. 144)

[55] H. Speier, "Die neuen Ausgrabungen unter der Petruskirche in Rom" (in R. Herbig, *Vermächtnis der antiken Kunst*, 1950, pp. 199 ff.).
[56] W. Seston, *op. cit.*, p. 155, emphasizes this point.

Reconstruction of the Monument
Located under the Church of St. Peter

It should be explicitly noted that we have here only a conjectural reconstruction on the basis of data from the Vatican. Only little of the monument can still be seen, and for all details we are thus far reduced to suppositions. See *Espl. Vat.*, 1951, I, Plate G (where there is also given an attempted reconstruction of the upper storey), and A. Ferrua, *La Civiltà Cattolica*, 1952, p. 25, Fig. 3.

water channel covered over with bricks. On the front side, that is, on the east of the wall, is found a shallow niche, 72 centimetres wide and about 1.40 metres high. On both sides of the niche the wall is painted red. About 74 centimetres in front of the niche two pillars were erected. These support a slab of travertine, which serves as a kind of roof and is fitted into the wall. Above this slab is found a wider and deeper niche—a sort of second storey. It, however, can no longer be exactly reconstructed. Since several bricks of the channel bear the stamp of Marcus Aurelius Caesar, this small monument can be dated in the second half of the second century, *if it actually was built at the same time as the channel.* This would agree well with the statement in which Gaius reports that he can show the "trophy" of Peter on the Vatican Hill. In this connection, to be sure, we must not forget that this text *by itself* does not permit us to decide whether the "trophy" is the place only of the martyrdom, or of a grave, or even merely of a memorial.[57] Since Constantine obviously oriented his entire basilica with reference to this place, it may be assumed with some probability, from the conclusions reached above concerning the unsuitable terrain, that we really are dealing with that "trophy" of Gaius.[58] This presupposes, of course, that the channel and the monument can both be dated in the same year (*Espl. Vat.*, 1951, I, pp. 103 f.).

Later, towards the end of the third century, a gray wall was erected on the north side of the monument. This occurred in connection with the extension of the cemetery and the building of numerous mausoleums in the vicinity. On the ancient red west wall, but especially upon the later north wall just mentioned, a large number of pilgrim inscriptions have been written. They date from a relatively late period, give the name of Christ in the form of the monogram, and express the wish that the deceased may "live in Christ."[59] It is remarkable that the name of Peter is never found, whereas in the graffiti on the Appian Way Peter and Paul are invoked. This fact

[57] This is not sufficiently taken into account in *present-day* discussion. The excavations can perhaps settle that controversial question, but may not *start* from it, as though the text of Gaius *in itself* rendered certain one or the other interpretation of the word *tropaion*.

[58] The report of the *Liber Pontificalis*, according to which Pope Anicletus had already erected a *Memoria* for Peter in the first century, has thus finally been proved false. K. Heussi, " 'Papst' Anencletus I. und die Memoria auf dem Vatikan" (*Deutsches Pfarrerblatt*, 1949, pp. 301 ff.), has already emphasized that this statement cannot be trusted.

[59] *Victor cum sui (s), Gaudentia vibatis in Christo. Paulina vivas, Nicasi vibas in Christo,* etc. (*Espl. Vat.*, 1951, I, p. 129; II, Plate LVII, a, b; LVIII, a, b).

does not really make it insuperably difficult to identify the edifice with the "trophy" of Peter that Gaius mentioned; nevertheless, it is astonishing, especially since, as already noted, even the Christian inscriptions of the later mausoleums never refer to Peter. These graffiti, in any case, should be studied much more carefully than appears to have been the case thus far. Whether they date before or after Constantine seems to me to be very important; it could even influence the dating of the monument itself.

Provisionally, however—though not at all with certainty—we may assert, for the reasons given, that the "trophy" of Gaius appears to have been found. If this is true, it is the single positive result of the excavations as far as they concern Peter; the result is thus a confirmation of the literary testimony of Gaius, which, however, takes us back only to the end of the second century. Even apart from the meaning of the word "trophy," however, there was no reason to doubt the correctness of his testimony. Previously, to be sure, it was disputed whether by the word "trophy" Gaius understood only the place of execution or a monument or a grave. If the identification of the "trophy" with the columnar monument should finally prove correct, then by "trophy" we should understand not only a place but also a building found there; even if not the grave, it is a memorial monument. It must further be assumed, then, that a similar monument is located under the Church of St. Paul; this, however, must be confirmed by excavation.

What was *under* this "trophy" of Peter, however, and whether in particular it concealed a real grave, is another question. It is not answered even by the identification of the "trophy," although reports in newspapers and illustrated magazines flatly assert that it has been. It is true that before the niche is a cavity 80 centimetres wide and 80 centimetres long; it was covered with a thick slab. Is this square place, which H. Grisar saw more than fifty years ago, to be called "the grave of Peter"? The dimensions could lead one at first to suppose that at a *later* time his relics had been brought here. I really cannot understand how anyone can speak without qualification of a "discovered grave of Peter," since in any case *no remains of a grave survive*. The most that one could say would be that one may *conjecture* the earlier existence of a normal grave at a deeper level, *if that grave was really crossed over later by the red wall* (*Espl. Vat.*, I, p. 139).

But what are the reasons cited to support this assumption? Around the empty square space are found a row of graves in the ground.

Three of them lie rather deep, and two of them date from a very ancient period. The one in which was buried a small boy, whose skeleton is present, was crossed over and damaged in the building of the red wall. The other is situated at the same depth, and is covered with a seal which bears the stamp of Vespasian, and so was used at the earliest in the year 70. We thus see that none of these graves surrounding the spot reaches back into the Neronian period, although they still belong to the first century. Accordingly it is not proved that in Nero's time this place was already used as a burial ground. Nevertheless, the great depth of these graves is pointed out, as is the further fact that burials in the earth took place only here. One points also to the striking poverty of these graves; to the fact that the orientation of the threshold before the niche differs from that of the wall; and to the remains of a wall which could have served to protect the side wall of the supposed grave. All these indications, so it is said, prove that even in the first century Christians had themselves buried here around the grave of Peter. But are they really Christian graves?

In the extension of the niche beneath the ground some *bones* were admittedly found (*Espl. Vat.*, 1951, I, p. 121, Fig. 87). But it cannot occur to anyone to wish to found a proof on this fact; the Pope himself, as already mentioned, has candidly conceded this. For it is not astonishing that bones are found in a plot containing graves. On the other hand, attention has been called to the fact that later, in the time of Constantine, a small marble box, 77 centimetres long and 30 centimetres in breadth and depth, was embedded in the graffiti-covered north wall. This box was discovered in the excavations. It contains an unidentifiable mass of earth and all sorts of remains. The assertion that at a certain time it was emptied, but once had contained bones of the apostle, is a hypothesis that cannot be demonstrated. Constantine, according to this assertion, had the bones placed in the box as far as they were still preserved.[60] In that case, it becomes necessary to assume that they had then been brought from some other place, and specifically, in accordance with the theory of the transfer, from the Appian Way.[61] Thus would be explained the fact that the grave assumed to lie under the memorial structure contains neither skeleton nor urn. This latter fact, on the other hand, has been explained by

[60] A. Ferrua, "A la recherche du tombeau de S. Pierre" (*Etudes*, 1952, pp. 44 f.). There is an exact description in *Espl. Vat.*, 1951; see Vol. I, p. 162; Vol. II, Plate LVII, b.

[61] A. Ferrua, *op. cit.*, p. 45.

saying that the grave was plundered in later centuries, and especially by the Saracens in the year 846.[62] According to the most recent hypothesis, one would have to assume that this small casket placed in the wall was also plundered. Or must we suppose that the place had already been destroyed by the elephants which, according to Aelius Lampridius (ch. 22), Elagabalus brought to the Vatican Hill?

Even Roman Catholic scholars probably had little expectation that one would find genuine relics of Peter, although the pious Roman Catholic from the common people, who like many others has believed for centuries that he kneels above the bones of the Prince of Apostles in the present Church of St. Peter, was able to cherish this illusory hope. From the scientific point of view it can only be asked whether at the time of Constantine Peter's bones were still really there. Concerning that we know absolutely nothing.[63]

He who reads without prejudice the report of the most recent excavations must concede that if one assumes that the bones of Peter had rested under the monument discovered, the entire archaeological question concerning the grave of Peter becomes only more complicated than it already was. Prompt witness of this is the fact that one of the leaders of the excavations, in an essay published soon after the appearance of the official report, discusses the assumption—with the most extreme caution, to be sure, and only as a query—that the bones had already been transferred once from the Appian Way to the Vatican Hill. (On account of the small dimensions of the square cavity before the wall, he says), there forces itself upon one the memory of the ancient tradition according to which Peter, after his martyrdom, was first buried not here, but on the Appian Way together with Paul.[64] He thus suggests the old thesis that has been rather generally rejected.[65] Be that as it may, the author goes on to say that in the second half of the second century the relics of Peter were deposited on the Vatican Hill in a small urn. There they supposedly remained until 258, when they were (again) transferred to

[62] *Ann. Bertiniani ann. 846.*—The graves of the apostles were spared by the Goths in the year 410 and by the Vandals in 455.

[63] According to C. Cecchelli, "La Tomba di S. Paolo" (*Capitolium*, 1950, p. 122), the heads of the apostles had already been brought to the Lateran by Constantine. However, other defenders of the genuineness of these relics date their transfer at a much later time.

[64] A. Ferrua, *op. cit.* (*Etudes*, 1952, p. 43). But in the above mentioned article in *La Civiltà cattolica*, p. 17, he seems rather to approve the rejection of this theory.

[65] See above, p. 128. In other points the articles of Ferrua, especially the one in *Etudes*, are more reserved than the official publication.

the Appian Way, and finally, under Constantine, were brought back a second time.

This complicated hypothesis shows clearly what difficulties result when one assumes that the bones of Peter had rested at the place so constituted as the recently published report describes.

On the assumption that Peter had been buried here, the most recent excavations raise more new questions than they answer old ones. Did the wall painted red really *cross over* the supposed "grave of Peter" as well as that of the boy? *Is such a site of the "trophy" conceivable?"* Is it certain that *Christians* lay in the surrounding graves? Does not a libation tube which was found argue rather for pagans?

We have seen how difficult it is to hold the theory that the bodies were transferred to the Appian Way about the year 258. Even more difficult is the theory of an original burial on the Appian Way.

At the moment I ask only the question whether everything is not explained much more simply if we assume that perhaps the pillar monument was the "trophy" of Gaius, but was so regarded at first only in the sense of a memorial monument erected at the place of the martyrdom. With this idea, to be sure, the thought of the grave may have been connected very early, even if one had no relics. For somewhere on the Vatican Hill—possibly in a common grave—the victims of the Neronian persecution will have been buried. Is it not possible that in the cavity under the "trophy" we are dealing only with a *cenotaph*, in much the same way, perhaps, as we must assume there was one on the Appian Way?[66] In that case the three memorial sites, on the Vatican Hill, on the Highway to Ostia, and on the Appian Way, were all three not burial places but memorial or cult sites, at which Christians celebrated the memory of the apostles, since they did not possess a real grave. The fact that in addition to the separate cult sites there also arose the common one on the Appian Way *could* be explained, as said, by the fact that in the pagan cemeteries on the Vatican Hill and on the Highway to Ostia assemblies were hindered and the need was felt of holding a celebration for both apostles at *one* place. Or it *could* even be that at first one of the schismatic churches of the third century had honoured here the memory of the apostles. In such a case we might be driven to think of the Novatian group, who likewise appealed to the primacy of Peter; this suggests itself especially since the liturgical sources possibly

[66] For the designation *sepulchrum* for cenotaph, see Tacitus, *Annals*, II, 83.

point in this direction.[67] The memorial site would then have been taken over by the great Church at a later time.

These, we grant, are only hypotheses; but without hypotheses we can reach no conclusions in this question. They seem to me, however, to do more justice to the archaeological evidence, in so far as they take into account only such objects as have actually been found.[68]

In order to prove that the bones of Peter really rested in the supposed grave under the present dome, we would need more certain indications than have been produced by the most recent excavations. Indeed, we actually must say that in this case particularly convincing and absolutely irrefutable arguments would have to be presented, since *the reasons which speak* a priori *against the possibility that Christians buried Peter in the neighbourhood of Nero's garden are almost overwhelming*. How could the Christians undertake an interment here in the terrible days of the Neronian persecution?[69] Did any possibility exist of distinguishing the body of Peter from the others? Is it not to be assumed that the bones of those executed, in case their ashes were not scattered on the Tiber, were thrown into a common grave?

Furthermore, how can Christians in Rome have had any interest in *relics* in the first century? In the time of Nero the Christians expected the world to end soon. In any case, we do not have even the slightest trace of a cult of relics before the martyrdom of Polycarp, and so at the earliest the middle of the second century, and then we still are not dealing with Rome but with Smyrna.[70] In *Rome* no one

[67] See above, p. 130.
[68] The failure, moreover, of the graffiti and the Christian inscriptions of the cemetery to mention the name of Peter could perhaps find an explanation in this way. For it is indeed striking that in the graffiti of the Appian Way Peter and Paul are invoked, while here they are not. The Memorial on the Vatican Hill was different from that on the Appian Way in that it did not serve merely for the cult of the apostle; the Vatican Hill was also known from times past as the place of execution of *other* victims of the Neronian persecution. May not the form the inscriptions took have been affected by the memory that Peter was here executed with many other Christians, and in any case was buried near them? No doubt the remembrance of Peter may have dominated over that of the nameless multitude, but it is at least possible that Christians thought also of these others and perhaps for this reason did not mention the name of Peter. Nevertheless, I do not wish to assert that the failure to name the apostle can be explained only in this way.
[69] So rightly K. Heussi, "Das Grab des Petrus" (*Deutsches Pfarrerblatt*, 1949, pp. 82 ff.).
[70] According to the most recent theory (H. Grégoire, "La véritable date du martyre de S. Polycarpe, 23 févr. 177," in *Analecta Bollandiana*, 1951, pp. 1 ff.; *Les persécutions dans l'empire romain*, 1951, pp. 28, 106 f.), the martyrdom of Polycarp should be dated later, in the year 177.

took an interest in the graves of the martyrs in the first two centuries. Indeed, prior to the third century there was no interest whatever in the graves; even the graves of the Bishops of Rome exist only from the beginning of the third century, and then in the Catacombs of Callistus.[71] If prior to this time emphasis was already placed in Rome on the possession of the mortal remains of martyrs and bishops, how then does it happen that we hear nothing of a grave either of Ignatius of Antioch, whose desire to be *completely* consumed by the wild beasts (Rom. 4:2) can scarcely have been fulfilled,[72] or of the martyr bishop Telesphorus, or of Justin, who nevertheless suffered the martyr death in Rome and were highly honoured there?[73]

In reality this interest first arose in Rome about the time when Gaius wrote to Proclus, when Callistus appealed to the nearness of Peter's grave, and when Bishop Fabian created in the Catacomb of Callistus a resting place for the bishops. This, then, occurred in the first half of the third century. It occurred in connection with the necessity of proving the apostolicity of the Roman tradition, after this tendency had arisen somewhat earlier in the east.[74]

This, however, concerns only the question of the grave. Regarding the location of the *places of execution*, the question stands otherwise. It is clear without further argument that the memory of the place of execution long continued, especially when it concerned victims of the terrible Neronian persecution. Even this memory would perhaps have been lost in the course of time, if in the third century there had not been an interest in finding the very graves of Peter and Paul, who had long been regarded as the founders of the church. Naturally one looked for them where the *execution* was located by the tradition, which still remained alive and for a part of the Neronian victims was fixed in writing by Tacitus.[75] Now at this time, that is, in the *third Christian century*, a pagan cemetery had existed at this place or in its vicinity for at least a hundred years. This

---

[71] See above, p. 135.

[72] The fact that in the fourth century (Chrysostom, *Homily on the Martyr St. Ignatius*, Migne, *P. G.*, Vol. 50, pp. 587 ff., and Jerome, *De viribus illustribus*, Migne, *P. L.*, Vol. 23, pp. 632 ff.) we hear that his remains were brought to Antioch only proves that in a time when the cult of relics was flourishing the question as to the remains of Ignatius was raised.

[73] This point, which seems to me decisive, is rightly stressed also by E. Schäfer, "Das Petrusgrab" (*Evangelische Theologie*, 1951, pp. 472 f.).

[74] It is not by chance that the lists of the bishops of Rome, the *Depositio Martyrum*, and the *Depositio Episcoporum*, begin in the first half of the third century.

[75] *Annals*, XV, 44.

we know from the latest excavations. Thus there was so much the more occasion to *connect the place of execution and the later cemetery* as the place of burial.

The same development is probably to be assumed for the tradition as to Paul's grave, which also was located in a pagan cemetery, situated in the direction of the place of execution at the Three Fountains. For St. Paul's Church also is situated in the area of a pagan necropolis. Paul as a Roman citizen probably was not executed at the same place as Peter and the other victims.

We come accordingly to the following result, which can also be regarded as the conclusion of this entire section concerning Peter the Martyr: The archaeological investigations do not permit us to answer in either a negative or an affirmative way the question as to the stay of Peter in Rome. The grave of Peter cannot be identified. The real proofs for the martyrdom of Peter in Rome must still be derived from the indirect literary witnesses, and from them we have reached the conclusion that probably Peter actually was in Rome and suffered execution under Nero. The excavations speak in favour of the report that *the execution of Peter took place in the Vatican district.*

*   *   *

In summary of our entire historical section, to the end of which we now have come, we must say that during the life time of Peter he held a pre-eminent position among the disciples; that after Christ's death he presided over the church at Jerusalem in the first years; that he then became the leader of the Jewish Christian mission; that in this capacity, at a time which cannot be more closely determined but probably occurred at the end of his life, he came to Rome and there, after a very short work, died as a martyr under Nero.

We must keep in mind these historical results as we now turn to the theological question of the primacy of Peter and his significance for the later Church.

Part II

THE EXEGETICAL
AND THEOLOGICAL
QUESTION

THE PROBLEM

WE SHALL start here with the exegesis of the saying of Jesus in Matthew 16:17 ff.: "You are Rock, and upon this Rock I will build my Church. . . ." In a first chapter we deliberately limit ourselves to the *strictly exegetical question*: What place do these words occupy in the framework of the Synoptic tradition? Are they really genuine words of Jesus or were they only ascribed to him by the Church? In the former case, what did Jesus intend to say by them? In that connection a special problem results from the fact that in the Greek the statement of Matthew 16:18 refers to the future: I *will* build my Church. Moreover, the imperative in the two parallel sayings most closely related to ours, the command in Luke 22:31 f.: "Strengthen your brothers," and the commission of the Risen One in John 21:16: "Feed my lambs," refer to the time after the death of Jesus. Does this mean to say that in the promise of Matthew 16:18 Jesus reckons with centuries, with the Church of *all* generations? Or does it mean that he has in mind only the Church which was then to be built in the Apostolic Age, that is, in the life-time of Peter after Christ's death? This question also is first of all a purely exegetical and historical one.

After answering this question, however, we must examine in a second *doctrinal and theological chapter* the question whether, even if the exegesis should conclude that Jesus thought only of the time of Peter, there is a legitimate possibility of extending that promise and that commission beyond the period of the foundation that Jesus had in view and applying it to the entire period of the later Church down to the present day.

Here in this quite concrete application arises the problem of the New Testament conception of time, which I have discussed elsewhere.[1] Is the period when the foundation was laid normative for the later period, in such a way that it represents the permanent unique foundation upon which the entire later structure rests once for all? Or is it normative in the sense that what happened at the beginning

[1] O. Cullmann, *Christus und die Zeit. Die urchristliche Zeit- und Geschichteauffassung,* 2nd ed., 1948 (Eng. Tr., *Christ and Time,* 1950).

is continually repeated in an analogous way during the entire period of the Church, so that the promises and commissions which Jesus gave for the period of the apostolic foundation should be handed on, without hesitation or change, as commissions valid for Christians who live in later years?

I note in advance that we must not make the matter all too easy for ourselves by answering too hastily with a clear-cut Yes or No. For in reality the problem is too complex to permit a solution in this simple manner. It is impossible for us to say in advance, in a generalizing way, that everything which Jesus said may be referred only to his time and the time of his immediate disciples, and so can have no validity for later generations. But on the other hand, it is also much too simple when it is declared that everything which Jesus said to an apostle concerning the Church can only be understood as said also to a whole chain of bishops, who can be designated as successors of *this specific apostle*. An application to the future is conceivable which respects the historical uniqueness of the situation in which the Church was founded. In reality, therefore, the problem presents itself in the following way: *How is the unique element to be marked off from that which is constantly repeated?*

This means, however, that we must raise the fundamental question concerning the essential difference between the apostolic office and the office of bishop. Can the uniqueness and unrepeatable quality which belong to the apostolic office in the New Testament be reconciled with an extension of a specifically apostolic commission to later bishops? Here, too, we propose to be on our guard against thinking that the question is already solved in advance.

In conclusion, however, we have to discuss also the very important problem whether it is justified for a saying addressed to an apostle to be *geographically* limited to bishops of a *particular* city. In other words, can that utterance be extended chronologically on the one hand, while at the same time it is limited in its spatial application? Is it actually to be held that the principle of a succession tied to one bishop's see is the only possible view? Or is this view legitimate at all? From the viewpoint of exegesis this question would scarcely be asked if the Roman Catholic Church did not proclaim as a dogma that Peter as the Prince of Apostles handed on his succession to the chain of *Roman* bishops. Can *such* a dogmatic extension of the saying of Jesus be reconciled with the results of exegesis and with what we know of the history of Primitive Christianity? Can that saying of Jesus legitimately be limited to the future bishops of a particular city, when the Scripture says not a word on this point, and does not even consider it necessary to mention the stay of the apostle in this city, and when in addition the historical tradition concerning a Roman episcopal office of Peter is of such a character as we have shown it to be?

To what extent, finally, does the actual *historical role* that the Roman church and its bishops played in the second and third centuries justify the Bishop of Rome in making a theological and indeed exclusive claim to the saying that Jesus addressed to Peter? Is it legitimate to give such absolute validity to a situation which only appears during the course of ancient church history, but is neither present nor hinted at when the apostles are founding the Church? In other words, the Roman church does not play a leading role at all during the lifetime of the apostles. At the earliest it begins to play such a role in Christendom at the turn from the first to the second century. Even then this role has no theological foundation. Is it possible to derive from the fact of this later role the standard that in all subsequent times, even down to the end of the period of the Church, only the bishop of this city may stand at the head of the entire Church? Is it permissible to take this position and then interpret the saying of Jesus to intend the limitation just described, as though there were no other possible way of applying it to the present?

As a marginal issue, the purely theological question may also arise whether the appeal to a *dogma* is sufficient here. In this case of the primacy of the Roman bishop, it is not just any dogma that is involved, but the one that *gives the basis of the claim of the Roman Catholic Church* that it alone is justified in proclaiming any dogmas whatever.

These questions are intended to state the problem and to show how the theological problem is connected with the exegetical one.

Usually the only possible fulfilment of the saying to Peter that is even considered is the Roman Catholic one. With a certain unquestioning confidence that the issue is self-evident, some give an affirmative and some a negative answer. We, however, shall study whether exegesis does not lead to another solution, so that the apostle Peter actually has for the Church of all times a "fundamental" importance in the etymological sense, but in a way that corresponds with the meaning and purpose of that saying as well as with the basic New Testament view.

Chapter One

THE EXEGETICAL QUESTION:
THE MEANING OF
MATTHEW 16:17-19

THE INTERPRETATION of Matthew 16:17 ff., like the discussion of the historical question concerning the stay of Peter in Rome, has been blurred all too often by confessional prejudices. Just as it is not permissible, in dealing with the question whether Peter was in Rome, to solve it in one way or the other on the basis of one's attitude toward the papacy, even so the discussion of the question as to what Christ meant by his words to Peter concerning the Church must not be burdened in advance by one's judgment regarding the later papal claim. As in the former question, so also here one must react against the conscious or unconscious popular view—as though, for example, one who recognizes the genuineness of that saying somehow makes a concession to this papal claim, or as though one who challenges its genuineness deals a particularly effective blow to this claim to power.

The history of interpretation which we prefix to the study of our passage teaches us that the confessional standpoint has quite often coloured the exegesis, and that usually the result is fixed in advance and then subsequently read into the text.

1. *The History of the Leading Interpretations*

We lack a detailed history of the way in which our section has been interpreted throughout the centuries, from the ancient Church Fathers down to our own day. Such a work would be of the greatest value not only for exegetes but also for the historians of doctrine and of the Church. To be sure, we find, in the older commentaries and also in books on church history, references to the interpretations that the Church Fathers and the Reformers gave. There is lacking, however, a complete and connected presentation of the patristic interpretations of the saying. Only with reference to more recent study are we in a substantially more favourable situation; in recent commentaries, and also in articles in journals, the various contributions that the last fifty years have made to the understanding of our text have already become in part the subject of systematic survey.[1]

We cannot pretend to give here even an approximately complete survey of the history of the exegesis of Matthew 16:17 ff. Of the older explanations I shall mention only those which are particularly typical. I shall speak somewhat more in detail of the more recent ones, but at first will report only their conclusions. In our interpretation of the text we shall come back to individual arguments of earlier exegetes.

The first attempts at explanation are still free from the ecclesiastical and political tendency to use the saying for or against the claim of the Roman Bishop. Only at the beginning of the third century, in the west, does this interest in the saying of Jesus become prominent.

In the first two centuries we find very few traces of any use of Matthew 16:17 ff. The first certain evidence of such a use occurs in *Justin's Dialogue* (100,4; 106,3),[2] and further in the *Pseudo-Clementina*. *Origen* starts from his distinction between letter and spirit in order to explain that the letter directs this saying concerning the Rock to Peter, while the Spirit has in mind everyone who becomes such as Peter was.[3]

When we come to the explanation of *Tertullian* mentioned above,[4] we already find ourselves in the area of exegesis influenced by ecclesiastical politics. In his struggle against the author of that edict concerning the extension of penance, whom we may identify with the

---

[1] See J. R. Geiselmann, *Der petrinische Primat (Mt. 16, 17), seine neueste Bekämpfung und Rechtfertigung*, 1927, and especially K. L. Schmidt, Article on ἐκκλησία in G. Kittel's *Theologisches Wörterbuch zum N. T.* (this article has now appeared also separately in English translation under the title, *The Church*, 1950, in the series, *Bible Key Words* From Gerhard Kittel's *Theologisches Wörterbuch zum N. T.*). On the latest literature see R. Bultmann, "Die Frage nach der Echtheit von Mt. 16, 17-19" (*Theologische Blätter*, 1941, pp. 265 ff.), and A. Oepke, "Der Herrenspruch über die Kirche: Mt. 16, 17-19 in der neuesten Forschung" (*Studia Theologica*, Lund, 1948-1950, pp. 110 ff.).

[2] See E. Massaux, *Influence de L'Evangile de S. Matthieu sur la littérature chrétienne avant S. Irénée*, 1950. The possibility of use he accepts for Ignatius and the Odes of Solomon.

[3] Origen on Matt. 16:18: "For rock means every disciple of Christ."

[4] *De pudicitia*, 21. See above, p. 121.

highest probability as the Roman Bishop Callistus,[5] he explicitly rejects the interpretation that "the power to bind and loose has passed on to this bishop, that is, to the entire Church that is near to Peter."[6] This, he says, would "twist the obvious purpose of the Lord, who committed this to Peter *personally*."[7] And Tertullian proceeds: "What does all that have to do with the Church, and particularly with you, psychic one? According to the person of Peter this authority belongs to spiritual men . . ." From this we probably may conclude that Callistus (217–222) had already referred Matthew 16:17 to himself,[8] perhaps indeed with special appeal to Peter's grave.[9]

---

[5] The expressions *pontifex maximus* and *episcopus episcoporum*, which Tertullian uses in the same passage to designate the author of the edict, which he calls an *edictum peremptorium*, are best suited, even though they are ironical, to Callistus, whom Hippolytus also reproaches in his *Philosophoumena* for his lax exercise of penance. This in any case is more natural than it is to follow P. Galtier ("Le véritable édit de Calliste," *Revue d'Histoire ecclésiastique*, 1927, pp. 465 ff.; "Ecclesia Petri propinqua, A propos de Tertullien et de Calliste," *Revue d'Histoire ecclésiastique*, 1928, pp. 40 ff.; *L'Eglise et la rémission des péchés aux premiers siècles*, 1932, pp. 139 ff.) in ascribing the edict to a Carthaginian bishop Agrippinus (see also G. Bardy, "L'édit d'Agrippinus," *Revue des Sciences religieuses*, 1924, pp. 1 ff.). The great majority of scholars identify the bishop addressed with Callistus; so P. Batiffol, *L'Eglise naissante et le Catholicisme*, 1927, p. 350; *Cathedra Petri*, 1938, pp. 175 ff.; H. Koch, *Kallist und Tertullian*, 1920; *Cathedra Petri*, 1930, p. 6; E. Caspar, *Geschichte des Papsttums von den Anfängen bis zur Höhe der Weltherrschaft*, Vol. I, 1930, p. 26, and especially A. Harnack, "Ecclesia Petri propinqua" (*Sitzungsbericht der Berliner Akademie der Wissenschaften*, 1927). M. Goguel, *L'Eglise primitive*, 1947, holds on the contrary that the theory of P. Galtier is possible, but he does not make a definite decision.

[6] On the expression *ad omnem ecclesiam Petri propinquam* see above, p. 121, the hypothesis of W. Köhler, "Omnis ecclesia Petri propinqua, Versuch einer religionsgeschichtlichen Deutung" (*Sitzungsbericht der Heidelberg Akademie der Wissenschaften*, 1937–38). Harnack's proposal (*op. cit.* in the preceding note) to take *omnem* as a scribal error for *romanam* is purely hypothetical, and is rejected even by most Roman Catholic scholars. See Batiffol, *Cathedra Petri*, 1938, p. 178. Contrariwise K. Adam, "Neue Untersuchungen über den Ursprung der kirchlichen Primatslehre" (*Tübinger Theologische Quartalschrift*, 1928, pp. 169 ff.).

[7] For the text of this passage see above, p. 121, note 92.

[8] A different view is taken by K. Heussi, "Die Nachfolge des Petrus" (*Deutsches Pfarrerblatt*, 1949, pp. 420 f.). According to him Callistus appealed to Matt., ch. 16, only to prove the right of *all* bishops to forgive sins.

[9] According to E. Caspar, "Primatus Petri" (*Zeitschrift der Savigny-Stiftung für Rechtsgeschichte*, 1927, pp. 253 ff.), Callistus did not appeal to Matt. 16:17 ff. Tertullian first did so, to oppose Callistus; but he did not suspect what spirits he was conjuring up. In this way, much as Cyprian later did without intending to do so, he gave the Roman episcopal see the weapons with which it would henceforth defend its primacy. Against this theory M. Goguel, *L'Eglise primitive*,

Tertullian completely rejects that application of the saying to later bishops, and indeed not only to those of Rome but to bishops generally.

In doing so he stands in opposition to Cyprian; the latter also is unwilling to see any ground for the primacy of the Roman Bishop over the remaining bishops derived from the saying of Jesus, but he does consider that the whole body of bishops is addressed in Peter. When Jesus says only to Peter that he is the Rock, he thereby points simply to the necessity of the unity of the Church.[10] Cyprian developed his view, which he already had championed at an earlier time, mainly in connection with his dispute with the Bishop Stephan (254–257).[11] The latter, therefore, evidently appealed, as Callistus did, to Matthew 16:17 ff.; he as Bishop of Rome proposed to derive from it his primacy over the entire Church. *Firmilian*, Bishop of Caesarea in Cappadocia, in a letter to Cyprian, opposes this interpretation of Stephan in which the Roman Bishop claims that he is entitled by succession to the *cathedra* of Peter.[12]

These explanations are burdened with tendencies drawn from ecclesiastical politics. For a time, the saying of Jesus to Peter plays scarcely any role in grounding the papal claim. Then, from the beginning of the Middle Ages, it is regularly used by the popes, as

1947, pp. 195 f., makes the point that on this view it would be remarkable that this effect of the argument of Tertullian and Cyprian does not show itself until so much later.

[10] *De catholicae ecclesiae unitate*, cap. 4–5; *Epistolae* 33, 59, 73, 75, 76, 81, etc. Concerning Cyprian's exegesis, see J. Chapman, *Revue Bénédictine*, 1902–3; *ib.*, 1910; and K. Adam, "Cyprians Kommentar zu Mtth. 16, 18–19 in dogmengeschichtlicher Beleuchtung" (*Tübinger Theologische Quartalschrift*, 1912); H. Koch, *Cyprian und der römische Primat*, 1910; *Cyprianische Untersuchung*, 1926; especially *Cathedra Petri*, 1930.

[11] By using all of the writings of Cyprian a unified interpretation of the saying to Peter can be made, in so far as he always recognizes the primacy of Peter as a sign of unity, but on the other hand always refuses to derive from it for the later Bishops of Rome a pre-eminent position over the other bishops, who are all successors of Peter. However, it is not quite clear how he connects with this view the "pre-eminence" (*principalitas*) he recognizes for Rome (*Epistola* 59, 14). P. Batiffol, *Cathedra Petri*, 1938, emphasizes in all parts of his book this idea, that according to Cyprian Rome is "the chief church, whence the sacerdotal unity has arisen" (*ecclesia principalis, unde unitas sacerdotalis exorta est*). (See on this point H. Koch, *Cyprian und der römische Primat*, 1910; *Cathedra Petri*, 1930.) If *principalis* were really to be thus understood, that Jesus with the words "you are Peter" founded *this* church, then Cyprian's exposition could scarcely be regarded as *entirely* consistent and unified.

[12] In connection with Cyprian, *Epistola* 75, 17.

11

though no other understanding of it were possible. Yet it is note-worthy that the outstanding ancient commentators who concerned themselves with Matthew 16:17 ff. without discussing questions directly related to church politics considered other possibilities of interpretation. Thus *Chrysostom* explains that the rock on which Christ will build his Church means the faith of confession.[13] Accord-ing to *Augustine*, Jesus meant by the rock not Peter but himself, an explanation which Luther will follow.[14] In his *Retractationes*[15] Augustine writes that earlier, under the influence of Ambrose, he referred the word "rock" to Simon. However, he goes on, it does not say, "You are the rock," but "you are Peter"; the rock is men-tioned only in the following sentence, and there it seems best to refer the word to Christ. He leaves the decision to his readers. A similar embarrassment is to be observed in other writers, for example *Cyril of Alexandria*. We thus see that the exegesis that the Reformers gave —though, as we shall see, it is questionable—was not first invented for their struggle against the papacy; it rests upon an older patristic tradition.

We mentioned earlier the striking fact that the Reformers at-tached little significance to the question whether Peter was in Rome or not, even though Luther had doubts about the matter. We find among them rather an intensive concern with the saying of Jesus in Matthew 16:17 ff., and their specific interest is in polemic against the Pope. *Luther*, on the one hand, like Augustine, interprets the rock to mean Christ himself: "Thus this rock is the Son of God, Jesus Christ himself and no one else."[16] From this basis he establishes the connection with Peter; he emphasizes that the word directed to Peter has in view (not his person but) only his faith in Jesus the Rock: "You are . . . the rock man, for you have recognized the true man who is the true Rock, and you have named him as the Scripture names him, that is, Christ."[17] "Not upon the rock . . . of the Roman Church is the Church founded, as some decrees explain it, but upon the faith which Peter confessed for the entire Church."[18] *Calvin*

---

[13] See J. Chapman, *Early Papacy*, pp. 72 ff.

[14] Augustine, *Sermons* 76, 147, 149, 232, 245, 270, 295.

[15] I, 21, 1.

[16] *Wider Das Papsttum vom Teufel gestiftet* (Weimar edition, 54; E. Mülhaupt, *Luthers Evangelien-Auslegung*, Vol. 2, pp. 545 f.).

[17] *Ib.*, Mülhaupt, p. 548.

[18] "Resolution Lutheriana super propositione XIII de potestate papae 1519" (Weimar edition, 2; E. Mülhaupt, *op. cit.*, Vol. 2, p. 525). Further passages in Mülhaupt, *op. cit.*, Vol. 2.

argues quite similarly: the words which the Roman Catholic teaching refers to the person of a man were in reality spoken only of Peter's faith in Christ. Hence the designation "rock" is addressed both to Simon and to the other believers. The bond of faith in Christ is the basis on which the Church grows.[19] Likewise for *Zwingli* Peter is only the type of him who believes in Christ as the sole Rock.[20] It is only a variation of all these interpretations when Melanchthon refers the saying to preaching and the preaching office.[21] Thus in the final analysis all the Reformers agree that Peter was named "Rock" by Jesus not as a person but only as a believer. The true Rock of the Church, they hold, is Jesus Christ.

We pass over the following centuries and come to recent times. We speak first of two typical interpretations which are rather closely connected with the Reformation view, but seek to give it a more solid exegetical basis. First of all, there is the interpretation of *Th. Zahn*. Like the Reformers, he emphasizes the faith of Peter, but on the other hand he also takes account of the fact that Peter was the *first* confessor and so occupies a special position in the foundation of the Church.[22] The commentary of *Strack-Billerbeck* connects more closely with the Reformers. It starts from the assumption that the Greek text was a mistranslation from an Aramaic original text. The correct English translation of the original would be as follows: "I say to you, yes to you, Peter: On this rock I will build my Church."[23] The word "rock" in this passage, therefore, would not mean Peter. Jesus did not say: "You are the rock," but rather: I say to you, Peter," etc. When he then proceeds: "On this rock I will build my Church," he speaks of his own Messianic dignity, his own divine sonship, in which men must believe.

Toward the end of the nineteenth and at the beginning of the twentieth century, however, another interpretation dominated in Protestant scholarship. The saying, it was held, was not spoken by

[19] See Calvin, *Commentaire*, ad loc.

[20] Among other places, his sermon on providence (Zwingli, *Hauptschriften*, Vol. II, p. 195); "Concerning the True and the False Religion" (Zwingli, *Hauptschriften*, Vol. 9, pp. 158 ff.).

[21] *De potestate et principatu Papae*.

[22] See Th. Zahn, *Das Evangelium des Matthäus*, 4th ed., 1922, ad loc.

[23] *Kommentar zum N. T. aus Talmud und Midrasch*, Vol. I, pp. 732 ff. Jesus, on this view, said: גם אנ' אמר לך אתה פטרוס. The translator by mistake understood אתה as the subject of a new sentence, when it was only the repeating of the second person singular pronoun already contained in לך. This is also the view of G. Gloege, *Reich Gottes und Kirche*, 1929, pp. 274 f.

Jesus at all. It was ascribed to him later, and this was done at a time and place where one had an interest in glorifying Peter. Even today the discussion of our passage often revolves around this question of "genuineness" or "spuriousness." Can this saying have been spoken by Jesus, or was it only created by the Church after his death? This question, as already noted, should be independent of that concerning the justification of the papal claim. As a matter of fact, even today the battle lines are not so drawn in this matter that the genuineness is recognized only by Roman Catholic scholars, while Protestant scholars contest it. Rather the discussion on this issue—as on the question of Peter's stay in Rome—takes place among Protestant exegetes themselves. Indeed, even in the area of Protestant exegesis it is not true that only the exegetes who rightly or wrongly are called "conservative" defend the genuineness of the saying, while the interpreters who rightly or wrongly are given the liberal label oppose it. On this point we should recall above all that even such radical critics as *D. F. Strauss* and *F. Ch. Baur* regarded the genuineness as quite obvious.

It was New Testament scholars, and above all *H. J. Holtzmann*, who toward the end of the nineteenth century first denied vigorously that Jesus uttered the saying; he could not possibly have so spoken, because he had no intention of founding a Church. The passage, on this view, appears to have received its present form only in the second century. The church consciousness which comes to expression in it is already basically Catholic in character. Indeed, Holtzmann actually goes so far as to explain that we here have to do with a first stirring of the Roman self-consciousness.[24] The entire course of critical study at the beginning of the twentieth century is then dominated by this conception, and it would take too long to cite here the names of all those who regard the saying as irreconcilable with the teaching of Jesus. The chief reason for denying that Jesus said it is always said to be the mention of the "Church." How can Jesus have spoken of the Church? After all, he preached only the Kingdom of God. It was only after his death that something quite different, that is, the Church, appeared. According to the famous word of A. Loisy: "Jesus announced the Kingdom of God, but what appeared was the Church."[25] It was to justify subsequently this unexpected development that this saying was ascribed to Jesus. So we hear from

[24] *Handkommentar*, I, *ad loc.*

[25] *L'Evangile et l'Eglise*, 1902, p. 111. See also *Les évangiles synoptiques*, 1908.

Johannes Weiss and *E. Klostermann* to *M. Dibelius, B. S. Easton, M. Goguel,* and many other representatives of New Testament scholarship, and from historians of this generation,[26] that the saying cannot come from Jesus. The only exception, apart from such conservative scholars as *Th. Zahn*[27] and *A. Schlatter,*[28] is *A. Schweitzer,* who recognizes the genuineness of Matthew 16:18; he takes his starting point, it is true, from the same contrast between an earthly Church and the Kingdom of God, but identifies the Church here with the Kingdom of God and interprets the passage in a purely eschatological way.[29] Among opponents of the genuineness, the representatives of the school of comparative religion, for example, *A. Dell,*[30] *H. Gressmann,* and *R. Reitzenstein,* attempt to explain the statement of Matthew 16:17 ff. not only from the tendency to legitimitize the later Church, but also from motifs found in comparative religion.

A. Harnack takes a somewhat less radical attitude. To be sure, he too holds that Jesus cannot have spoken the promise with reference to the Church. This saying rather was coined at a later time, and probably in Rome, as it strove for the primacy. But in contrast to his predecessors Harnack denies to Jesus, in the entire section, only this one sentence concerning the Church; the remaining parts of the utterance addressed to Peter he regards as genuine. With these words Jesus assured Peter of immortality: "You are Peter, and death will not conquer you." This is how the words concerning the gates of hell are to be understood. Jesus said nothing to Peter, however, concerning the building of the Church. This part was rather inserted later into the original promise.[31] Since Harnack did not intend to put forth his explanation as a mere conjecture, he attempted to determine an original text in which those words concerning the Church, and only those words, had actually been lacking. This text, he held, was the Diatessaron of Tatian. This latter assertion,

---

[26] See also J. Grill, *Der Primat des Petrus,* 1904, p. 79; J. Schnitzer, *Hat Jesus das Papsttum gestiftet?,* 1910, p. 82; F. Heiler, *Der Katholizismus. Seine Idee und seine Erscheinung,* 1923, pp. 39 ff.

[27] See above, p. 163.

[28] *Der Evangelist Matthäus,* 1929.

[29] *Geschichte der Leben-Jesu-Forschung,* 4th ed., 1926, p. 416 (cf. Eng. Tr., *The Quest of the Historical Jesus,* 2nd ed., 1911, p. 369, note).

[30] *ZNW,* 1914, pp. 1 ff. See above, p. 19.

[31] "Der Spruch über Petrus als den Felsen der Kirche" (*Sitzungsbericht der Berliner Akademie der Wissenschaften,* 1918, pp. 637 ff.).

however, was refuted from the Roman Catholic side as early as 1922.[32]

We thus have seen that it is mainly the mention of the Church that has caused scholars to declare the passage spurious. So also it is precisely on this point that a change of opinion occurred in the period between the two world wars; the attempt was made to prove that in reality Jesus could very well have spoken of a Church, on the condition that in this connection one does not think of the Church in the modern sense, but of what the Aramaic equivalent meant to a Jew of that time. Here it is chiefly two scholars who must be named: *F. Kattenbusch*, who in his work on the place of origin of the Church proposes the thesis that the Son of Man idea leads to that of a "People of the Saints";[33] and then *K. L. Schmidt*, who in two decisive articles[34] seeks to determine the Aramaic expression which lies behind the Greek word for Church, and on this basis shows that the word fits perfectly as an utterance of Jesus, since it refers to the idea of the People of God, the remnant or the separate synagogue.

In this way the chief argument against genuineness seemed to be removed. At the same time, interesting studies by *J. Jeremias*[35] emphasized by other arguments the Semitic character of the word and its roots in Jewish conceptions of the cosmic rock. Hence there now occurred a swing back to an extensive agreement among Protestant exegetes in favour of accepting the genuineness. It finds expression, for example, in the book of *O. Linton* concerning "The Problem of the Primitive Church in Recent Study."[36] The late Roman Catholic New Testament scholar from Fribourg, *F. M. Braun*, O.P., in his exceedingly instructive book, "New Light on the Church," also con-

---

[32] See especially S. Euringer, "Der locus classicus des Primates (Mt. 16, 18) und der Diatessarontext des heiligen Ephraim" (*Festgabe für A. Ehrhard*, 1922, pp. 141 ff.); also, A. Kneller, *Innsbrucker Zeitschrift für katholische Theologie*, 1920, pp. 147 ff.; J. Sickenberger, "Eine neue Deutung der Primatstelle (Matt. 16, 18)" (*Théologique Revue*, 1920, pp. 1 ff.) ; and against A. Harnack also Ed. Meyer, *Ursprung und Anfänge des Christentums*, Vol. I, p. 112.

[33] *Festgabe für A. Harnack*, 1921, pp. 143 ff. The collective meaning of the Son of Man concept is also emphasized by T. W. Manson, *The Teaching of Jesus*, 1931, p. 211, and R. Newton Flew, *Jesus and his Church*, 1938. See also H. Odeberg, *The Fourth Gospel*, 1929, pp. 39 f.; N. A. Dahl, *Das Volk Gottes*, 1941, p. 90.

[34] "Das Kirchenproblem im Urchristentum" (*Theologische Blätter*, 1927, columns 293 ff.); "Die Kirche des Urchristentums" (*Festgabe für Ad. Deissmann*, 1927, p. 259). See also especially *Theologisches Wörterbuch zum N. T.*, Vol. III, Article on ἐκκλησία, 1936 (English translation, *The Church;* see note 1 of this chapter).

[35] *Golgotha*, 1926, pp. 68 ff.; *Angelos*, 1926, p. 109.

[36] *Das Problem der Urkirche in der neuern Forschung*, 1932.

firms this new consensus among Protestant scholars.[37] So it might seem that the question as to genuineness has finally been settled along this line.

In the year 1941, however, a reaction again occurred. It came from *R. Bultmann*, in connection with my remark in my monograph on "The Kingship of Christ and the Church."[38] I had said that the challenge to the genuineness of Matthew 16:17 ff. cannot be justified on scholarly grounds. In a rather long essay in *Theologischen Blätter*,[39] Bultmann seeks to undermine this statement; he defends anew the assertion of spuriousness that he had championed earlier. He seeks to refute F. Kattenbusch and K. L. Schmidt; he points to the absence of the word "Church" in the teaching of Jesus, and above all tries to demonstrate that Jesus spoke only of a Kingdom to come in the future, not of a Church that is now being realized. In so doing, he, like his earlier predecessors, believes that in the last analysis he must think in terms of a modern understanding of the word "Church." Even Bultmann, however, had already conceded in previous studies that the saying must have been coined and ascribed to Jesus at a very early time, since its character is entirely Semitic and so it comes from the period of debates concerning the law in Palestine.

Thus the question was raised anew by R. Bultmann. In the subsequent debate *W. G. Kümmel* took a prominent role with his much discussed essay on "The Church Concept and the Consciousness of History in the Primitive Church and in the Mind of Jesus."[40] He likewise comes to the conclusion that the saying was not uttered by Jesus but was only ascribed to him later by the Church. His arguments, however, are essentially different from the earlier ones. His starting point is that in Primitive Christianity, as with Jesus, there was a tension between the eschatological future and the present, but that the tension was solved in a different way in each case. In the case

---

[37] *Neues Licht auf die Kirche*, 1946 (German translation of *Aspects Nouveaux du problème de l'Eglise*, 1942, enlarged and revised by the author). On p. 85 Braun names as representatives of this consensus: F. Kattenbusch, K. L. Schmidt, H. D. Wendland, G. Gloege, W. Michaelis, J. Schniewind, F. Leenhardt, R. Otto, A. Fridrichsen, R. Newton Flew, O. Cullmann. The list could easily be extended, for example by those whom Braun often cites: O. Linton, J. Jeremias, etc.

[38] *Königsherrschaft Christi und Kirche*, 1941, p. 22.

[39] "Die Frage nach der Echtheit von Matth. XVI, 17–19" (*Theologische Blätter*, 1941, pp. 265 ff.).

[40] *Kirchenbegriff und Geschichtsbewusstsein in der Urgemeinde und bei Jesus* (*Symbolae Biblicae Upsalienses*), 1943. Even earlier W. G. Kümmel had opposed the genuineness, in *Die Eschatologie der Evangelien*, 1936, p. 16.

of Primitive Christianity, the Church was regarded as the already present fulfilment; for Jesus, on the contrary, the already present fulfilment was connected only with his person. The two solutions, according to Kümmel, could not have stood side by side in the mind of Jesus.

Others have challenged the genuineness with still other arguments. For example, *Emanuel Hirsch* does so after the manner of the older critics and without considering the recent statement of the problem.[41] *J. Haller* completely rejects the recent studies and discards the saying without offering any real exegetical foundation.[42] *H. Strathmann*[43] regards the saying, in connection with his somewhat schematic geographical division of the roles of the evangelists, as the creation of the church at Antioch.[44] *E. Stauffer* takes a special position; while he regards the utterance as a saying of the Lord, he assigns it not to the Incarnate Jesus, but to the Risen One, who spoke the words on the occasion of his first appearance, which was granted to Peter.[45]

N. A. Dahl[46] and *O. Michel*[47] do not deny the genuineness categorically, but take an extremely cautious attitude. *R. Liechtenhan*, on the contrary, while he carries on a debate with R. Bultmann and continues the ideas of Kümmel, nevertheless uses these ideas in a different way. He represents the view that Jesus' eschatological expectation concerning the future included the foundation of his Church; towards the setting and form of the saying, however, he takes a critical attitude.[48] Especially does the last major work, which comes from *A. Oepke*,[49] offer anew a full defence of the genuineness. In doing so, it emphasizes mainly the idea of the People of God, an

---

[41] *Frühgeschichte des Evangeliums*, II, 1941, pp. 306 ff.

[42] *Das Papsttum*, 2nd ed., 1951, pp. 4 f., 473 f. The saying, he contends, could only have originated after the year 70, when events proved that the temple rock had no permanence. This unexpected conclusion J. Haller draws from the above mentioned work of J. Jeremias.

[43] "Die Stellung des Petrus in der Urkirche. Zur Frühgeschichte des Wortes an Petrus Mt. 16, 17-19" (*Zeitschrift für systematische Theologie*, 1943, pp. 223 ff.).

[44] See above, p. 25, note 35.

[45] "Zur Vor- und Frühgeschichte des Primatus Petri" (*ZKG*, 1943-44, pp. 1 ff.

[46] *Das Volk Gottes. Eine Untersuchung zum Kirchenbewusstsein des Urchristentums*, 1941, p. 165.

[47] *Das Zeugnis des Neuen Testaments von der Gemeinde*, 1941, pp. 9 f., 22 f.

[48] *Die urchristliche Mission*, 1946 (*Abhandlungen zur Theologie des Alten und Neuen Testaments*).

[49] "Der Herrnspruch über die Kirche, Mt. 16, 17-19, in der neuesten Forschung" (*Studia Theologica*, 1948-50, pp. 110 ff.).

idea solidly rooted in Jewish conceptions; on the other hand, by showing the rhythm in which these verses are constructed, it seeks to ascribe the saying to the Logia Source and at the same time to show its organic attachment to the narrative framework as it appears also in Mark.

Thus at the present time the question is once more in flux, and we can scarcely speak any longer of a consensus of opinion. A statistical study of the position that thirty-four modern authors take on this question has shown that they divide into two approximately equal groups.[50]

Up to this point we have mentioned only Protestant scholars. The genuineness of the saying naturally cannot be challenged by Roman Catholic exegetes. In general, the modern Roman Catholic commentators limit themselves to offering a searching detailed exegesis. It is noteworthy that we find very little concerning the point which one would gladly find discussed by precisely these scholars—concerning the question, that is, whether and how it accords with the purpose of Jesus to refer these words to bishops as successors, whether and how, indeed, the promise of Jesus contains any idea whatever of a succession. *F. M. Braun*, in debate with K. L. Schmidt in the above mentioned work,[51] is the only one who ever takes up the question. He does not, indeed, discuss it in an exegetical way; this the scope of his book scarcely permitted. In the Roman Catholic *commentaries* the presence of the idea of succession is for the most part not examined; it is rather presupposed as an undiscussed fact. And yet this should be proved, for it certainly is not at all self-evident, and he who reads the saying without prejudice will never by himself get the idea that Jesus here speaks—in a sort of prophetic way—to successors of Peter. The Roman Catholic exegetes really owe a more thorough explanation on this point than one usually reads in their commentaries.

I choose as examples two recent Roman Catholic commentaries which have dealt with the Gospel of Matthew. They are by P. Dausch and M. J. Lagrange. In *Dausch*[52] we read but a single sentence concerning the specific question that here interests us: "since, according to the second half of verse 18, the Church founded upon Peter is to be unshakable in its stability and in its duration, and since it is almost universally conceded that Peter came to Rome and died

[50] See A. Oepke, *op. cit.*, p. 111, note 1.
[51] See above, pp. 166 f.
[52] *Kommentar zum Matthäusevangelium*, 1936, *ad. loc.*

there, the primacy is already assured on this basis alone." *F. M. Lagrange*, however, deals with this question somewhat more in detail.[53] After an intensive criticism of Harnack, he mentions the objection of the "Anglicans" that the passage speaks only of Peter, not of any possible successors. Why this objection is ascribed only to the Anglicans is not clear. In reality we are dealing here with a question which Protestants of all denominations have raised long since and repeatedly in opposition to the Roman Catholic presupposition. Lagrange replies that in this saying Jesus did not limit the duration of the Church. As long as there is a Church, it will have the same foundation, even if the head and the members change. There thus exists, he claims, a "successive unity" in the leadership of the Church. Jesus will see to it that in order to provide the foundation for the Church there will be at all times shepherds of the quality of Peter, that is, of the same faith. History proves that this has been the case, and this confirms the trustworthiness of the Lord's saying.[54] Concerning this retreat from exegesis to later history, which we find almost universally among Roman Catholic scholars,[55] we shall speak in the closing chapter. For in any case it can be considered only as a confirmation and not as a justification of the exegesis.

2. *The Narrative Framework of Matthew 16:17–19*

We now undertake, on the basis of a careful examination of the text, to explain the verses under discussion. First of all we must give close attention to the context in which they stand. This very context raises questions, especially since Mark and Luke have the same narrative framework, but without the crucial verses which here concern us. These momentous words concerning the rock on which Jesus will build his Church thus stand in but one of our four Gospels, the Gospel of Matthew. For many this fact still constitutes what we may call the first external occasion for challenging the genuineness. This argument, however, should certainly be discarded. The fact that a saying belongs to the so-called special material of Matthew is no justification at all for even raising the question of genuineness. How many pearls we would have to discard as spurious from Jesus'

---

[53] *Evangile selon S. Matthieu*, 5th ed., 1941, *ad loc.*

[54] J. Sickenberger also omits any discussion of successors in his explanation of Matt. 16:17 ff. in *Biblische Zeitfragen*, 1929, pp. 16 ff.

[55] See for example K. Pieper, *Jesus und die Kirche*, 1932, and K. Adam, *Wesen des Katholizismus*, 1934.

Sermon on the Mount—to name only this one example—if we were to let ourselves be guided by this principle![56]

The point has been made that the historical framework, which is found also in Mark and Luke though without these verses, is interrupted by this section in Matthew in a rather unfortunate way. We therefore propose to begin by studying this argument. Do the verses fit the narrative framework or not? On this point one thing must be noted in advance; even if it should prove true that the section with which we are concerned breaks the narrative framework, or in chronological respects is actually irreconcilable with it, we still could not draw from that fact the conclusion that the words are spurious, that is, that they were not spoken by Jesus. This conclusion would rather warrant only the preliminary conclusion that a unit of tradition, handed down separately, has been inserted here by Matthew in a setting in which it did not originally belong.

First, however, we must look more closely at this historical framework. It deals with the famous confession of Jesus by Peter at Caesarea Philippi, and we propose to read this narrative in the form in which it stands in the Gospel of Mark. On the whole, Matthew gives it, apart from variations in detail, in the same form that Mark has; only he introduces in this framework the promises of Jesus to Peter.

While the story of Peter's confession of Jesus is common to all three Synoptics, it is probably presented most vividly and in most effective simplicity in Mark. Precisely in this Gospel, moreover, it has a quite central position. One is inclined to trace the story back to a direct participant, that is, to the chief participant, to Peter himself, in case the notice of Papias is correct, according to which the evangelist Mark was the interpreter of Peter, and in his Gospel reported the stories from the life of Jesus which Peter cited in his sermons as illustrative examples.[57] In any case, Matthew and Luke, in the parallel passages, do not possess the same freshness as does Mark, in whose Gospel a certain animation marks this entire narrative. This animation permits us in a way to share in the excitement of those who were present at the event itself.

[56] It therefore seems to me unnecessary to follow the explanation that Eusebius gives in his *Demonstratio evangelica*, 3, 5. He explains the silence of the Gospel of Mark, which goes back to Peter, by the humility and modesty of the apostle. This is the interpretation given by Roman Catholic exegetes such as P. Dausch, *Kirche und Papsttum—eine Stiftung Jesu*, 1911.

[57] Eusebius, *Ecclesiastical History*, III, 39, 15 f.

Mark is conscious of the fact that in this moment something of special importance must have happened. Even the beginning of the conversation must have been an impressive moment. Previously Jesus had commanded silence and had done everything to prevent any discussion of his Messianic calling from arising. Now on his own initiative, though in the narrow circle of disciples, he starts a conversation concerning this question to which previously he had carefully avoided making so much as the merest allusion. Now he is the very one who asks: "Who do the people say that I am?" Then he asks further—and here we note how both the questioner and the persons questioned are inwardly moved—"And you, who do you say that I am?" Then comes the answer of Peter, which again in its modest brevity embodies the emotion of the disciple: "You are the Christ." Matthew, who has a slight tendency to edifying liturgical paraphrase, may well have weakened somewhat the effect of this answer when he gave it the fuller form: "You are the Christ, the Son of the Living God." This expansion appears rather a weakening of the Marcan text, even if we must be somewhat cautious in making such judgments, which rest upon subjective impressions. The Lucan text also was not content here with the simple wording of Peter's answer as we read it in Mark. It says: "The Christ of God." In contrast, the simple words: "You are the Messiah," are more powerful in their simplicity and sound more original. What the demon-possessed man had already said to Jesus in Capernaum: "Jesus the Messiah," this we now hear from the mouth of the disciple who is the representative and spokesman of the others. In the name of all he utters the great word that up to this time no disciple had dared to speak in the presence of Jesus. Among themselves the disciples may have discussed it when Jesus was absent, and the confession of Peter will have rested upon their firm conviction.[58]

They knew that they were not mere disciples of a rabbi, as were all other disciples. They were certain that their teacher was more than a rabbi, and they had the proud consciousness, which emerges in other passages, that they formed the following of the Messiah. One speaks a great deal of the self-consciousness of Jesus. We could also speak of the self-consciousness of the disciples.

According to Mark, Jesus at first answers nothing in response to this confession, and this is very significant. The disciples still do not

[58] W. Michaelis, *Das Evangelium nach Matthäus* (*Prophezei*), Part II, 1949, p. 339, assumes on the contrary that Peter previously had suspected nothing of this kind; Jesus' words presuppose a sudden disclosure.

know in what way he conceives this Messianic calling. Jesus says neither Yes nor No. He simply commands the disciples not to tell this to anyone, that is, not to tell anyone that he is the Christ. Only when he shall suffer will the people recognize in him the Messiah. The disciples, however, must now be the first ones to be taught in what sense he is the Messiah. This instruction follows in verses 31 f. It is attached to the commandment to say nothing to anyone concerning his Messianic calling, and it likewise explains this command. This is *the entirely natural continuation of the narrative*. In view of the importance of the occasion the passion prediction necessarily followed here, and it explains all the commands to be silent. This prediction and the protest of Peter by no means form a new narrative. Neither are they a sort of epilogue. Rather, they give *the point of the entire event at Caesarea Philippi*.[59] Now that the word "Messiah" has been uttered, and Jesus has not rejected this title but also has not accepted it, he must inform the disciples of the restricted sense in which alone he applies the word to himself: Messiah—yes, but in a quite different way from what you think; Messiah, but as a suffering, rejected, executed one. Mark adds that Jesus now spoke openly—he "said everything."[60]

And then follows—not at all a new narrative or an appendix but—

[59] This must be emphasized in opposition to R. Bultmann, "Die Frage nach dem messianischen Bewusstsein Jesu und das Petrus-Bekenntnis" (*ZNW*, 1919–20, pp. 165 ff.), and *Geschichte der synoptischen Tradition*, 2nd ed., *ad. loc.*, whose view is that the Marcan narrative of the event at Caesarea Philippi closes with the command of silence (in this point, but only in this point, he agrees with K. L. Schmidt, *Der Rahmen der Geschichte Jesu*, 1919, pp. 217 ff.). He then further asserts that the report in Mark is a torso; the original narrative, which to be sure was only created by the Church, demands the continuation that we read in Matthew. Mark shortened the account here due to his "anti-Petrine" attitude (see on this point above, p. 25), and so robbed the story of its conclusion. Quite similar, though with acceptance of the genuineness of the Matthean narrative, is the judgment of W. Michaelis, *Das Evangelium nach Matthäus*, Part II, p. 339. A. Schlatter, *Der Evangelist Matthäus*, 1929, *ad loc.*, actually goes so far as to explain the Marcan omission of Jesus' words of Matt. 16:17–19 as an effort to make a belated connection of the passion prediction with the confession of Peter. In reality the final verses offer the key to the understanding not only of what happened at Caesarea Philippi but also of the so-called "messianic secret." Hence the central position of our section in the Synoptic Gospels. Only in Matthew do the verses which contain the passion prediction and the protest of Peter seem a sort of afterpiece, more or less separated from the preceding narrative by the words ἀπὸ τότε ("from that time"). This very fact speaks in favour of the originality of the Marcan narrative.

[60] παρρησίᾳ ("freely," "openly," "plainly").

the *real point* of the story, in which the protest of Peter proves that even the innermost group of disciples had not grasped the real meaning that the Messianic calling had for Jesus. Peter, too, shared completely the diabolical conception of the Messianic calling, as the devil had represented it in person in the temptation story, when he offered to Jesus the kingdoms of the world. The idea of a suffering Messiah was entirely foreign to Peter, and *according to Mark it was entirely foreign to him when he uttered that confession, "You are the Messiah."* This fact must be emphasized, that even when he spoke that confession, according to Mark, he still had not grasped *its essential meaning*. And even now he does not grasp it. He reacts against this idea of the suffering of the Messiah, and so great is his astonishment and his emotion that he dares to "rebuke" Jesus. Nowhere else do we hear that a disciple did this. But this shows how great the astonishment of Peter must have been; it was so much the greater since Jesus has finally for once spoken with his disciples concerning his Messianic calling and evoked the confession of his Messianic role. Peter's position as a disciple, indeed, will also be affected if Jesus is a suffering Messiah; in that case he, like the others, is the disciple of a suffering and rejected Messiah, and for them, too, everything is quite different from what they have conceived it to be.

Jesus, however, turns around, and Mark now notes very acutely that in the words he addresses to Peter, he also has in view the other disciples, for what he says applies also to them. Jesus knows that they, too, share that false conception of his Messianic role and consequently of their discipleship. The example of the sons of Zebedee, for example, proves that.

And then Jesus utters the unusually strong words: "Depart from me, Satan!"[61] Thus he uses the word that he had hurled at the devil himself at the time of the temptation (Matt. 4:10). The devil is now making use of Jesus' own disciple, Peter; that is his greatest trick. Nevertheless, Jesus recognizes it, and here too Mark portrays with special vividness how he accompanies this harsh word to Peter with the simultaneous look at the other disciples. He who tries to force upon Jesus another Messianic task than the one he has received from God, he who thereby seeks to turn him from this task he has received from God, is a tool of Satan!

[61] We may leave undiscussed the question whether ὕπαγε ὀπίσω μου is to be understood literally, that is, (depart) "after me," in the sense of a summons to follow him as a disciple. I do not believe that it has a meaning essentially different from the simple ὕπαγε ("depart") in Matt. 4:10.

The originality of this Marcan narrative, in comparison with the parallels in Luke and Matthew, appears not only in its unclouded clearness, which really is striking, but also in various points of detail. Thus this entire story does not play in Matthew the dominating role that it has in Mark. In Matthew, that is, the disciples have already at an earlier time confessed before Jesus his majesty, at the time of the walking upon the sea (Matt. 14:33). Matthew thereby reduces in advance the importance of the story here reported.[62] In Mark its unique significance rests upon the very fact that here for the *first* time the disciples speak with Jesus with regard to what he is in their eyes.

Here it is seen that the arrangement of material, which of course is due to the evangelists, can become important in giving significance to the individual narrative. It is, so to say, a commentary on the part of the evangelist. So for the understanding of this narrative concerning Peter's confession, it makes a difference whether or not there already appears at some earlier point in the story a narrative in which the disciples confess the Messianic role of Jesus. Matthew, by introducing the disciples' saying: "You are the Son of God," in a chapter that *precedes* this sixteenth chapter of his work, has really robbed this event of its unique significance. Mark, on the contrary, has plainly preserved the memory of the fact that in order to understand this event it is essential to realize that what happened here had not yet happened at any previous time. Therefore in his arrangement of material he saw to it that in his Gospel no narrative preceded in which the disciples had already made a confession of Jesus as the Messiah.

Details within the narrative itself also seem to point to the conclusion that Matthew had a shallower grasp than Mark of the bearing of the event. For example, Matthew formulates the opening question of Jesus in a way that already anticipates the answer: "Who do the people say that *the Son of Man* is?" In Mark this is put in a form that is certainly more original, "Who do the people say that *I* am?"[63]

By this, we do not mean to say in any *a priori* way that verses 17–

---

[62] W. Michaelis, *Das Evangelium nach Matthäus* (*Prophezei*), p. 338, seeks to minimize the significance of this fact by writing that at this point Matthew was conscious that he was anticipating.

[63] Too far-fetched is the explanation of R. Graber, *Petrus der Fels*, 1949, p. 31. He takes the contrary position and gives Matthew the preference here. He holds that Mark and Luke here replaced the expression "Son of Man" by the first person singular, because the mention of the Son of Man, which points to Daniel and alludes to the people of God who will defeat the world powers, seemed to them too dangerous in this passage.

19, which concern us and are found only in
creation of the Primitive Church. Nevertheles
must also be considered when we now put the
chief objective in making a closer examina
framework: Does Jesus' saying to Peter, wh
follows Peter's confession of Jesus, fit harmo
work? Do these verses 17–19 really belong t
they spoken on this occasion, or on the contr
belong in another context and were they first
by Matthew? Even in the latter case, as we h
fully genuine, that is, spoken by Jesus but on

We must consider, at least theoretically,
that it was Matthew who inserted into the fra
narrative these words of Jesus to Peter. This
by the entire manner in which the evangelist
ticular, have arranged the material transmitt
or already written tradition. It is the lastin
on "Form Criticism" to have proved that th
like all oral tradition, contained only sin
chronological or geographical connections be
of the evangelists, who assembled these singl.
consists in the fact that they combined then
Thus they are not only collectors but also ar
tion it can be shown that each one proceede
in his own way, and it is particularly i
Matthew and Luke in this regard. Matthew i
follows a plan based on considerations of co
is, he connects with one another the stories
belong together in their theological significa
ings concerning the Law (Sermon on the M
ing John the Baptist (Matt., ch. 11), parable
against the Pharisees (Matt., ch. 23), etc. I
cern to Matthew whether he thereby pres
sequence; from the start he has written his
point of view. The evangelist Luke, on th
himself says in his prologue, to report the
logical sequence.

Hence it is not only justified but actuall
not whether the words are genuine, that
whether Matthew, who alone includes the
chronological setting, or whether here too

The originality of this Marcan narrative, in comparison with the parallels in Luke and Matthew, appears not only in its unclouded clearness, which really is striking, but also in various points of detail. Thus this entire story does not play in Matthew the dominating role that it has in Mark. In Matthew, that is, the disciples have already at an earlier time confessed before Jesus his majesty, at the time of the walking upon the sea (Matt. 14:33). Matthew thereby reduces in advance the importance of the story here reported.[62] In Mark its unique significance rests upon the very fact that here for the *first* time the disciples speak with Jesus with regard to what he is in their eyes.

Here it is seen that the arrangement of material, which of course is due to the evangelists, can become important in giving significance to the individual narrative. It is, so to say, a commentary on the part of the evangelist. So for the understanding of this narrative concerning Peter's confession, it makes a difference whether or not there already appears at some earlier point in the story a narrative in which the disciples confess the Messianic role of Jesus. Matthew, by introducing the disciples' saying: "You are the Son of God," in a chapter that *precedes* this sixteenth chapter of his work, has really robbed this event of its unique significance. Mark, on the contrary, has plainly preserved the memory of the fact that in order to understand this event it is essential to realize that what happened here had not yet happened at any previous time. Therefore in his arrangement of material he saw to it that in his Gospel no narrative preceded in which the disciples had already made a confession of Jesus as the Messiah.

Details within the narrative itself also seem to point to the conclusion that Matthew had a shallower grasp than Mark of the bearing of the event. For example, Matthew formulates the opening question of Jesus in a way that already anticipates the answer: "Who do the people say that *the Son of Man* is?" In Mark this is put in a form that is certainly more original, "Who do the people say that *I* am?"[63]

By this, we do not mean to say in any *a priori* way that verses 17–

---

62 W. Michaelis, *Das Evangelium nach Matthäus (Prophezei)*, p. 338, seeks to minimize the significance of this fact by writing that at this point Matthew was conscious that he was anticipating.

63 Too far-fetched is the explanation of R. Graber, *Petrus der Fels*, 1949, p. 31. He takes the contrary position and gives Matthew the preference here. He holds that Mark and Luke here replaced the expression "Son of Man" by the first person singular, because the mention of the Son of Man, which points to Daniel and alludes to the people of God who will defeat the world powers, seemed to them too dangerous in this passage.

19, which concern us and are found only in Matthew, are a later creation of the Primitive Church. Nevertheless, the point just made must also be considered when we now put the question that was our chief objective in making a closer examination of this narrative framework: Does Jesus' saying to Peter, which only in Matthew follows Peter's confession of Jesus, fit harmoniously into *this framework*? Do these verses 17-19 really belong to this event, and were they spoken on this occasion, or on the contrary did they originally belong in another context and were they first inserted in this passage by Matthew? Even in the latter case, as we have said, they may be fully genuine, that is, spoken by Jesus but on another occasion.

We must consider, at least theoretically, the second possibility, that it was Matthew who inserted into the framework of the Marcan narrative these words of Jesus to Peter. This necessity is made clear by the entire manner in which the evangelists, and Matthew in particular, have arranged the material transmitted to them by the oral or already written tradition. It is the lasting merit of the works on "Form Criticism" to have proved that the oral gospel tradition, like all oral tradition, contained only single units, without any chronological or geographical connections between them. The work of the evangelists, who assembled these single units of the tradition, consists in the fact that they combined them each in his own way. Thus they are not only collectors but also arrangers. In this connection it can be shown that each one proceeded to arrange the material in his own way, and it is particularly instructive to compare Matthew and Luke in this regard. Matthew in grouping his material follows a plan based on considerations of content and theology; that is, he connects with one another the stories which seem to him to belong together in their theological significance: miracle stories, sayings concerning the Law (Sermon on the Mount), sayings concerning John the Baptist (Matt., ch. 11), parables (Matt., ch. 13), sayings against the Pharisees (Matt., ch. 23), etc. It is of no primary concern to Matthew whether he thereby preserves the chronological sequence; from the start he has written his Gospel from this other point of view. The evangelist Luke, on the contrary, strives, as he himself says in his prologue, to report the events in their chronological sequence.

Hence it is not only justified but actually imperative to ask first not whether the words are genuine, that is, spoken by Jesus, but whether Matthew, who alone includes them, has put them in their chronological setting, or whether here too he has simply connected this section with Peter's confession of Jesus because *in its content* it seemed to him to fit here. In the latter case, to Peter's confession of Jesus as the Messiah there corresponds, so to speak, a confession of Jesus to Peter as the rock of his Church.

First of all, we must recall that in Matthew the giving of the name Cephas—Rock seems first to occur at this point. In Mark, on the contrary, Jesus, as we have seen,[64] gives this name to Simon at an earlier time, when he forms the group of the Twelve (ch. 3:16); and in the Gospel of John he actually gives it at the very first meeting (ch. 1:42). One may say, of course, that in Matthew 16:17 Peter does not *receive* this name for the first time, but that here it is only *explained* to him, after being given to him at an earlier time.[65] In that case there would be no direct chronological conflict between Mark and John. It is noteworthy, however, that Matthew has not reported the giving of the name on any earlier occasion. He thus appears to be of the opinion that this did not take place until the moment when Jesus also explained the name by telling of his purpose to build his Church upon this rock.[66] Then we should assume that although it was accepted as unquestioned fact that Jesus gave to Peter the title Cephas, there was no definitely fixed tradition concerning the time at which he did this.[67] So if Matthew really identified the giving and the explanation of the name, it might be so much the more natural for him to seek for these verses, which he found in the tradition, a place where they seemed to him to fit in view of their content; this was the principle he followed in arranging material.

But however that may be, Matthew by his very act of grouping material according to its content created a chronological connection: the utterance of Jesus, in the light of this context, appears in this Gospel as an *answer* to Peter's confession of Jesus, and it receives in this way a particular meaning. In Mark and Luke, however, the

[64] See above, p. 21.

[65] This is stressed especially by Th. Zahn, *Das Evangelium des Matthäus*, 4th ed., 1922, *ad loc.* He points to the fact that the Matthew passage lacks the formula customary in *giving* names (Gen. 17:5, 15; 32:28; Matt. 1:21, 25; 2:23; Luke 1:13, 31, 59–63; 2:21).

[66] W. Michaelis, *op. cit.*, pp. 340 f., is also of the opinion that Matthew here intends to tell of the *giving* of the name. He thinks that John 1:42 and Mark 3:16 are intended only as a reference to this later time.

[67] See M. J. Lagrange, *L'Evangile selon S. Matthieu*, 5th ed., 1941, p. 324: "the tradition of the change of name was attested by all, but there was less certainty concerning the occasion." See also Lagrange's judgment concerning the originality of the setting that Mark presupposes for the giving of the name. See above, p. 21, note 21.

narrative of the confession of Peter does not lead to that answer of Jesus. On the contrary, Jesus is silent about it and commands silence. Hence we must ask whether Matthew, when he gave this sequence of content and chronology to the unit of tradition that he alone transmits, did not connect two originally separate groups of sayings, of which the one does not really fit as an echo or answer to the other.

We have seen, in fact, that in the narrative framework Peter plays the role of one who does not understand the Messianic role of Jesus. He rather shares that very conception of the Messiah which Jesus regards as a temptation from Satan. To be sure, he utters the words: "You are the Messiah." But the continuation of this story makes clear how abysmally deep is the misunderstanding that separates Peter from Jesus even here. Indeed, we must actually say that the entire story leads on to this continuation; *this is its point*: "Depart from me, Satan!" We have seen that the parallel to the temptation story is clear. In both cases the devil seeks to persuade Jesus to fulfil a Messianic role radically different from the one with which he knows he is entrusted.

Thus the conclusion of the narrative framework shows that he who spoke those words: "You are the Christ," was a tool of Satan, not indeed in uttering the confession of the Messiah but rather *in his conception of these words*. This time Satan comes to Jesus in the person of Peter. Therefore Jesus says to his disciple: "You are not thinking of the things of God but of the things of men."

When one considers the meaning of this narrative framework, it becomes difficult indeed *a priori* to assume that *in this very context* Jesus said to Peter: "You are inspired by the Father in Heaven; he has given you a special revelation." But this is what we read in verse 17. This certainly does not fit well with what we have just established to be the intent in the narrative of Peter's confession. Precisely at this point the quite vivid portrayal of Mark seems to be interrupted and also twisted, if it is followed by the saying of Jesus concerning Peter the rock. For the fact that in the narrative of Mark Jesus at first says nothing at all in reply to this confession of Peter, and so does not take any position with regard to it, corresponds completely to the attitude he maintains towards the title of Messiah in the entire Synoptic tradition; he always manifests a notable *reserve* toward this title, without explicitly rejecting it.[68] One can trace this

---

[68] Jean Héring, *Le Royaume de Dieu et sa venue*, 1937, pp. 111 ff., goes further in saying that he rejected the title. The irreconcilability of Matt. 16:17 ff. with the narrative framework of Mark 8:27 ff. he also emphasizes strongly (p. 127, note 2).

in the hearing before the High Priest. He knows that the title of Messiah, used without qualification and addition, can give rise to grave misunderstandings. Thus the silence of Jesus, as Mark presupposes it in our passage, can scarcely be explained as an accidental or deliberate omission of a saying of Jesus; it rather has theological significance.[69]

I therefore consider it exegetically probable that Matthew found in an ancient oral tradition the words with which Jesus explains the title Cephas; in accord with his constant method of arranging material he sought for this separately transmitted unit of tradition a place that was fitting *from the point of view of its content*; he thought that he had found it in the story of the confession of Peter at Caesarea Philippi. It may have been chiefly the correspondence of the statement of Peter: "You are the Christ," with the statement "You are Peter," that led him to insert verses 17–19 in this place. We shall discover later (p. 182 f.) further reasons for the insertion at this point.

A further trace of the fact that originally these words did not stand in this context could be found in the fact that in verse 17 the object is lacking. It does not say in that verse: "*This* (namely, that I am the Christ) has been revealed to you not by flesh and blood but by my heavenly Father." The demonstrative pronoun "this," which we usually add in the translation, is lacking in the Greek text. In the original tradition also some object certainly must have stood here; it cannot have been lacking even in a separate unit of tradition. However, one can ask whether the fact that it is lacking in Matthew is not to be explained by saying that the unit originally had another introduction. This part of the saying of Jesus, which in content belongs to Matthew 11:27, could actually have been placed at this point by the Evangelist to connect it with the narrative framework.

The very reverse has been asserted—that verses 17–19, as far as geographical location is concerned, stand in a setting entirely suitable to them.[70] Indeed, it has actually been asserted that the Marcan

---

[69] This is in opposition to Héring, *op. cit.*, p. 125, who takes account of this possibility. Mark, he says, already interpreted the silence in the sense of an unqualified acceptance of the Messianic title; I on the contrary believe that Mark correctly understood the meaning of this silence, that is, he also regarded it not directly as a sharp rejection, such as J. Héring ascribes to Jesus, but as an attitude of *reserve*. This reserve is in full harmony with the "Back, Satan"; nevertheless, there exists in our narrative a heightening, which leads from this silence to that climax.

[70] On the geographical question, see O. Immisch, "Matthäus 16, 18" (*ZNW*, 1916, pp. 18 ff.).

narrative is a torso in its present form, that is, without the verses that Matthew alone contains. It is said to require just such an answer as the explanation of Jesus which we read in Matthew. Since Jesus himself evoked the Messianic confession of his disciples, the narrative cannot have ended with the mere command not to tell about it. Matthew 16:17 ff. would thus present the original and natural conclusion.[71] This view, however, overlooks the fact that the conclusion of the Marcan narrative is *not* the command to keep silent. It is rather those words of Jesus to Peter: "Depart from me, Satan!"—and they are also taken over by Matthew. The attempt has also been made to show that the answer of Jesus has been constructed in exact parallelism to Peter's confession. Just as in that confession it says: "You are the Christ," so here: "You are Peter." But as we have already said, it could very well be that it was just this rather formal analogy that led Matthew to combine the two units. Of course it is not excluded that even at an earlier stage of the tradition the two groups of sayings were united as they are in Matthew; but this is not probable.

On the basis of what has been said, however, we must at least take into account the strong possibility that the disputed verses did not belong originally in the context in which Matthew has put them. This opinion says nothing concerning genuineness or spuriousness.

If the event of Caesarea Philippi is not really the original framework of these traditional words, then the question arises whether, if we provisionally assume their genuineness, it still is possible to discern their setting. The most favoured theory in this case is that while the saying was indeed spoken by Jesus, it was spoken not by the Incarnate Jesus, but rather by *the Risen One*, on the occasion of an appearance to Peter alone. On this view, the entire incident was transferred back into the life of the Incarnate One at a later time.[72] Many things favour this possibility. It really is striking that the very first and so possibly the most important appearance of Jesus, that is, the one to Peter, is nowhere narrated in the New Testament. And yet it is clearly presupposed—for example, in the oldest text that we possess, in the earliest summary of the Christian faith, in I Corinthians 15:5. We have seen that in this passage the appearance to Peter stands first in a chronological enumeration of those who have seen

---

71 So R. Bultmann, W. Michaelis, A. Schlatter (see above, p. 173, note 59), and also Th. Zahn, *ad loc.*

72 So chiefly E. Stauffer, "Zur Vor- und Frühgeschichte des Primatus Petri" (*ZKG*, 1943-44, pp. 1 ff.); R. Bultmann, *Theologie des Neuen Testaments*, 1948, p. 46 (Eng. Tr., *Theology of the N. T.*, I, p. 45). See above, p. 61.

the risen Lord. Furthermore, we have found in Luke 24:34 the mention of the fact that the Lord appeared to Simon; indeed, the way in which it is mentioned shows that here too we must be dealing with the first of the appearances. We have noted that the significance of this fact for the position of Peter in the Primitive Church simply cannot be overestimated, and we have also attempted to find an explanation of the fact that no narrative account of this most important of all appearances has been preserved.[73]

A trace of such a narrative could indeed exist in ch. 21 of the Gospel of John. To be sure, we have here an appearance before *several* disciples in Galilee. But the dialogue that begins in verse 13 takes place essentially between the Risen One and Peter. The beloved disciple comes in, so to speak, quite incidentally. Therefore it may justifiably be asked whether, although the missing narrative of this appearance of Jesus to Peter alone is not reproduced, it is not at least utilized. For the dialogue refers in its first part only to the relationship between Christ and Peter, and to the commission which is given to Peter. We have spoken of the hypothesis that the lost conclusion of Mark lies behind this passage.[74]

Was it not this narrative, taken up into John, ch. 21, which Matthew found in a somewhat different version, transferred back into the life of the Incarnate One, and so connected with Peter's confession of Jesus at Caesarea Philippi? The very content of the dialogue between Jesus and Peter in John 21:15 ff. might favour this hypothesis. It deals indeed with the same question as Matthew 16:17 ff.; that which in Matthew is a promise appears here in the imperative, as a commission of the Risen One to Peter: "Feed my lambs."

It must be conceded that this hypothesis is attractive. At the least, we may reckon with the possibility that it is correct. Yet after all it is only a hypothesis. For we possess no conclusion of Mark which narrates the appearance to Peter alone, and John, ch. 21, does not say that its account deals with such an appearance.[75]

On the other hand, it is improbable to me that Jesus never *during his lifetime* explained the title "Rock." For it is quite certain that it was during his lifetime that he gave the title to Peter. It is true that "Sons of Thunder," the title of the sons of Zebedee, is also nowhere explained. But that may be connected with the fact that the gospel tradition naturally had less interest in them. In reality, Jesus must have explained their title also. On this ground I cannot

[73] See above, pp. 61 f.   [74] See above, pp. 59 f.   [75] See above, pp. 60 f.

agree with the above mentioned hypothesis without further evidence.

But must we not consider another occasion *within* the lifetime of Jesus when the explanation of the title could have been given? It has been supposed that there might have been a situation *similar* to that of Caesarea Philippi.[76] At that time, however, Jesus did not speak of his suffering; rather, the simple confession of his divine sonship stood in the foreground, so that verse 17 was entirely in place. One could think, for example, of John 6:66; this hypothesis has actually been proposed,[77] and its possibility must be recognized.

In this case, however, we are not restricted to a pure hypothesis. Rather, we have in one of the Synoptic Gospels a parallel text that contains the commission to Peter to strengthen his brothers, and gives it in another setting, namely that of the Last Supper. This is Luke 22:31 ff., a passage already often mentioned. It presents an exact parallel to Matthew 16:17 ff., not indeed in its literal wording, but in its meaning. It is embedded in the prediction of Peter's denial: "Simon, Simon, Behold, Satan has asked for you in order to sift you in the sieve like wheat. But I have prayed for you that your faith may not waver, and do you, when you have turned, strengthen your brothers." Peter then said to him: "Lord, with you I am ready to go even to prison and death." Jesus replied: "I tell you, Peter, the cock will not crow today until you have denied me three times."

This dialogue thus contains three things: (1) The vow of Peter that he will go with his Lord to prison and to death. (2) The prediction of Peter's denial. (3) The command of Jesus to Peter to strengthen his brothers after his conversion.

Was not this the true context also of our saying in Matthew 16:17 ff.?[78] If so, we could easily understand how Matthew could hit upon the idea of connecting it with Peter's confession at Caesarea Philippi. There, too, the chief thing reported is a confession of Peter, even though it is of another kind than in this passage, where it has taken the form of a declaration that he is ready to stand courageously for his Lord. On this view Matthew could have had a further reason for introducing the saying in the place where we now read it. Simon, together with the other disciples, is here brought into connection

---

[76] So K. L. Schmidt, "Die Kirche des Urchristentums" (*Festgabe für Ad. Deissmann*, 1927, p. 283).

[77] So Bernhard Weiss (*Meyer's Kommentar*, 10th ed., 1910), *ad loc.*

[78] A similar yet somewhat different position is taken by R. Liechtenhan, *op. cit.*, pp. 9 ff.

with *Satan*, and this occurs specifically with reference to the suffering of Christ, which is indirectly in view also in the prediction of the denial. Was this, perhaps, also a contributing factor in the choice of the scene of Caesarea Philippi, where Peter is addressed at the end as Satan? We cannot of course assert this with certainty.

I am inclined to presuppose that the framework of the Passion story as Luke gives it was the setting also for the saying reproduced by Matthew. My reason is that ch. 21 of the Gospel of John, which in many respects appears to be a still more direct parallel to Matthew 16:17 ff. ("feed my sheep"), seems consciously to refer to a tradition according to which there occurred during the lifetime of Jesus a scene such as Luke 22:31-34 portrays. The dialogue between the Risen One and Peter, in John 21:15 ff., presents a direct replica of that dialogue in Luke 22:31-34 between the Incarnate One and Peter, and probably can only be understood in the light of the latter passage.[79] It is striking that we find here exactly the same connection between vow, prediction, and command that we have in Luke 22:31-34, except that in John these words correspond to the post-resurrection situation. For the first time since the prediction of the denial Peter again stands before his Lord, but now he stands before the Risen One. In place of the three-fold denial by Peter comes now his three-fold assurance: "Yes, Lord, you know that I love you." To the vow of Peter that he will go with the Lord to prison and to death corresponds the prophecy of the martyrdom. In place of the command to strengthen his brothers there comes here the command to feed the sheep of Christ.

Some scholars, as we have seen above, assume that the basis for Matthew 16:17 ff. was a resurrection appearance to Peter, which has been used in John 21:15 ff.[80] On the basis of the inner and formal relationship between Matthew 16:17 ff., Luke 22:31 ff., and John 21:15 ff., I also assume a relationship between John 21:15 ff. and Matthew 16:17 ff. But I do so in the reverse sense; John 21:15 ff. attests a knowledge of a narrative from the passion story of the Incarnate One; according to this narrative Jesus, after the Last Supper, on the evening before the crucifixion, and on the occasion of Peter's assurance that he will follow his Lord to death, predicts the denial,

---

[79] This is contested by M. Goguel in *L'Eglise naissante*, 1947, p. 192, and *Jésus*, 1950, p. 390 (see above, p. 60), probably in connection with his unconvincing thesis that the denial of Jesus by Peter is unhistorical ("Did Peter Deny his Lord? A Conjecture," *Harvard Theological Review*, 1932, pp. 1 ff.).

[80] See above, p. 181.

but at the same time predicts also Peter's conversion and the founding of his flock on Peter as the rock. This connection is present in
Luke 22:31-34. The wording of the Lucan passage, to be sure, does
not agree with that of Matthew 16:17 ff.; this is the only weak point
in the theory here proposed. But as far as the wording is concerned,
Matthew may very well have had at his disposal here a special
tradition which originally belonged in the same framework as the
words of Luke 22:31 ff. The Synoptic tradition offers examples
enough of this. The author of John 21:15 ff., who shows a knowledge of this connection, seems to have known this special tradition
of Matthew. For the picture of "the sheep that Peter is to feed" implies that of the "flock," and this concept, as we shall see, is closely
related to the one of the "Church" of Matthew 16:18.[81]

We thus reach the conclusion that the saying in Matthew 16:17 ff.
probably belongs to the Passion story; it was originally transmitted
in connection with the prediction of Peter's denial, but was placed
by Matthew in another setting. We shall see later[82] that the immediate nearness of the death of Jesus, and above all the connection
with the Last Supper, make the saying concerning the "Church"
particularly intelligible. We are dealing here with an exegetical
probability, to the acceptance of which I am led by the undeniable
difficulty that results for exegesis from the insertion of Matthew
16:17 ff. into the framework of the narrative of Peter's confession at
Caesarea Philippi. This is not without significance for determining
the meaning in detail of the verses in question. Nevertheless, I note
expressly that *the interpretation as a whole that is given in what follows
does not stand or fall with the acceptance of this theory concerning the
original setting.*

3. Genuineness and Meaning of the Saying

We must first test whether the reasons that have been urged against
the genuineness are valid. The assumption of earlier opponents of the
genuineness, that the verses were lacking originally even in Matthew
and were inserted into the text only later under the influence of
Roman claims, we can leave undiscussed.[83] It is refuted by the

[81] See below, p. 197.

[82] See below, p. 190. The theological relation to the Passion is emphasized very
strongly, though to be sure on the basis of the narrative framework, by Karl
Barth, *Kirchliche Dogmatik*, II, 2, 1942, pp. 482 ff.

[83] K. L. Schmidt, *Die Kirche des Urchristentums*, p. 281, rightly calls it "too clumsy
to be taken seriously."

textual tradition and the history of the use of these words. So today the thesis of spuriousness is still defended only in the form that Matthew has reproduced here a saying that was not uttered by Jesus but created by the Church. In that case, however, it must be demanded at the start that the defenders of this thesis make clear the circumstances and reasons that led the Church to create such a saying as early as the days before Matthew was written.

This demand is the more urgent since the great antiquity and the Palestinian origin of the section may today be considered beyond question. This is shown by the quite Semitic linguistic character of this section. On this point, in fact, almost all scholars are united, whether they accept or reject the genuineness.[84] We have observed that even Bultmann, who is particularly emphatic in denying that Jesus spoke these words, has always claimed that the Palestinian church must have created the saying. Above all it is emphasized here, and probably correctly, that the saying could hardly have arisen first in the Greek Dispersion, because in the Greek, and so in the gospel text as we have it, the word play here plainly intended is not contained at all. Only in the German translation is it restored: "You are rock (Fels), and upon this rock (Felsen) I will build my Church." In Greek Simon's title reads *Petros*, with the masculine ending. We have seen that the name *Kepha* was reproduced in Greek by *Petros*. But Jesus says that he will build his Church upon this *Petra*. The words that should correspond do not really correspond here. In the Aramaic, however, we have both times the same word *Kepha*: "You are *Kepha* and upon this *Kepha* I will build my Church." Thus here the name and the thing are exactly identical. Therefore we must assume that the saying was originally coined in Aramaic.[85]

The Semitic character is confirmed by various other observations: the designation of the father of Peter as *bar-yônâ*;[86] the expression "flesh and blood" for "men";[87] the word pair "bind and loose";[88] then also the strophic rhythm—three strophes of three lines each—which is found similarly in other sayings of Jesus, for example,

---

[84] So also A. Harnack, "Der Spruch über Petrus als den Felsen der Kirche: Mtth. XVI, 17 f." (*Sitzungsbericht der Berliner Akademie der Wissenschaften*, 1918, pp. 637 ff.).

[85] M. Goguel, *L'Eglise naissante*, 1947, p. 189, note 4, finds this argument indecisive, since in a play on words the correspondence need not be complete.

[86] See above, p. 22, on the thesis of R. Eisler in *Jesous basileus ou basileusas*, p. 67.

[87] In the N. T. in I Cor. 15:50; Gal. 1:16; Eph. 6:12; Heb. 2:14. Frequent in Jewish literature (Sirach 14:18), but not yet in the O. T.

[88] אסר and שרא. See below, pp. 204 ff.

Matthew 11:7–9 and 11:25–30;[89] and further the illustration of the rock as foundation, to which there is an exact parallel in the rabbinical literature, where Abraham is mentioned as the rock of the world.[90]

The fact that only the Palestinian Matthew gives the saying also points to the Palestinian origin of the tradition.[91] Still another consideration can be cited to show that the tradition is very early. The story would scarcely have been handed on at a time when Peter no longer stood at the head of the Jerusalem church and James was already the leader there. The saying must thus have been transmitted at a time when Peter was still in Jerusalem.[92] The very early character of the tradition, which is vouched for by the Palestinian character of the verses, naturally does not prove beyond question that the utterance must come from Jesus, but it nevertheless is an important *presupposition* for that conclusion.

We have seen that the *chief objection* to its genuineness concerns the mention of the "*Church.*" Jesus, it is said, cannot have spoken of the Church, since he proclaimed only the coming Kingdom of God.

The first thing to note, in reply to this claim, is that it is correct that the word for "Church" (*ekklesia*) occurs in the Gospels only *one* other time. This, too, is in the Gospel of Matthew, ch. 18:17: "If (the brother who has sinned) does not listen to you, tell it to the Church." The genuineness of this passage also is vigorously disputed; in addition, the meaning here is not the same.

[89] See J. Jeremias, *Angelos*, 1926, pp. 107 ff., and especially A. Oepke, *op. cit.*, pp. 150 f.

[90] See the rabbinical explanation of Isaiah, ch. 53, in Strack-Billerbeck, *Kommentar zum N. T. aus Talmud und Midrasch*, Vol. I, p. 733; J. Jeremias, *Golgotha*, p. 73: "When God looked upon Abraham, who was to appear, he said: Behold, I have found a rock on which I can build and base the world. Therefore he called Abraham a rock."

[91] H. Strathmann, "Die Stellung des Petrus in der Urkirche" (*Zeitschrift für systematische Theologie*, 1943, pp. 255 ff.; see above p. 25), in connection with his view of the geographical origin of each Gospel, assigns this saying to the Antiochene tradition. In opposition to this, W. Michaelis, *op. cit.*, p. 353, makes the point that in Antioch Greek was spoken.

[92] W. Michaelis, *Das Evangelium nach Matthäus*, p. 350, actually thinks that the reason Luke did not include this saying was that it found its fulfilment only in the earliest period. Others, however, are of the opinion that it was precisely later Palestinian disputes between Peter and James (relatives of Jesus) that could have given occasion to the creation of the saying. (So K. Goetz; R. Bultmann thinks of debates in Palestine over the Law; M. Goguel of discussions that took place after 70). But we know too little of such disputes to explain on this basis the origin of the saying. According to J. Jeremias, the early character of the saying is clear also from the fact that we find such early traces of its use, in the N. T. itself: Gal. 1:16–18 and 2:9.

These statistics concerning the use of the word, however, cannot be decisive. The issue in question is rather whether not only the word but also the thing that the word designates is lacking. That is how we must put the question. In this connection it has justly been recalled[93] how striking it is that in the entire letter of Paul to Rome the word "cross" does not occur a single time, although the letter treats of the atoning death of Christ from beginning to end. It has further been pointed out that in the Gospel of John also the Greek word for Church (*ekklesia*) is nowhere found, and yet it cannot be doubted that this Gospel speaks of the Church; indeed, the peculiar character of this Gospel consists precisely in the fact that it connects the historical Jesus with the Church.[94]

The problem lies elsewhere. First of all we must be on our guard against falling into the mistake of most exegetes, who think that they must oppose the genuineness of the utterance because it mentions the "Church." They assume it to be self-evident that the word for "Church" can only designate an organized Church in the later sense. Then they seek to show that Jesus cannot have held this anachronistic view of the Church. Such a procedure, however, must be rejected.

We first must emphasize that the Greek word for Church, *ekklesia*, *does not designate anything like a Christian creation*, but belongs to the Jewish sphere.[95] We still find the word in this original meaning in the New Testament, in Acts 7:38: "It is this (Moses) who was in the *ekklesia* in the wilderness with the angel . . ." In this passage *ekklesia* means the people of Israel whom Moses led through the wilderness. In the Greek translation of the Old Testament, the Septuagint, *ekklesia* occurs about a hundred times, and in these cases it usually translates the Hebrew *qahal*, which, when connected with the genitive *Yahweh*, "of God," always designates the people of Israel with a reference to redemptive history. There is a series of still other Hebrew and Aramaic words that can be rendered in Greek

---

[93] See A. Oepke, *op. cit.*, p. 114.

[94] See O. Cullmann, *Urchristentum und Gottesdienst* (Eng. Tr., *Early Christian Worship*, 1953, pp. 38 ff. (cf. *Les sacrements dans l'Evangile johannique*, 1951, pp. 9 ff.). On the question of the Church in the Gospel of John, see also E. Gaugler, "Die Bedeutung der Kirche in den johanneischen Schriften" (*Internationale kirchliche Zeitschrift*, 1924, pp. 97 ff.).

[95] See L. Rost, *Die Vorstufen von Kirche und Synagoge im Alten Testament*, 1938; further, O. Michel, *Das Zeugnis des Neuen Testaments von der Gemeinde*, 1941, pp. 5 ff.; J. Y. Campbell, *Journal of Theological Studies*, pp. 130 ff.

by *ekklesia*.[96] All of these expressions, of which some can also be translated into Greek by *synagoge*, refer to Israel as the people of God; one of them (*kenishta*) can also mean "separate synagogue."

We must start from the meaning "people of God" when we ask the question whether or not Jesus can have spoken of the Church. Let us then put in place of the all too modern word "Church" the expression "people of God": "on this rock I will build my people of God." In this sense Jesus did not have to create anew the concept used. It already existed; indeed, it was *quite common* in Jewish thinking. Every Jew was certain that he was a member of this *ekklesia*. As soon as a group within late Judaism became conscious that the role of the people of God, to which Israel as a whole had proved disloyal, was being realized in them and through them, the concept of the *ekklesia* in its Semitic form necessarily moved into the foreground. This was especially true in the Jewish "congregation of the New Covenant," which has become so well known through the recent discoveries near the Dead Sea.[97] The ancient prophetic idea of the "remnant" of Israel (Isa. 7:3; 10:21) leads directly to such a revitalization of the people of God consciousness in small separate communities.

[96] Hebrew equivalents: *qahal, Edhah, ṣibbur, kᵉneseth;* Aramaic: *qahᵃla, ṣibbura*, and most frequently *kᵉnishta*. On all lexicographical questions it is sufficient to refer to K. L. Schmidt's basic article on ἐκκλησία in G. Kittel's *Theologisches Wörterbuch;* it carries further the older but helpfully orienting compilation of H. Cremer, in H. Cremer-Kögel, *Biblisch-theologisches Wörterbuch des neutestamentlichen Griechischen*, 11th ed., 1923. There is much in favour of *kᵉnishta* as the basic word (K. L. Schmidt). Whether however it is to be preferred because it likewise designates the building I would assert with less confidence, since indeed the figure of the building is included in the general idea of the people of God, and so is also implied by the phrase *qehal Yahweh*. (See on this point Ph. Vielhauer, *Oikodome, das Bild vom Bau in der christlichen Literatur vom Neuen Testament bis Clemens Alexandrinus*, 1939.) I would prefer, with M. J. Lagrange, *Commentaire, ad loc.*, to leave open the question as to which Aramaic word should be considered most likely. Indeed, it is not of basic importance, for the important thing is that all of these words belong to the thought world of the people of God. Lagrange considers both *qahᵃla* and *kᵉnishta* as possible Aramaic equivalents, Zahn *kᵉnishta*, Bultmann and Michaelis *qahᵃla*. Schlatter points to the Hebrew words *qahal* and *edhah*.

[97] Examples taken from the earlier discovery (see L. Rost, *Die Damaskusschrift*, in *Kleine Texte*, 1938): *edhah* in vii, 20; x, 4, 8; xiii, 13; *qahal* in vii, 17; xi, 22 (S. Schechter's edition). See also O. Michel, *Das Zeugnis des Neuen Testaments von der Gemeinde*, 1941, pp. 17 ff. With regard to the new discovery see among others K. G. Kuhn, "Die in Palästina gefundenen hebräischen Texte und das Neue Testament" (*Zeitschrift für Theologie und Kirche*, 1950, pp. 194 ff.). See above, p. 64.

Above all, the Jewish Messianic expectation includes the conception of a Messianic community and is inconceivable without it.[98] Here we should recall the Son of Man designation; in the Book of Daniel (ch. 7:9–28) it refers to "the people of the saints," and on the basis of the idea of representation is applied to a single personality. But an eschatological community is the essential possession also of the Messiah of the official Jewish hope.

In so far as we, in agreement with the entire gospel tradition, ascribe to Jesus the Messianic consciousness in any form whatsoever, we should have to assume, even if we had no text on the subject, that his thinking included the idea of the eschatological people of God that belonged to him. If he considered himself to be the Danielic Son of Man (Mark 14:62 and parallels), he also knew that according to Daniel 7:18, 27 the Son of Man represents the "people of the saints."[99] The concept of representation, which is indispensable for the understanding of the Old Testament redemptive history, is fundamental for Jesus' knowledge of his own redemptive work. When he speaks of the people of God that he is founding he certainly thinks of the "remnant of Israel," which will represent this people in its entirety and about which the Gentiles will be gathered.[1]

Compared with the ancient Jewish idea of the people of God, the new feature which Jesus brought is that this *ekklesia*, this people of God, is reconstituted in view of the end. It is reconstituted on the basis of what he conceives to be his special Messianic deed, the suffering of the Servant of God. In the creation of this new people of God built upon this basis consists his specific work on earth.

In this *Jewish* sense there is an "ecclesiology" even in the thinking of Jesus, and it is solidly anchored in his "Christology." Therefore we can understand it when a scholar such as Bultmann, who denies that Jesus had any Messianic consciousness, also challenges the

---

[98] Enoch 38:1; 53:6; 62:8; 83:8; 84:5.

[99] To have centred attention on this idea is the lasting merit of F. Kattenbusch, "Der Quellort der Kirchenidee" (*Festgabe für Harnack*, 1921, pp. 142 ff.). T. W. Manson and R. Newton Flew hold the same idea; see above, p. 166, note 33.

[1] K. L. Schmidt and F. Kattenbusch also assume that the "remnant," the "separate congregation," represents Israel in its entirety. For this reason I consider unjustified the criticism that Oepke, *op. cit.*, pp. 114 ff., 140, who here agrees with R. Bultmann, makes against K. L. Schmidt and F. Kattenbusch. The idea of a Pharisaic separation is not at all essential to the idea of the remnant; the former only presents the danger to which the latter *can* lead. The fact that the group of Jesus comprises precisely the *lost* sheep excludes all Pharisaism. See below, p. 190.

genuineness of the word concerning the *ekklesia*. He who, on the contrary, is of the opinion that Jesus regarded himself as the Messiah, even if in the special sense of the Son of Man and the Suffering Servant of God—and this today includes the great majority of exegetes—should refrain even on this basis from rejecting too quickly the genuineness of Matthew 16:17 ff.; as Messiah Jesus must have had in view a community.[2]

Connected with this special way in which Jesus conceived his Messianic work is the fact that the people of God is no longer simply identical with the Jewish nation. Even the prophetic idea of the remnant and the preaching of John the Baptist had already purified the conception of the people of God in this sense. Jesus knew himself to be sent to the "lost sheep of the house of Israel" (Matt. 10:6; 15:24), but this very limitation to the *lost* sheep finally breaks through every national restriction and likewise excludes every Pharisaic-sectarian separation. It is true that the redemptive road to the founding of the people of God goes by way of Israel. But the very reduction to this fellowship within Israel creates the presupposition for the realization of the people of God that is to include all mankind.

The Messianic reconstitution of the people of God aims at the "new covenant," which Jesus announces and likewise establishes *at the Last Supper*, on the evening before his death. Covenant and people of God belong together.[3] If my theory is correct that Jesus gave the promise of Matthew 16:17 ff. in the setting indicated by Luke 22:31 f., and so in connection with the Last Supper and the words spoken there, then *in this context* the prediction of the building of the *ekklesia* stands out in unusually bold relief. The connecting of the new building with Jesus' Messianic work of suffering unto death then becomes particularly clear. But it also is clear on other grounds.

Jesus speaks of his *ekklesia*. To me this does not seem, as has been claimed, irreconcilable with the fact that in Judaism the concept involved was the people *of God*, the *qehal Yahweh*, the *ekklesia* of the Lord (Num. 16:3; Deut. 7:6). It is possible, in fact, for the Messiah-

---

2 See P. Volz, *Die Eschatologie der jüdischen Gemeinde im neutestamentlichen Zeitalter*, 1934, p. 49. This is very strongly stressed also by F. J. Leenhardt, *Etudes sur l'Eglise dans le Nouveau Testament*, 1940, p. 16. See also O. Linton, *Das Problem der Urkirche in der neuern Forschung*, 1932, p. 148: "The Messiah is not a private person. Essential to his rule is a Church."

3 See L. Rost, *Die Vorstufen von Kirche und Synagoge im Alten Testament*, 1938, pp. 18 ff. On the Church and the Last Supper see F. Kattenbusch, *op. cit.*

Son of Man to speak of *his ekklesia*.[4] In this capacity he also can say that he will "build" this people. There is no contradiction here with the fact that this building is the work of God.[5]

If one reads the words of Matthew 16:17 in the light of this essentially Jewish idea and takes account of the fact that in the time of Jesus *qahal—ekklesia* was a quite common concept, firmly rooted in Jewish thinking, one really cannot *on that basis* deny the genuineness of the saying. I therefore maintain my statement, which Bultmann took as the starting point of his recent denial of this genuineness; I hold that there is no scientific justification for this denial. For sound scientific method requires that we explain the concepts first of all according to the sense that they have in the environment to which the writing belongs whose text is to be explained. It is not right to start from a later concept of the *ekklesia* and then conclude that it cannot possibly be ascribed to Jesus. It must first of all be asked whether there is not an *ekklesia* concept that corresponds to the Jewish thinking whose categories Jesus took over.

Furthermore, it can be shown that this very image of the *rock* is connected in Judaism with the idea of the community. Reference has properly been made to the conception of the holy rock. But we can discern a still more precise context if we recall that in the *Book of Daniel*, which Jesus must have known, the Son of Man concept, so central for him, is connected with the conception of the Messianic "people of the saints," which brings to an end the world empires. In the same Book of Daniel (ch. 2:34 f., 44 f.) we read of a block of stone which is *interpreted to mean an empire* that will shatter all empires.[6] This block of stone separates from the mountain, smashes the statute of Nebuchadnezzar, and then grows into a great mountain, which fills the entire world. Already in Judaism this stone had been referred to the Messiah.[7] Still more important for our study, however, is the fact that the saying of Jesus in Luke 20:17 f. certainly has in mind this passage of Daniel: "What means this saying of Scripture: The stone which the builders rejected has become the cornerstone? He who falls on this stone will be shattered; on whomsoever

---

[4] Matt. 13:41 speaks of the "Kingdom of the Son of Man."
[5] The difficulty seen here by K. L. Schmidt, *Die Kirche des Urchristentums*, p. 288, I do not feel. Yet E. Klostermann, *Das Matthäusevangelium*, p. 140, also finds it objectionable that Jesus says "my" Church.
[6] To have shown these connections is the merit of Joachim Jeremias; see his book, *Golgotha*, pp. 77 ff.
[7] Strack-Billerbeck, *Kommentar zum N. T. aus Talmud und Midrasch*, Vol. I, p. 877.

it falls, it crushes him."[8]—In the designation of Abraham as the rock we have already found a Jewish preparation for the view that Jesus, and later the apostles,[9] become the rock, the foundation.[10]

Moreover, the image of the *building* of a community is fully intelligible from the Jewish manner of thinking and expression.[11] The Old Testament speaks of the *House* of Israel (Num. 12:7; Ruth 4:11; Amos 9:11; etc.) Jesus also uses this expression in Matthew 10:6 and 15:24. Therefore the illustration, in its application to the Church, is quite common with the writers of the New Testament books, particularly in I Timothy 3:15, which speaks of the house of God, which is the *ekklesia* of the living God, and further in I Peter 2:5 (the spiritual house), Ephesians 2:22, Hebrews 3:2 ff.; 10:21. We must further recall that the idea of "edifying"[12] is common in application to the fellowship (Amos 9:11 f.; in the New Testament particularly Acts 9:31). Paul also uses it, originally not in the specific individualistic and pietistic sense, but in the meaning that the illustration contains of the building up of the Church.[13] Of especial importance for our question, however, is the fact that Jesus himself, as we shall see,[14] speaks in another saying concerning the fellowship founded by him; he here uses the analogous illustration of the *temple* that he will rebuild.

*   *   *

In our passage it is presupposed that the people of God will be formed while the present age still lasts. The future "I will build" could perhaps mislead us to identify its realization with that of the purely future Kingdom of God which comes at the end. But what follows, the saying concerning "binding and loosing," and par-

---

[8] The verb λικμᾶν is explained only by Dan. 2:34 f., 44 f. R. Graber, *Petrus der Fels*, 1948, p. 29, shows that the relation to the Daniel passage is much closer when seen from Matthew 21:42 ff. than it is from the parallel Lucan passage, from which J. Jeremias starts. This, however, is the case only if vs. 44, which is lacking in good textual witnesses, is original. The discussions of R. Graber are perhaps particularly fitted to prove this originality. R. Bohren, *Das Problem der Kirchenzucht im Neuen Testament*, 1952, pp. 32 ff., believes that he sees another connection, which however has in view only the prophet. This is Jer. 1:18 f.: "I make you today an iron pillar and a bronze wall . . . they will fight against you, but will not overcome you."

[9] See below, pp. 216 f.   [10] See above, p. 186.

[11] For all details I refer to the careful study of Ph. Vielhauer, *Oikodome, das Bild vom Bau in der christlichen Literatur vom N. T. bis Clemens Alexandrinus*, 1939.

[12] οἰκοδομεῖν.   [13] I Cor. 8:1-10; Rom. 14:19; 15:2, 20.

[14] See below, pp. 198 f.

ticularly the contrast between earth and heaven, shows that Jesus means a people that already appears in this age.

This very fact, however, leads many to deny that Jesus spoke this saying. Is it possible that Jesus, who certainly announced the Kingdom which comes at the end, actually expected the realization of the people of God *in this present age*? In the last analysis this problem of time stands in the background of the entire debate. In considering it, we wish to distinguish from one another the following limited questions: 1. Did Jesus lay the foundation of a Messianic fellowship even in his life-time? 2. Did he expect that even after his death this age would still continue, and that then especially this fellowship would be built up, before the end would come?

As we begin to consider the first question, we should note at the outset that it is given a false perspective if it is placed in the form of an alternative: present *or* future Messianic community. The Jewish idea of the people of God—*qahal*—*ekklesia* cannot be forced into this alternative. Rather it includes both present and future. Particularly, however, it must be considered that for Jesus, in view of his Messianic selfconsciousness, present and future, promise and fulfilment, even if distinguished, nevertheless do not represent opposites; on the contrary, in his person the fulfilment has already been anticipated. Particularly in reference to the Messianic community we must not say: present *or* future, promise *or* fulfilment.

Perhaps the quite one-sided view of Albert Schweitzer is responsible for the fact that many are still unable to see the problem except in the form of an either-or alternative. Before Schweitzer the scholars, in their presentation of the teaching of Jesus, were all too quick to push eschatology into the background or completely discard it. They described it by using the slogan: "a concession conditioned by contemporary Jewish ideas." Thus they held that the essential thing in it was only the relation to the contemporary situation. For this reason the reaction of Albert Schweitzer was entirely necessary. But it in turn succumbed again to the temptation to survey the entire teaching of Jesus in a false time perspective; it presented his teaching as though Jesus expected everything from the future. In reality it is the very tension between "already fulfilled" and "not yet fulfilled" that is characteristic of the New Testament conception of time.[15] This conception, indeed, runs through the entire New Testament; it already marks the attitude of Jesus in the Synoptic

[15] See O. Cullmann, *Christus und die Zeit*, 1948, pp. 72 ff. (Eng. Tr., *Christ and Time*, 1950, pp. 84 ff.).

Gospels.[16] Even in Jesus' own preaching the Kingdom of God is on the one hand still not present, for it comes only at the end; and yet in the presence of Jesus it has already broken in: "If I cast out demons by the Spirit of God, then the Kingdom has already come to you" (Matt. 12:28). "Tell John what you hear and see: the blind see again, the lame walk, lepers are cleansed, the deaf hear, the dead rise, and to the poor the good news is preached" (Matt. 11:4 f.).

Thus there can be no doubt that Jesus himself reckons with such an anticipation of the Kingdom of God; in him the decision has already occurred, even if the completion is expected only in the final time. It would curtail the preaching of Jesus to accept as valid only the one or the other aspect. He who regards as decisive only the sayings concerning the future should ask himself what it is then that really distinguishes Jesus at all from other prophets. Promise was uttered by all prophets, even promise for a near future. But the new thing with Jesus is the very fact that even now there is a fulfilment.

It is doubtless universally conceded that after the death of Jesus, in *Primitive Christianity* and for *Paul*, this tension between present and future, promise and fulfilment, really exists. But in Primitive Christianity this does not mean, as the adherents of Albert Schweitzer in particular assert, a reinterpretation or falling away from the position of Jesus, who had spoken only of the future; rather, this tension is *already present for him*. There does exist on this point a certain difference between Jesus and the Primitive Church; Jesus is conscious that the fulfilment is present *in his person*, while the Primitive Church sees the fulfilment *in the Church*. But there is no conflict here at all. Rather, the fulfilment in the person of Jesus leads directly to the fulfilment in the Church, and the fulfilment in the Church points back in turn to the fulfilment in the person of Jesus.[17] Therefore it is not merely possible that Jesus also sees the people of God already beginning to be constituted in his day; we would almost have to postulate this even if we had no clear texts to prove it.

A direct contradiction between the future Kingdom of God and

[16] See W. G. Kümmel, *Verheissung und Erfüllung* (*Abhandlungen zur Theologie des Alten und Neuen Testaments*, 1945).

[17] This must be given unqualified emphasis in opposition to W. G. Kümmel's much esteemed essay, *Kirchenbegriff und Geschichtsbewusstsein in der Urgemeinde und bei Jesus*, 1943 (see above, pp. 167 f.). The point to note is that he sees here an irreconcilable parallelism of two related forms of the historical consciousness, and draws from this the conclusion that Matt. 16:17 ff. is spurious. The conclusions which W. G. Kümmel here draws seem to me in reality to contradict his own premises.

the already realized people of God is only a construction built on the basis of modern thinking. For Jesus the two aspects certainly do not coincide, but they do not form opposites, as we are inclined to believe on the basis of a modern thought pattern. The higher concept that even in Judaism unites both aspects, present and future, is this very idea of the "people of God." It is used here equally with reference to its present and its future realization, and as soon as the conviction is present that the end has already been anticipated, even if the completion is still to come, the distinction practically loses its importance.

Thus the foundation of the earthly people of God dates back in the time of the Incarnate One, even if it is really "built up" only after his death. Jesus created the foundation for this people of God even in his lifetime. In order to prove this by texts, we again must refuse to be misled into regarding as decisive only the occurrence of the word *ekklesia*. We must investigate whether the thing is not actually present in passages where the word is lacking. In this connection particular reference has properly been made to the forming of the group of the Twelve. The attempt has indeed been made to deny that Jesus did this and to transfer its origin into the later time of the Primitive Church.[18] But there really exists no necessity for doing this, and what is more, it is quite impossible to see how this group could have arisen as late as the time of the Primitive Church; on the contrary, it was necessary rather to take pains to re-establish it after the defection of Judas. But what could the establishing of this group mean if not the founding of the people of God which is to prepare for the Kingdom of God? The reference to the Jewish idea of the people of God is here quite plainly present. The number Twelve, indeed, must be connected with the number of the twelve tribes of Israel.

The most important thing, however, is not merely the *choice* of the twelve disciples; it is above all the *mission* they received from Jesus, that is, the role that he gives to this fellowship. It cannot be sufficiently emphasized that the command he gives in sending them forth refers to the identical *Messianic* functions that *Jesus himself* fulfils in his role of the "Coming One." Here it is confirmed that even in the present age the Messiah needs for his preparatory work a

---

[18] So, following many others, R. Bultmann, "Die Frage nach der Echtheit . . ." (*Theologische Blätter*, 1941). On the contrary, the significance of the Twelve as a preliminary stage of the Church is emphasized with special force by G. Gloege, *Reich Gottes und Kirche im N. T.*, 1929, and also by H. D. Wendland, *Die Eschatologie des Reiches Gottes bei Jesus*, 1931.

community, and that the group of the Twelve represents at least the start of the future Messianic *ekklesia*. We have seen that in his answer to the Baptist Jesus cites these facts as a sign that with his coming *the time of redemption has already broken in*: "the blind see, the lame walk, lepers are cleansed, the dead rise, to the poor the good news is preached." In a strikingly parallel manner Jesus commands his disciples when he sends them forth: "Go to the lost sheep of the house of Israel and proclaim that the Kingdom of Heaven has come near . . . heal the sick, raise the dead, cleanse the lepers, cast out demons" (Matt. 11:4 f.; 10:7 f.). The analogy between this command and the answer to the Baptist deserves further consideration. For here it becomes clear that for Jesus not only his own coming but *also the existence and the work of the group of disciples is already the fulfilment and inbreaking of the time of redemption*. The same deeds that he himself does they also are to accomplish, as proof that the prophecy has already been fulfilled in him.[19] Thus the forming and the sending forth of the group of disciples is quite closely connected with his Messianic conviction. When he also says, on the other hand, that they will not have completed visiting the cities of Israel before the Son of Man comes (Matt. 10:23)—a saying which moreover permits various interpretations[20]—it still remains true that the work of the group of disciples is a Messianic work, and that thus, even in the lifetime of Jesus, the fulfilment does not occur only in his person; rather, in these men the people of God has already begun to be realized.[21] We should understand in this way the saying concerning the fishers of men (Mark 1:17 and parallels) and that concerning the work in the harvest (Matt. 9:37 f.); and the parable of the fishnet (Matt. 13:47 ff.) confirms the provisional and yet anticipatory character of the catch of fish.

Where such things happen as Jesus enumerates in his answer to the Baptist (Matt. 11:4 f.), the question whether the Kingdom of God is future or present loses all point.[22] The anticipation of the Kingdom

---

[19] It is connected with this, as H. Riesenfeld points out in *Ämbetet i Nya Testamentet*, n. d., pp. 17 ff., that the metaphors with which Jesus' functions are described are transferred to the apostles.

[20] See O. Cullmann, *Le retour du Christ, Espérance de l'Eglise selon le Nouveau Testament*, 1943, pp. 23 f.

[21] This should be stressed against A. Loisy, *L'Evangiles Synoptiques*, p. 9, with whom R. Bultmann, *op. cit.*, column 275, allies himself when he writes that the fact that Jesus gathered disciples has nothing to do with the Church.

[22] Wherever the Kingdom of God is *a living reality*, this is the case. Think of Blumhardt.

of God thus occurs here even in the lifetime of Jesus; the foundation of the people of God is laid, even if it also remains true that the real building is only carried out after the death of Jesus, on the basis of the new covenant. This *ekklesia* that is "built" after the death of Jesus will be an anticipation of the Kingdom of God, but the group of disciples in the lifetime of Jesus is on its part an anticipation of that *ekklesia*.

Jesus regards the narrower and the wider group of disciples as a fellowship with a particular task. As such it already represents a realization. This is clear also from other passages; it appears, for example, when he speaks of his true family (Mark 3:33 ff. and parallels), and especially when he addresses the disciples as a "flock," as he does in Luke 12:32: "Fear not, little flock, for it has pleased your Father to give you the Kingdom;" and further in Matthew 26:31: "I will smite the shepherd and the sheep of the flock will be scattered." With this agrees also the already mentioned "lost sheep of the house of Israel" (see also Matt. 9:36). We know from the Damascus Document that also in the Jewish "community of the New Covenant," which has now become better known, the concept of the shepherd was common, and that the *ekklesia* concept is in reality expressed by this image.[23] In the remaining writings of the New Testament the designations flock, shepherd, sheep, and feeding almost always refer to the Church. We should think here above all of the Gospel of John: John 10:1 ff.; 21:16 ff., but also of I Corinthians 9:7 and Acts 20:28.[24]

*　　*　　*

The fellowship that Jesus founded even in his lifetime does of course point to the *future*. Only after his death will it develop, will it be "built up" in the real sense. We have seen that the Messianic consciousness must lead to the founding of the Church. For Jesus, however, this consciousness involves the necessity of his death. Therefore his death is the real starting point of the new people of God. The establishing of the Lord's Supper[25] can only mean that the new fellowship is founded by his death. But here the question arises whether for Jesus the time immediately after his death is the time of the complete fulfilment or whether, before the end comes, the time

23 See above, pp. 63 f., 188.
24 R. Bultmann, *op. cit.*, column 268, denies that in the Synoptic passages the idea of a group is present; in the Gospel of John, he claims, the words have a quite different meaning.
25 See above, p. 190.

of anticipation begun by his earthly work will still continue for a while, and continue as the period of the Church. Matthew 16:17 ff. implies this second assumption. Before we deal with the question whether this agrees with the general expectation of Jesus as we are able to deduce it from the Synoptic Gospels, we still must study a very important utterance of Jesus. It seems to me to be an exact parallel to Matthew 16:17 ff., and it also refers to the time after the death of Jesus. I refer to the saying that Jesus spoke concerning the *temple* and that obviously played a decisive role in his so-called trial.[26] To be sure, it was—at least according to Mark 14:57 f.— false witnesses who accused Jesus of having said: "I will destroy this temple made by hands and in three days build up another not made by hands." Later also, however, at the cross, a similar saying is ascribed to him by the passers-by. Moreover, it is possible to explain wherein the *false* witness probably consisted, if we take into account another saying of Jesus, which stands in Mark 13:2. A disciple there says to Jesus: "Behold what great stones and what great buildings!" Jesus answers him: "There will not remain one stone upon the other which will not be destroyed." He thus clearly predicts here the destruction of the temple. It therefore is probably true that what Jesus really said was worded in the way that the Gospel of John (ch. 2:19) actually puts it into his mouth on the occasion of the cleansing of the temple: "*Destroy* this temple, and in three days I will build it up." The falsified feature in this saying, accordingly, as it is ascribed to the false witnesses in Mark, would be only the change of person in the first half of the sentence. Jesus would not have said: "*I* will destroy," but "the temple will be destroyed." In the second half of the sentence, on the contrary, the first person seems quite in place: "I will rebuild it."

26 M. Goguel, *Jésus*, 2nd ed., 1950, pp. 330 ff. (Eng. Tr., *The Life of Jesus*, 1933, pp. 507 ff.), speaks in support of the genuineness of this saying, but does not connect it with Matt. 16:17 ff. (He relates it, on the contrary, to the parable of the vinedressers; extension to the Gentiles.) As arguments in favour of genuineness he points out that the prediction of the destruction of the Temple cannot be a prophecy "*ex eventu*," since indeed the temple was destroyed in 70 by fire, not by earthquake, as the saying of Jesus presupposes ("there will not remain one stone upon another"); he further cites the fact that to Stephen also a similar saying is ascribed (Acts 6:10 ff.). M. Goguel assumes that Judas informed the Jewish magistrates of this utterance of Jesus. A high estimate of the saying about the temple and its significance for Primitive Christian thinking is found in Marcel Simon, "Retour du Christ et reconstruction du Temple dans le pensée Chrétienne primitive" (*Aux sources de la tradition chrétienne, Mélanges M. Goguel*, 1950, pp. 249 ff.).

Only in the Gospel of Mark do we read "another not made by hands," after it has been said previously of the temple at Jerusalem that it "was made by hands." But whether this precision is original or not—there is no real reason why it should not be so—in any case Jesus had in view a fellowship when he announced that he would again erect the destroyed temple. We have already seen, indeed, that it was already common in Jewish terminology to apply to the people the image of the building. In the New Testament area this usage is quite common; the Church is the temple or the "spiritual house," as it is called in First Peter (ch. 2:5 ff.).[27] It is possible that the author of the Gospel of John, when he went on to apply the saying about the temple to the body of Christ, likewise thought of the Church.[28]

In any case, however, it must be assumed, in keeping with the Synoptic tradition, that Jesus proclaimed the building of a temple not made by human hands. By this he can only have meant the new people of God that he intended to found.[29] For our study this saying about the temple is the more important since here, exactly as in Matthew 16:18, the illustration of the building occurs. *We thus have here a direct parallel to the saying concerning the ekklesia,* and if it plays so small a role in discussions of our question, this results only from the fact that scholars let themselves be misled by statistics of word usage, and so no longer pay attention to the essential idea.

*   *   *

By his saying concerning the temple, as well as by the words of institution of the Lord's Supper, Jesus announces a new fellowship for the time *after his death.* With this agrees the fact that in Matthew 16:17 ff. he speaks in the future tense: "I *will* build my *ekklesia.*" We have seen that according to this saying this future must still fall in this age, since otherwise the contrast between heaven and earth would have no meaning. This very fact, however, gives occasion for the final objection which is raised against the genuineness of the passage. It is claimed that if Jesus spoke of a future realization of the people of God, to follow after his death, he can only have meant its final realization in the Kingdom of God. Those other promises, such

[27] See above, p. 192.

[28] See O. Cullmann, *Urchristentum und Gottesdienst* (Eng. Tr., *Early Christian Worship,* pp. 71 ff.

[29] Concerning the Jewish Messiah and the rebuilding of the temple see Enoch 90:28 ff. On this point see J. Engnell, *Studies in Divine Kingship,* 1943; E. G. Kraeling, "The Real Religion of Ancient Israel" (*Journal of Biblical Literature,* 1928, p. 138). H. Riesenfeld, *Jésus transfiguré,* 1947, p. 59.

as the saying concerning the temple, must in such a case be understood to mean that with the death of Jesus the consummation of the Kingdom of God already occurs. Since, however, in Matthew 16:17 ff. the *ekklesia* is already realized in the present age, it is alleged that there exists here a contradiction, and therefore this saying cannot come from Jesus.[30]

The question thus arises: Did Jesus then expect any intermediate period between his death or resurrection and his return? If it is really true, as Albert Schweitzer asserts, that Jesus expected the Kingdom of God to come at the moment of his death, then indeed there would no longer be any place for a period of the Church. The people of God would pass over directly into the final Kingdom of God. We cannot discuss this problem in its full extent, and I mention only a few outstanding points. First of all, we have no text which really supports Schweitzer's hypothesis. For Jesus his own death undoubtedly constitutes the central event in the redemptive process that leads to the Kingdom of God. But he sees the tension between present and future; it is already present in his lifetime, and he knows that by his death it is not yet removed.[31]

It is sufficient to recall the necessity of the *Gentile mission*, which Jesus often emphasized and which must be carried out only after his death, before the coming of the end (Mark 14:62). That will be the specific task of the little flock in the period after his death and before the end; it is to build up the people of God in such a way that the Gentiles find acceptance in it. What Jesus has already revealed as proclamation, the inclusion of the Gentiles in the people of God, is to become reality after his death. Therefore the redemptive history must still continue for a period after his death, because the command given at the sending forth of the disciples is not yet fully carried out; it can only be fully carried out when Jesus has died and arisen.[32] The establishing of the new covenant at *the Last Supper* probably pre-

---

30 So R. Bultmann, "Die Frage nach der Echtheit von Mtth. 16, 17-19," *Theologische Blätter*, 1941.

31 See on this point W. Michaelis, *Der Herr verzieht nicht die Verheissung*, 1942; W. G. Kümmel, *Verheissung und Erfüllung*, 1945, pp. 38 ff.; O. Cullmann, *Christus und die Zeit*, pp. 131 f. (Eng. Tr., *Christ and Time*, pp. 149 f.).

32 E. Peterson, in his highly regarded essay, "Die Kirche," 1929 (now printed in the collection, *Theologische Traktate*, 1951), is right when he sees in this the real essence of the Church. So also O. Cullmann, *Christus und die Zeit*, 2nd ed., 1948, pp. 138 ff. (Eng. Tr., *Christ and Time*, pp. 157 f.); in this matter I stress strongly the retention of the eschatology, while in the view of E. Peterson it is, so to speak, dissolved in the Church.

supposes, even if the explicit command to repeat the rite should not be original, a continuation of the Messianic time of preparation that has begun in the earthly work of Jesus.

Moreover, the promise of Mark 14:28, whose genuineness usually is not contested, is probably only correctly understood by assuming that in it Jesus did not consider that his death was identical with the consummation: "but after I have risen I will go before you into Galilee." Here belong further the sayings concerning fasting (Mark 2:18 ff.): "When the bridegroom is taken from them, then they may fast." Also in his answer to the high priest (Mark 14:62 and parallels), Jesus distinguishes between the moment when the Son of Man will sit at the right hand of God and the one when he will come again on the clouds of Heaven. To be sure, Jesus scarcely reckons with a duration of millenniums, but he does assume that there will be a rather brief period of time between his resurrection and return. That, however, does not concern us in our study.[33] The important thing here is that he anticipates after his death also some period within which the Kingdom of God is prepared, and if it has already been anticipated, it is nevertheless not yet completed. In this period of time falls the building of the *ekklesia* of which Jesus speaks in Matthew 16:17 ff.

*　　*　　*

Now that we have thus established from every angle that Jesus spoke of a building of the new people of God, and have seen in what sense he did so, we still have to explain the further sayings connected with this subject. The question as to who is meant by the rock we postpone until we have discussed the remaining points, since it will lead us directly to the doctrinal question.

In the saying we first hear that the gates of Hades will not prevail against this *ekklesia* which Jesus will build upon the rock. By Hades is meant the realm of the dead[34]—and not chiefly the realm of sin and damnation.[35] This is the truth in the thesis according to which

[33] See O. Cullmann, "Das wahre, durch das Ausbleiben der Parusie gestellte Problem" (*Theologische Zeitschrift*, 1947, pp. 177 ff.).

[34] So also E. Klostermann, *Das Matthäusevangelium, ad loc.*, and A. Schlatter, *Der Evangelist Matthäus, ad loc.*

[35] R. Bohren, *Das Problem der Kirchenzucht im Neuen Testament*, 1952, pp. 63 f., assumes rather that from the gates of hell stream forth spirit hosts who fight to prevent the building of the Church. W. Vischer, *Die evangelische Gemeindeordnung*, 1946, sees both united. So does M. Meinertz, *Theologie des Neuen Testaments*, Vol. I, 1950, p. 75. On the entire subject see especially W. Bieder, *Die Vorstellung von der Höllenfahrt Jesu Christi*, 1949, pp. 43 ff.

this passage speaks of the triumph that the resurrection brings over death.[36] Whether a translation error for "porter" is present here may remain undiscussed.[37] It is possible. Nevertheless, the image of the gates of the realm of the dead is already found in Israelite and Jewish writings: Isaiah 38:10; Psalms 9:13; 107:18; Job 38:17[38]; Wisdom of Solomon 16:13; III Maccabees 5:51; Psalm of Solomon 16:2. The idea is that the gates of the realm of the dead, which close behind all men, will no more be opened, that the realm of the dead will no more permit its dead to escape. Matthew 16:18 states, probably with the same figure and in dependence on it, that before the attack of the Church the gates which otherwise stand firm against every attempt, however strong, to storm them, lose their previously unconquerable power; before the Church they must open. If this is the case, the *ekklesia* is here thought of as the attacker. One could indeed seek also to regard the gates as the attackers.[39] When we think that the *ekklesia* is conceived in this illustration as a building, this might seem almost likely. But the question whether the *ekklesia* or the world of the dead is thought of as the attacker can hardly be answered with certainty.[40]

It is clear, on the contrary, that according to this saying *the ekklesia is included in the function of Jesus*, which consists of his victory over

---

[36] A. Harnack, "Der Spruch über Petrus als den Felsen der Kirche, Matth. XVI, 17 f." (*Sitzungsbericht der Berliner Akademie der Wissenschaften*, 1918, pp. 637 ff.), deletes the saying concerning the Church. He prefers to see here only a prediction of the resurrection of *Peter*; he replaces αὐτῆς ("it") by σου ("you"). (See above, p. 165.) This, however, is impossible, because the explanation of the name Peter requires the figure of the building. (So rightly M. J. Lagrange, commentary on Matthew, p. 324.) Whether αὐτῆς ("it") is to be connected with ἐκκλησία ("church") or with πέτρα ("rock") was already considered by the Church Fathers (Origen); πέτρα is too far removed, and on the basis of content also ἐκκλησία must be the word meant here. (See M. J. Lagrange, commentary on Matthew, p. 327.)

[37] R. Eppel, *Aux sources de la tradition chrétienne, Mélanges offerts à M. Goguel*, pp. 71 ff., holds that πύλαι ("gates") would represent שַׁעֲרֵי, while πυλωροί ("gatekeepers," "porters") would represent שֹׁעֲרֵי (reference to Job 38:17, LXX). In another way Ed. Bruston, *Les promesses de Jésus à l'apôtre Pierre*, 1945, pp. 10 ff., assumes here a translation error for "assaults of the abyss."

[38] The LXX, to be sure, reads πυλωροί ("gatekeepers," "porters") here. See the preceding note.

[39] R. Eppel, *op. cit.*, p. 72, appeals to J. Dutlin, "The Gates of Hades" (*Expository Times*, 1916, pp. 401 ff.), in pointing out that the verb κατισχύω ("prevail") fits an attack rather than a defence.

[40] For the conception of the gates as the attacking force, see Th. Zahn, commentary on Matthew, p. 542, and M. J. Lagrange, commentary on Matthew, p. 326.

death by his death and resurrection. The task that was given to the disciples during Jesus' lifetime as a Messianic function,[41] the conflict with death, whether in the form of healings of the sick or raisings of the dead (Matt. 10:7 f.), is here promised to the entire *ekklesia*. The foundation that is laid in Peter thus has to support a building that means victory over death. It is predicted that the *ekklesia* founded upon Peter as the rock will indeed exist in the time when death still rules, and so will exist in the present age,[42] but it will nevertheless share already in the resurrection power that marks the Kingdom of God. We shall remind ourselves, when we discuss and reach a conclusion concerning the essential nature of an apostle, that in the New Testament the apostles are first of all witnesses of the resurrection who are entrusted with a commission.

The illustration of the building, and likewise that of the door, give occasion to use that of the *keys* of the Kingdom of God. Mention has just been made of the gates of Hades; now the doors of the Kingdom of Heaven are in mind. Just as Hades is the realm of the dead, so the Kingdom of Heaven is that of life in the resurrection. This illustration of the keys seems to have been common. In Revelation 1:18 it is said of the Son of Man that he has the keys of death and of Hades, manifestly in order to open them for those imprisoned within. In Revelation 3:7 it is said, with a reference to Isaiah 22:22, that the Holy One has the "keys of David," with which he irrevocably opens and closes (see also Rev. 21:25). In Matthew 16:19 it is presupposed that Christ is the master of the house, who has the keys to the Kingdom of Heaven, with which to open to those who come in. Just as in Isaiah 22:22 the Lord lays the keys of the house of David on the shoulders of his servant Eliakim, so Jesus commits to Peter the keys of his house, the Kingdom of Heaven, and thereby installs him as administrator of the house.[43] There exists a relation between the house of the *ekklesia*—whose building was mentioned just before, and whose foundation is Peter—and the heavenly house whose keys he receives. The connecting element here too is the idea of the people of God.

Here again Peter is connected with the resurrection. The so-called

---

[41] See above, pp. 195 f.

[42] This confirms the view that it is not simply the coming Kingdom of God that is meant here.

[43] On the illustration of the steward of the household see Mark 13:34; Luke 12:42; 16:1 ff.; I Cor. 4:1; I Pet. 4:10. Th. Zahn, *Das Evangelium nach Matthäus, ad loc.*, is hardly right when he thinks here not of admission but only of authority over secret chambers.

power of the keys makes him, so to speak, the human instrument of
the resurrection. He is to lead the people of God into the resurrection
Kingdom. That is the task which he will have to carry out on earth
after the death and resurrection of Jesus. In this connection we must
think of that other saying of Jesus which rests upon the very same
illustration; it is his saying to the Pharisees: "you close the door to
the Kingdom of Heaven" (Matt. 23:13). The Pharisees might indeed
boast that they on the contrary open the door to the Kingdom of
Heaven. But it is not they, it is rather the called rock, Peter, who has
this office. As in Matthew 23.13, in the saying against the Pharisees,
so here too may be in mind the *mission* that Peter will carry out by his
preaching, and by which he will open access to the Kingdom of
Heaven, while the Pharisees "rush over sea and land to make a single
proselyte, and when he has become one, they make of him a son of
Hell who is twice as bad as they are" (Matt. 23:15).[44] It is characteristic that in Matthew this utterance follows right after the one on the
opening of the Kingdom of Heaven, and this justifies us when we
also connect with the apostolic mission the giving of the "keys of the
Kingdom of Heaven" in Matthew 16:19.

Just as this saying concerning the keys of the Kingdom of Heaven
connects directly with the one that deals with the "building" of the
ekklesia and with the gates of the realm of the dead, so also the words
concerning "binding" and "loosing" must be understood in connection with what precedes. This must be considered first of all in
regard to the way the expressions "on earth" and "in heaven" correspond. These expressions are to be understood first of all not in a
spatial but in a temporal sense. What Peter does for the *ekklesia* is
effective for the coming Kingdom of Heaven. Here again it is seen
how close is the connection between the Messianic present and the
future, between the already realized fulfilment and the consummation still to come.

What do the expressions "bind" and "loose" signify? According
to Rabbinical usage[45] two explanations are equally possible: "pro-
hibit" and "permit," that is, "establish rules";[46] or "put under the

---

[44] The connection with Matthew, ch. 23, has been pointed out by J. Schniewind,
  Das Evangelium nach Matthäus (*Das N. T. Deutsch*), 1927, *ad loc.*, and also by
  W. Vischer, *Die evangelische Gemeindeordnung*, 1946, pp. 24 f.
[45] אסר and שרא.
[46] So G. Dalman, *Worte Jesu*, I, p. 175 (Eng. Tr., *The Words of Jesus*, 1909, p. 214);
  E. Klostermann, *Das Matthäusevangelium*, *ad loc.*; likewise Th. Zahn, *Das
  Evangelium nach Matthäu.*, *ad loc.* (he denies any connection with John 20:23);
  and W. Michaelis, commen..ry on Matthew, *ad loc.*

ban" and "acquit."[47] Since for Jesus entrance into the Kingdom of Heaven is closely connected with forgiveness of sins (Matt. 18:18 and John 20:23), the latter meaning is doubtless chiefly in mind here, but without excluding the other, which is equally well attested by Rabbinical texts.[48] Indeed, the power to teach and to discipline cannot be sharply separated. Peter thus receives a share in the authority of Christ to forgive sins. To the functions that had been committed to the disciples even in the lifetime of Jesus, the same ones, as we have seen,[49] that Jesus himself exercises (Matt. 11:4 ff.; 10:7 f.), there is now added this highest office of forgiving sins, an office that Christ alone controls but commits also to Peter with a view to establishing the earthly people of God. In case the binding is meant to refer also to the demonic powers, there would be a further connection with the preceding illustration.[50]

I recall at this point that this promise is given not only to Peter, but in almost the same words to the other disciples as well: "Truly I tell you, all that you shall bind on earth will be bound in heaven, and all that you shall loose on earth will be loosed in heaven" (Matt. 18:18); "If you forgive the sins of any, they will be forgiven; if you retain the sins of any, they will be retained" (John 20:23). This is important for the question as to the character of the pre-eminence with which Peter is certainly distinguished here. The "binding" and "loosing" he shares with the other disciples. This corresponds completely with what we have established in the historical section, in our chapter concerning the disciple Peter and his position among the Twelve. He is to be sure the first among them, but nevertheless is their representative in all things; he always speaks in the name of the others, and people turn to him in order to speak at the same time to all the disciples. This unique position comes to expression also in the fact that the promise of the effectiveness of his "binding" and "loosing" is given not only to him but also to the other disciples, but it is given to him in a special way, and only for him is it connected with the announcement that upon him as the rock the *ekklesia* is to be built. This corresponds with the historical fact which, as we have established, occurred after the death of Jesus; Peter, in the

---

47 So A. Schlatter, *Der Evangelist Matthäus, ad loc.;* J. Schniewind, *Das Evangelium nach Matthäus, ad loc.;* Ed. Schweizer, *Gemeinde nach dem N. T.,* 1949, p. 13.

48 See Strack-Billerbeck, *op. cit.,* Vol. I, p. 738, on Matthew, *ad loc.*

49 See above, pp. 195 f.

50 So R. Bohren, *Das Problem der Kirchenzucht im Neuen Testament,* 1952, pp. 52 ff., who agrees with F. Heiler, *Urkirche und Ostkirche,* 1937, p. 59. With a somewhat different turn, A. Dell, *op. cit.* (*ZNW,* 1914, pp. 38 ff.).

earliest period, stands at the head of the Primitive Church in Jerusalem, but soon gives up this position to act in dependence on James in organizing the Jewish Christian missionary work; this work he does in company with other disciples, but as its leader.

Read to Edg THIS Chapt.

*   *   *

This, however, leads us to the final exegetical question we must ask; it will also form the transition to the discussion of the doctrinal problem: Whom does Jesus mean when he says that upon the rock the new people of God will be built? The question could seem superfluous were it not that the really self-evident reference to the person of Peter has been contested, and often is still contested, from the Protestant as well as from the Catholic side.

The solution of the Reformers, that the rock is only the faith of Peter,[51] does not satisfy. In the first place, this explanation stands or falls with the very questionable connection of the words with the narrative framework, and we have seen that precisely in this story there is little concern with the faith of Peter, which here is anything but exemplary. But in addition to this, the text offers no real support for this interpretation. Rather, the parallelism of the two statements: "you are rock, and upon this rock I will build . . ." shows that the second rock refers to nothing different from the first one.[52] This is more clearly expressed in the Aramaic, where the same word *kepha* occurs both times, than it is in the Greek. The explanation that Jesus did not say at all: "You are Peter," but: "I say to you, yes to you, Peter,"[53] is purely hypothetical, in spite of the fact that it refers back to the Aramaic. There may indeed be some truth in the view that in the last analysis the rock means Christ himself (as in Matt. 21:42). But that is not what is said here; this passage says that Jesus' role as rock is transferred to a disciple.[54] So there remains only the one possibility, that by this saying Jesus actually meant the person whom he characterized by the name "rock." Indeed, if the saying

---

[51] See above, pp. 162 f.

[52] For this reason we must also pronounce unsatisfactory the thesis that G. Gander represents in his article "$\Pi ETPO\Sigma$-$\Pi ETPA$" (*Revue de Théologie et de Philosophie*, 1941, pp. 5 f.). He holds that *Kepha*, in Syriac *Kipha*, is a name of both persons and things, so that it refers to Peter only in the first but not in the second part of the sentence.

[53] Strack-Billerbeck, *op. cit.*, see above, p. 163.

[54] H. Riesenfeld, *Ämbetet i Nya Testamentet*, n. d., pp. 17 ff., shows how the metaphors which designate Jesus' own functions are transferred to the apostles.

were referred to the faith of Peter, one could no longer directly discern the connection with the giving of the name, and the saying certainly intends to point to this and even to explain it. The giving of the name, which is an established fact even apart from Matthew 16:17 ff., deals with the person of Peter, and not merely with his faith, just as the person of the sons of Zebedee is in view when Jesus gives them the title "Sons of Thunder."

For this reason all Protestant interpretations that seek in one way or another to explain away the reference to Peter seem to me unsatisfactory. No, the fact remains that when Jesus says that he will build his *ekklesia* upon this rock, he really means the person of Simon. Upon this disciple, who in the lifetime of Jesus possessed the specific advantages and the specific weaknesses of which the Gospels speak, upon him who was then their spokesman, their representative in good as well as in bad, and in this sense was the rock of the group of disciples—upon him is to be founded the Church, which after the death of Jesus will continue his work upon earth.

The Roman Catholic exegesis must be regarded as correct when it rejects those other attempts at explanation.[55] On its part, however, it proceeds in an even more arbitrary way when it tries to find in this text a reference to "successors." He who proceeds without prejudice, on the basis of exegesis and only on this basis, cannot seriously conclude that Jesus here had in mind successors of Peter; this was not his meaning when he said to Peter that he was the rock on which was to be built the fellowship of the people of God that leads to the Kingdom of God. We shall speak later concerning the doctrinal problem; we shall ask whether it cannot be said subsequently, in the light of church history, that the saying may be referred to certain successors. But at first we propose to keep this question clearly separate from the exegetical one, as all serious exegetes, including Roman Catholic ones, are accustomed to do when they deal with other Biblical passages.

On exegetical grounds we must say that the passage does not contain a single word concerning successors of Peter. It speaks on the one hand of *Peter* and on the other hand of the *Church*. Of these two words one, the *ekklesia*, refers to a fellowship which is to be built in the future, without any time limit being given. The other word,

[55] M. Meinertz, *Theologie des Neuen Testaments*, Vol. I, 1950, p. 74, does indeed make one concession to the Protestant interpretation when he writes, "the confession (that Peter makes) in faith is the presupposition." But naturally he nevertheless considers that it is the *person* of the confessing one that is addressed.

Peter, refers to a human person, whose earthly activity will necessarily be limited by his death. Accordingly it could be said that a single human person, who will die at a certain time, cannot be the foundation of a fellowship which is to continue for an indefinite period.

It is true that the duration of the Church is not limited in Jesus' words. However, neither is it *explicitly* extended to the period after the death of Peter, and this also must be noted in a saying addressed to the historical Peter. The question of duration is not considered at all; it is left open. In no case, however, is it justified to proceed as Roman Catholic scholars usually do. Since the period of building is not limited, they conclude too hastily that in the entire promise to Peter Jesus must have spoken also of the period after Peter's death, and therefore successors of Peter must also be addressed here.[56] *Peter's feeding of the lambs in John 21:16 ff. is certainly limited by his martyrdom!* So the statement "I will build my *ekklesia*" need not be extended beyond the lifetime of Peter. It could be that at the moment when he gave a promise to Peter in particular, Jesus limited himself to speaking concerning the initial building immediately after his resurrection; this need not mean that he thought the building would be completed in the lifetime of Peter.

But if we nevertheless assume that in *this first statement* Jesus thought of a period embracing many generations,[57] this does not mean at all that the rock—Cephas—Peter mentioned in this sentence includes also successors of Peter. In this sentence it is *only the work of*

[56] Even in so thorough and cautious an exegete as F. M. Braun, *Neues Licht auf die Kirche*, 1946, we read on p. 165: "Since . . . the apostles appear endowed with special and complete authority and since the operation of the Church, which is to continue to the fulfilment of the times, extends over an intermediate period of indeterminate duration, it would only be consistent, even apart from other considerations, if the 'new consensus' (see above, pp. 166 f.) would concede that the succession corresponds to Jesus' intention and that the apostles, after exercising their power for some years, transferred to others their authority as church leaders." In opposition to K. L. Schmidt, whom F. M. Braun cites on the same page, I prefer to avoid playing off a "prophetic succession" against the "apostolic succession." That an apostolic succession is directly or indirectly present in *other* passages of the New Testament, but in a sense still to be defined (see below, pp. 219 f.), I freely recognize. But I deny the more emphatically that Jesus spoke of such a succession in Matt. 16:17 ff. W. Michaelis, *Das Evangelium nach Matthäus*, p. 354, actually makes an argument for genuineness out of the failure to mention the succession; had the saying been invented later, the succession would have been mentioned.

[57] W. Michaelis, *op. cit.*, p. 346, believes it necessary to conclude from the illustration of the "building" that Jesus must have "had in mind a longer development."

building which belongs to an unlimited future, *not the laying of the foundation of the rock* on which is built! In the future Jesus will build upon a foundation which is laid in the time of his earthly career and in the time and person of the historical apostle Peter. We shall see[58] that in the entire New Testament the illustration of the foundation, which indeed is identical in meaning with that of the rock, always designates the unique apostolic function, which is chronologically possible only at the beginning of the building; see Ephesians 2:20; Romans 15:20; I Corinthians 3:10; Galatians 2:9; Revelation 21:14, 19. In Matthew 16:18 Peter is addressed in his unrepeatable apostolic capacity.

Everything that is said of Peter in this entire promise really concerns the Peter who then lived, even if the period of building that continues after Peter is explicitly in mind. The content of *the next sentence*, the giving to Peter of the keys, the power to bind and loose, also refers to the future. In this case, however, the reference is not to an unlimited future, but to the life of Peter following the death *of Jesus*. Here Jesus certainly speaks no longer of building during an unlimited period; he speaks rather of the specific rock itself, the apostolic foundation—represented by Peter—of the Church that is to be built. The preceding saying concerning building, which is not limited as to time, gives no exegetical justification for assuming an unlimited duration of time for the entrusting with the keys, the binding and loosing, which is given explicitly to Peter, the rock of the building. Whether and in what way these words directed to Peter may also be legitimately applied *subsequently* to the *later* Church we shall not discuss until the final chapter. On exegetical grounds it must be said that we have no right to see successors addressed in Peter. That would have to be indicated in some way. Wherever Jesus speaks elsewhere of the functions his disciples are to exercise, he plainly means only the disciples themselves and not their successors. And if in the first sentence, which deals with the building, Jesus really includes the period after Peter, this means only that the *unique* mission as rock which the historical Peter fulfils *in the redemptive history* is of such a character that its unique effectiveness continues even beyond his death, so that the historical Peter—and not any successors—is and remains the foundation even in this unlimited further building. When the Johannine Christ, in the high priestly prayer (John 17:20), speaks concerning the coming generations who

---

[58] See below, pp. 217 f., and H. Riesenfeld, *Ämbetet i Nya Testamentet*, n. d., pp. 17 ff.

will believe "through the word of the apostles," he does not speak also of successors to the apostles. He speaks of the *apostles themselves*, of what their once-given preaching signifies for the future Church.

That successors are not addressed is clear also from the Lucan parallel to Matthew 16:17 ff. We have seen that in that passage the command to strengthen the brothers is quite closely connected with the prediction of the denial. Peter must first be converted. Here it is certainly clear that in this section, which implicitly speaks of the future Church, Jesus did not include in his outlook any successors. What is said here is directed only to the historical Peter who denied Jesus.

To be sure, the sentence concerning the keys, concerning loosing and binding, speaks of functions of the historical Peter that continue in the Church. They refer to church leadership, and this indeed must continue to exist. That, however, does not mean that in this saying in Matthew 16:17 ff. Jesus is speaking of the leadership that *later* leaders will give. On the contrary, all that is said here deals with the leadership of him who, according to the preceding sentence, has also the unique mission, absolutely decisive for the Church and not to be repeated, of being the *rock*, of presiding as apostle over the Church immediately after the death and resurrection of Jesus.

As soon as any saying Jesus spoke to the disciples refers to a continued effect of the deeds of the apostles, the Roman Catholic exegetes speak of *successors*. It must be said with all emphasis, however, that continued effect need not mean continued effect *in* "*successors*."

In what he says Jesus certainly does not exclude the activity of other church leaders in later times. But in this *saying concerning the foundation* he does not speak of them; he speaks of Peter. Concerning men who are installed as leaders by apostles the New Testament actually does speak elsewhere, and we shall mention the passages later.[59] Here, however, in what Jesus says to Peter in Matthew 16:17 ff., nothing of the sort is said.

It therefore will not do to argue in the following way: The time of building that Jesus mentions in the first sentence is not limited. But the historical Peter will die. Consequently he cannot be the rock of a Church that continues to exist after him. Therefore Jesus must have successors in mind along with Peter.

It is also impossible to start from the second sentence to give an

[59] See below, pp. 219 ff.

exegetical defence for the reference to successors, and so to say something like the following: The power of the keys, and further the binding and loosing, which are entrusted to Peter, must be exercised also in the Church later built by Jesus. Consequently, together with Peter, successors also must be addressed who will carry out this binding and loosing and administer the keys. This also is too hasty a conclusion. Jesus will build not upon the keys, nor upon the binding and loosing, but *upon the apostle Peter*, to whom Jesus *at that time* committed the keys and the binding and loosing.

It must again be explicitly noted that the exegetical conclusion, that this passage speaks only of Peter, still says nothing concerning the possible application of the saying. It may be proper, however, for us to indicate a crucial point which stands *on the border line of exegetical study*. The Roman Catholic position concludes, from the continuance of the Church and from the continued necessity of church leadership, that successors are included in the person of the rock addressed, Peter. This conclusion appears to me connected with a failure to grasp the basic attitude of all New Testament thought. In opposition to Hellenism, it is characteristic of the thinking of Jesus as of all Biblical thinking that *what continues has its roots in the once-for-all unique event*. A historically unique event is the redemptive event; that is, it definitely cannot be repeated but is the *foundation* of a continuing situation whose ongoing life derives from this never-to-be-repeated event. This paradox lies at the basis of Jesus' sayings about the future, and finds a classic expression in the illustration of the rock and the *subsequent* building. In this sense we must also regard all the apostolic action, including the loosing and binding promised to Peter, as *the basic event*. It belongs to what happened once for all; it belongs, one may say, to the incarnation of Christ.[60]

But in saying this we have already stepped outside the field of exegesis. Our exegetical study has led us to the following result: The saying in Matthew 16:17 ff. is genuine. It was spoken by Jesus, not at Caesarea Philippi, but in another setting, possibly that of the passion story. Jesus promises Peter that he will build upon him the earthly people of God that will lead to the Kingdom of God; he promises that in this people Peter will have the leadership, both in missionary work and in organization. His immediate thought, just

---

[60] To use the illustration I gave in *Christus und die Zeit* (Eng. Tr., *Christ and Time*): the Apostolic Age belongs to the midpoint, to the *centre*, by which as norm we must measure everything else that occurs in the redemptive process on the time line.

as in John 21:16 ff., probably deals only with the time of Peter. But even if he explicitly had in view the period following Peter's death as the time of the building of the Church, what is said of Peter as the Rock refers only to him, the historical apostle; he represents once for all the earthly foundation, the beginning who supports the whole structure of the *ekklesia* that is to be built in the future.

Chapter Two

THE DOCTRINAL
AND THEOLOGICAL QUESTION:
THE APPLICATION OF
MATTHEW 16:17 ff. TO
THE LATER CHURCH

W<small>E NOW LEAVE</small> the exegetical standpoint and ask the doctrinal question. We connect the exegetical result with our knowledge both of the actual course of the history of the Christian Church and of the fact that there still exists today a Christian Church. On this basis we ask: Are we justified in going further? In the light of these facts can we attribute to the saying a significance that is at least a legitimate *extension* of the promise of Jesus? Roman Catholic theologians, indeed, are accustomed to concede explicitly that the Roman primacy cannot be based upon the exegesis of Matthew 16:17 ff. alone. They grant that this is possible only when this passage is connected with later history.

At the outset we must make a basic statement. It is our right and duty to apply to later generations and to our situation even those sayings of Jesus which deal directly with a unique situation and with specific persons of his time. This, of course, is no longer exegesis in the strict sense; but it may be called application of the exegesis. Preachers do this, and no one thinks of reproaching them with the *a priori* charge that in so doing they are untrue to the text. What Jesus says concerning prayer and almsgiving, for example, in the Sermon on the Mount is of course directed to the disciples who lived in his time; no one, however, will consider it unjustified or contrary to the mind of Jesus to apply his teachings on these subjects to all later Christians. Nevertheless, it must be added that this application must really extend in a straight line the basic idea contained in the saying. That is, it must agree with the exegesis and be grounded in the total witness of the New Testament.[1]

When, as is the case in Matthew 16:17 ff., the saying of Jesus does not have a content addressed simply to the wider circle of disciples, as are, for example, the instructions of the Sermon on the Mount, but refers rather to *quite specific functions*, then in the application the special character of these functions must be respected. This must be done in a two-fold way: on the one hand, the significance of the saying for the present may not be seen in the *repetition* of a function, if this is *basically* unique; and on the other hand, the application may not be arbitrarily *restricted*.

With regard to the former point, a role that Jesus promises to an apostle may not be transferred to men of later times, if it belongs to the very *meaning and nature* of the designated function that it can only be exercised by such men as have lived with the Incarnate One *during the earthly life of Jesus*. Indeed, this limitation in time must be taken into account even when—and indeed precisely when—the saying of Jesus in question assigns to this function a lasting significance for the later Church even down to the present time. We shall have to ask whether this is not the case for at least *one* aspect of the saying in Matthew 16:17 ff.

With regard to the latter point, a promise of Jesus may not be limited to a certain category of later Christians, for example, one strictly limited to one episcopal see, if the function in question is one that can and must be taken over by men of the post-apostolic period down to the present time, but according to Jesus' saying is neither explicitly nor by suggestion limited to one place or to be determined according to a particular *principle of succession*. We have to ask whether that sort of narrowing can be justified by the role in church history that the Christian church of one city has played and still plays for the entire Church.

Both of the viewpoints just named must be considered in the application of Matthew 16:17 ff. For we have seen that two things are promised to Peter: 1. He is the rock for the coming Church that is being built. 2. He holds the leadership in the Church whose building is begun. To this corresponds the fact that Peter plays in Primitive Christianity a double role: the unique one as apostle, and the one that is continued in the Church, as leader of the Church. Although the two promises are closely connected with one another, yet for

---

[1] Here a synthetic combination of the theological views of the various writings of the New Testament is both justified and essential.

their *application* they must be treated separately. This is because the previously posed question, whether too wide an extension or too narrow a limitation is being made, presents itself differently for each of them.

1. *The Laying of the Foundation of the Church*

Even in the course of the exegesis we established the fact that the laying of the foundation is to be understood in the temporal sense. As we now go beyond exegesis, we first must say that this saying, as far as it concerns the rock on which the structure is to be built, is directed to an apostle, not to a bishop. At the moment when Peter receives the promise of being the rock of the coming Church, he is addressed as one of the Twelve. According to the united witness of the New Testament, however, the apostolic office, particularly that of the Twelve, is a unique office not to be repeated. In the post-apostolic period there must always be church leaders, bishops, and missionaries in the Church of Christ, but never again can there be apostles. In the next paragraph we shall speak of the fact that often in the earliest period an apostle himself can be a community leader, at least for a certain time; indeed, Peter himself as apostle led the Primitive Church until he dedicated himself entirely to the mission. But even this will never exist again: there will never again be bishops who, like Peter, lead churches as *apostles*. The functions of leading and doing missionary work do indeed continue; they must continue in the Church. But the function of leading and doing missionary work as an apostle cannot continue. The saying concerning building the Church on Peter as the rock, however, designates an apostle as the basis of the Church that is to be built. When, as in the case of Peter, we are dealing with a church head and missionary who is likewise an apostle, the apostolic concept is necessarily the dominant concept.

We here must ask what the nature of the apostolic office is in the New Testament.[2] The apostle is given a special commission by Jesus as the Incarnate One or when he appeared after his resurrection; so, according to the rule in late Judaism, he is like Jesus himself, and is

---

[2] See K. H. Rengstorf, Article on ἀπόστολος in G. Kittel's *Theologisches Wörterbuch zum N. T.*, Vol. I, 1933, pp. 397 ff., and the essay by H. von Campenhausen cited above, p. 58, note 63. Further: Ed. Schweizer, *Das Leben des Herrn in der Gemeinde und ihren Diensten*, 1946, pp. 69 ff.; *Gemeinde nach dem N. T.*; and T. W. Manson, *The Church's Ministry*, 1948, pp. 31 ff.

bound to give accounting to him. Upon the fulfilment of his com-mission, he returns it to Jesus and cannot hand it on to another.

During Jesus' lifetime the content of the commission is the fulfil-ment of the Messianic function that Jesus himself fulfilled, the func-tion of preaching and healing the sick.[3] Since after the death of Christ the preaching is first of all witness to the resurrection of Christ, the apostle from then on must be a personal "witness of the resurrection of Christ" (Acts 1:22).

The necessity for an apostle to be a witness of the resurrection is clear from I Corinthians 9:1. In that passage Paul has to defend his apostolic office. He does it by pointing to the fact that he also, like the other apostles, has seen the Risen One. In Acts 10:41 Peter says: "Christ appeared to us who after his resurrection ate and drank with him." Thus after the death of Jesus there were more apostles than the Twelve. This follows clearly from the enumeration in I Corin-thians 15:5 ff., which speaks on the one hand of the Twelve, and on the other hand of *all the apostles*.

But the "having seen" must always be connected with a com-mission.[4] Concerning Paul we know this (Gal. 1:16). The Eleven also receive such a commission from the Risen One (Matt. 28:19), and so does Peter in particular (John 21:16 ff.). In the case of the Twelve, however, a further special condition must be fulfilled: they must in addition have lived with the historical incarnate Jesus. That is clearly said in Acts 1:21, where the substitute for Judas is chosen. The conditions that he must fulfil to belong to the circle of the Twelve are there clearly given: first of all, he, like all apostles, must be a "witness of the resurrection of Christ"; in the second place, he must have "gone in and out" with Jesus during his lifetime. In other words, the Twelve have the additional function of guaranteeing the continuity between the risen and the historical Jesus. Therein con-sists their unique function. They twice receive the apostolic commis-sion, first from the Incarnate One, then from the Risen One. Among them Peter is the most important. Only at that time could one be an eyewitness of the historical Jesus, an eyewitness of the resurrection. *There never will be such a witness again.* Upon one of these eyewit-nesses Christ intends to build his Church.

From the men of his time Jesus chose those who were to be his

---

3 In the lifetime of Jesus there are the smaller group of the Twelve and the larger one of the Seventy (Luke 10:1 ff.).

4 See A. Fridrichsen, "The Apostle and his Message" (*Uppsala Universitete Arsskrift*, 1947). See above, pp. 56, 63.

witnesses, and among them Peter, to whose witnessing he attached a particular value. We shall see that Peter, precisely on the basis of the *apostolic concept* just established, is actually the first among the apostles. It must be said at once, however, that according to the united testimony of the New Testament he shares this "fundamental" function with the other apostles. Thus in Ephesians 2:20, where exactly *the same illustration of the building* is used as in Matthew 16:18, Paul writes that the Church "is built upon the foundation of the apostles and prophets." So also Revelation 21:14 speaks of the "twelve foundations of the walls of the Holy City, on which the twelve names of the twelve apostles of the lamb are written," and with the same illustration Paul mentions the "pillars" in Galatians 2:9.[5]

From this it follows that the first Christians actually considered the apostles as such to be the foundation of the Church. Hence also, in the light of the total conception of the New Testament, which we have to consider in this doctrinal section, it is not at all arbitrary when in Matthew 16:17 ff. we see Peter addressed in his *apostolic capacity* and hence emphasize so strongly the apostolic concept. In any case, the illustration of the building in Ephesians 2:20 and Revelation 21:14 is connected with the apostolic function, and this is important. So also in Romans 15:20 the illustration of the foundation occurs to Paul: "that I may not build upon another foundation." (See also I Corinthians 3:10.) Perhaps the New Testament passages named actually refer to Jesus' saying concerning the rock in Matthew 16:17 ff. In that case we might say that we have here the oldest commentary on it.

In I Corinthians 3:11; 10:4; Matthew 21:42; and I Peter 2:4 ff. it is said that Jesus himself is the foundation stone or corner stone. This is doubtless the silent presupposition in all the other passages. But this does not prevent the apostles from being the foundation composed of human instruments of God and resting in turn upon Christ; nor does it prevent Peter from having the prominent role among them and for the Church of all later time.

Just as in Ephesians 2:20 and in Romans 15:20 the foundation is to be understood in a chronological way, so also in Matthew 16:17 ff. In Ephesians 2:20 and Romans 15:20, as well as in Revelation 21:14, it nevertheless is impossible, even as a later application, to think of successors of the apostles. Indeed, a recent study has actually proved

---

[5] James, although not belonging to the Twelve, very probably was regarded as an apostle. See below, p. 230, note 31.

that in contrast to other New Testament metaphors that were transferred from Jesus to the apostles and from them to the later offices,
the illustration of the Rock, of the foundation, is used solely for the
apostles. In this fact the uniqueness and unrepeatable character of the
apostolate comes clearly to expression.[6]

In the foundation that *all* the apostles form Peter is the specially
visible rock. Here again our earlier historical conclusion is confirmed;
he does indeed share his dignity with the other disciples, but within
the group he is particularly representative. Precisely in connection
with the concept of the apostle as the specially commissioned witness
of the resurrection it is also confirmed that Peter, with the other
apostles, forms the foundation and yet at the same time constitutes
the rock within this foundation. Peter, that is to say, was the *first* who
saw the Risen One on Easter. Probably he also received then confirmation of the apostolic commission,[7] and this is the more important since he was the one who had denied Jesus. He accordingly
is the apostle *par excellence*. In this essential relation as the outstanding
one, he is in a particular way what all the other apostles are. It is
interesting to note that here too his position as leader within the
apostolic circle rests upon a chronological distinction; *he is the first
one who saw the Risen One*, and according to John 21:15 ff. the special
apostolic commission given him by the Incarnate One is renewed by
the Risen One. We recall that Matthew, in his list of the apostles,
gives to Peter the title of honour, "first." Thus this also is a part of
the essential role of the apostle Peter. He is particularly qualified to
hand on the news that Jesus, who lived and died on earth, died and
rose for the salvation of the world.

Thus the events immediately after the death of Jesus confirmed the
saying concerning the rock, and if one seeks in the happenings of this
period a *confirmation and illumination of Jesus' saying*, he should seek
it in the fact that Peter is the first witness of the resurrection, and that
his apostolic commission is renewed by the Risen One. This is closely
connected with the result of the exegetical interpretation of the statement: "the gates of the realm of the dead will not overpower the
Church."[8] In the light of the Easter events this interpretation, con-

---

[6] See H. Riesenfeld, *Ämbetet i Nya Testamentet*, n. d., pp. 17 ff.

[7] So especially if the hypothesis is correct that a report concerning the first appearance of Jesus to Peter, such as perhaps was given in the lost ending of Mark, is
used in John 21:15 ff. See above, pp. 59 ff., 180 ff.

[8] See above, p. 202, note 36. Only in this form may we recognize a grain of truth
in the interpretation of A. Harnack—rejected above—that the promise of Peter's
resurrection is here given him.

nected with the promise that the Church is founded on Peter as the rock, receives a particularly strong confirmation in the fact that it is he who is the most important witness of the resurrection of Christ. We have seen that it is not the faith of Peter that is meant by the rock, as the Reformers taught, but rather his person. We now add that it is his person in so far as he had been chosen by the incarnate Christ and in so far as the Risen One appeared to him first of all.

Thus it is absolutely irreconcilable with the New Testament concept of apostleship when a saying on the founding of the Church that was addressed to an apostle is simply referred to future bishops. Elders and bishops certainly do take the place of the apostles, and one may call them successors, even if this expression opens the way to misunderstandings. But in any case it must not be forgotten for a moment that they occupy a completely different position, and they must not be regarded as successors in the sense of "continuers of the apostolic function." They are successors in the chronological sense, but not in their nature. *Their function follows that of the apostles, but as a fundamentally different one.*[9]

So we hear indeed in the New Testament that apostles installed church officers. Paul and Barnabas appointed elders in the cities of Lystra, Iconium, and Antioch (Acts 14:23); moreover, Paul, in his farewell to the elders of Ephesus, commits to them the "flock," especially in anticipation of false teachers (Acts 20:17 ff.). Tendencies towards a so-called "apostolic succession"—if we choose to use this ambiguous expression—are thus actually to be found in the New Testament,[10] but with the explicit reservation that this succession, as far as it concerns the essence of the apostolate, is not to be understood in the sense of a continuation. The apostles give over to those

---

[9] Against the Roman Catholic theologian M. Meinertz, *Die Theologie des Neuen Testaments*, Vol. I, 1950, p. 79: ". . . thus the apostolate requires a continuing present."

[10] This is quite strongly stressed by W. Mundle, "Das Apostelbild der Apostelgeschichte" (*ZNW*, 1928, pp. 36 ff.), an article to which Erik Peterson attaches special importance. See E. Peterson, *Theologische Traktate*, 1951, p. 296 (letter to A. Harnack) and p. 411 ("Die Kirche"). On the question of apostolic succession see also K. H. Rengstorf, "Das Wort Gottes und die apostolische Sukzession" (*Die Kirche Jesu Christi und das Wort Gottes*, edited by W. Zoellner and W. Stählin, 1937, pp. 187 ff.); A. M. Ramsey, "The Word of God and Apostolic Succession" (*Lutherische Kirche in Bewegung, Für Fr. Ulmer zum 60. Geburtstag*, 1937, pp. 179 ff.). See Ed. Schweizer, *op. cit.*, pp. 75 ff.; T. W. Manson, *op. cit.* (note 2 of this section), pp. 52, 54. The Anglican standpoint is represented by K. E. Kirk, *The Apostolic Ministry*, 1946 (especially the essay by G. Dix, "The Ministry in the Early Church").

men the leadership, *but not their own apostolic office.* For they knew quite well that they could not hand this on at all, since it could only be given by Jesus himself directly and *without mediation* (Gal. 1:12 ff.!). Therefore they did not install any "apostles" as successors in leadership, but rather "bishops" and "elders." In what way the latter in turn are to follow one another, the New Testament does not say at all, and since the authority of the bishop may not be identified with that of the apostle, the above named New Testament passages that speak of the installing of local church leaders by the apostles permit no deductions as to how bishops are to follow bishops in the future.[11] In the high-priestly prayer the Johannine Christ speaks of what will follow the apostles. After the petition for the apostles he goes on to speak of those who "believe through the word" (of the apostles; John 17:20). Thus the apostles are followed by the entire Church of the believers. Accordingly the Church has the power of control over the episcopal office, and it is to exercise it as the Holy Spirit guides it (Acts 20:28).

Foundation and building may not be interchanged. Elders and bishops are only *watchmen* who are to see to it that further building is really done on the foundation of the apostles; they are not themselves the foundation. A confusion of foundation and building is present, however, when one appeals to the fact that the apostles installed elders and bishops in order to claim for a bishop Jesus' saying to the rock apostle. Although Roman Catholic theology itself emphasizes very strongly the uniqueness of the apostolic office, it devaluates that office in this decisive point of the application of Matthew 16:17 ff. There will be no more men who, like Peter, have eaten and drunk with Jesus the Incarnate One, have seen his suffering and his death, and to whom, after the denial, Jesus has appeared as the Risen One three days after his death. Later we shall speak also of the fact that there also will be no more men who, like Peter, are leaders of the *first* Church of Christ, the original church at Jerusalem.

Therefore, in the light also of *the total New Testament witness concerning the apostolic office,* and in the light of *the events of the Primitive Church,* that part of the promise of Jesus that speaks of building on the rock Peter may receive subsequent interpretation and application

[11] This does not intend to say that the Scripture condemns the principle of succession. It does not express itself as to the How of determining the succession of bishops. Only this is certain, that the Holy Spirit operative in the Church is to be at work in the process. So rightly K. H. Rengstorf in p. 202 of the essay cited in the preceding note.

to the later Church only in such a way that this later Church rests once for all and in every generation upon the foundation that was laid *once*; it was laid, that is, at the beginning, at the midpoint of the times, in the time of revelation, when Christ lived on earth, died, and rose.

And now we ask further: But how can the foundation, understood in this chronological way, continue to play this role for the Church of all later times? How can every generation understand that for the Church Peter—and this really means Peter, not pretended successors—is "actually" Peter in the etymological sense? How can the Church today still be founded upon the historical person of the apostle Peter?

This is only possible if this very temporal uniqueness of the foundation formed by the apostles is respected, that is, if the historically unique effect of their person and their work continues to exist in our present as a concrete gift from the time of revelation. This unique gift, which constitutes the continuance of the apostles in the period of the Church, is the Apostolic Scripture. It is not confessional prejudice, but simply the Primitive Christian apostolic concept, that leads me to affirm this. Here in these writings we today, in the midst of the twentieth century, meet the person of the apostles, the person of the first among the apostles, Peter; in this way they continue to support, he continues to support, the structure of the Church. In the only New Testament text that explicitly speaks of the relation of the apostles to the Church that follows them—I refer to the already mentioned section of the high priestly prayer in John 17:20—the further working of the apostles is connected not with the succession principle but rather with the *word of the apostles*: "those who believe through their word."

Without apostles we would have no New Testament, no knowledge at all of Jesus the Risen One. Everything that we know of him we owe to them. And this—we repeat—is true of Peter in a special way. Papias tells that the Gospel of Mark was written according to the sermons of the apostle Peter, and so rests upon his testimony. If this report is correct, then it is also historical to say that the oral tradition lying behind the written Gospels goes back in the first instance to the apostle Peter, especially if we, in agreement with recent study, regard the Gospel of Mark as the oldest Gospel.

When we read the Gospels, we are thus in contact with the person of the apostles and the rock apostle. We today are no longer in the situation to hear for ourselves the eye witnesses of the historical life of Jesus and of his resurrection. We can no longer go to Jerusalem, as Paul did, to "make the acquaintance of Peter" (Gal. 1:18). Nor shall we meet the eyewitness Peter in any other city. But he does remain for us the rock, the foundation; he remains such in the Gospels and in a derived way in the Book of Acts and the letters, which rest entirely upon the first apostolic witness. Here the historical apostolic foundation of the revelation, on which Christ in every generation builds his Church anew, takes concrete form for us also, and *yet retains its unique and never repeated form*. Here the apostles continue to live, and so all Christian Churches, not only the Roman Catholic Church, should write upon their church buildings: "You are Peter, upon this Rock I will build my Church." "Built upon the foundation of the apostles and prophets." "I pray for those who believe through the word of the apostles." Every Christian Church should be *"ecclesia catholica et apostolica,"* a catholic and apostolic Church. A Church that is not apostolic is no longer a Christian Church. But it is perverse to wish to be content, for example, with the apostle Paul, as often happens in Protestant churches. It has become the custom to connect the apostle Peter only with the Roman Catholic Church, and the apostle Paul with the Protestant Church.[12] In reality every Church needs also the apostle Peter, because he as "first" among the twelve apostles has to guarantee the continuity with the incarnate Jesus.[13]

The application of the saying concerning the rock to the later period can thus be made in this sense, in full agreement with the exegesis, but also with the history of the beginnings of the Church.

The question that is asked from the Roman Catholic side is: Who guarantees in the present the scriptural link that leads back to the apostles? This question is justified in itself. But it may not be answered *on the basis of the saying concerning the rock*, on the basis of Matthew 16:17 ff., which is a "foundation saying"; for the rock is and remains the once-for-all foundation. To be sure, there must be guarantors, watchmen, shepherds, interpreters in the Church. But they are quite false to this their role if they refer to themselves the saying concerning the rock. They are indispensable materials of which Christ makes use in the further building of his Church. Their

[12] This is the usual and particularly favoured procedure at ecumenical conferences. In such a connection the eastern churches hold to the apostle John as their Patron.

[13] I wish to make this reservation also in regard to the book of J. L. Leuba, *L'Institution et l'evénement*, 1950, which otherwise offers a good historical basis for interdenominational conversations.

specific task is to take care that this rock remains unshaken in the place where Christ has put it, and that it remains just as he has put it. Thus watchmen, shepherds, bishops are instruments of the promise Jesus made to build his Church on Peter.[14]

2. *The Leadership of the Church*

It is a frequent error of Protestant theologians that they do not sufficiently consider in their theological application the continuation of the saying, in which Jesus clearly speaks of the leadership of the Church. Even if the power of the keys concerns primarily the missionary leadership,[15] yet the power to bind and loose, in both of its possible meanings,[16] definitely presupposes church leadership.

We have said already that the leadership of the Church by Peter is also *apostolic* leadership, and so belongs to the never to be repeated Rock role, the laying of the foundation. For we dare not forget that the *entire* promise is dominated by the saying about the rock; it indeed, in connection with the giving of the name, forms the point of departure. But on the other hand, we have pointed out many times that in contrast to the office of the apostle, that of the leader in the Church continues. Thus we here must pay attention to two things: on the one hand, to the non-transferable character of the leadership of the Primitive Church by Peter; on the other hand, to the fact that there must also be leadership later in the Church, so

[14] Richard Baumann, *Des Petrus Bekenntnis und Schlüssel*, 1950, in general formulates the problems correctly, but solves them too quickly along the lines of Roman Catholic teaching. In doing so he is concerned to base his argument entirely on the Scripture. On p. 49 he formulates the following objection against the conception according to which the Church of all time builds *further* on the foundation laid *once*, that is, at the beginning, so that in this building one "layer" or "story" rises on the other to the end of time. He says that in this case "that which is present in the first layer at the first Pentecost would be something unfinished, scarcely begun"; and that is "no house and no temple." This argument, however, is incorrect to this extent, that here the word "unfinished" is understood in the sense of "qualitatively uncompleted." It is not the case, however, that further building takes place because the building without the upper stories would be incomplete and would represent nothing finished. It is "unfinished" before the end of time simply in the chronological sense. A qualitative judgment is never included when reference is made to the end, to the fulfilment of the times. The building is already a complete whole in the lowest storey of the church structure; the number of storeys has only chronological significance. The foundation remains the same; it is so firm that it bears the uppermost storeys as well as the lowest ones.

[15] See above, pp. 203 f. [16] See above, pp. 204 f.

that Peter is in a certain respect the archetype and example for all future church leadership.[17]

Since we are dealing here with application, it is permitted and required that we connect Matthew 16:17 ff. with what we have learned from The Acts and the Letters concerning the actual role that Peter played in the Primitive Church. When we read the promise of Jesus in the light of the history of the Apostolic Age, it must be said that it was fulfilled in the sense that Peter actually is the head of the Primitive Church. As we have seen, he stands at the head of the Primitive Church of Jerusalem, though to be sure only in the very earliest time. For James will soon take over the leadership in Jerusalem. Nevertheless, Peter retains for all time the unique greatness and dignity of having been *in the first days of the Church of Jesus Christ* the leader of the Primitive Church and thereby of the entire Church of that time. This must stand first of all as a fixed fact in the redemptive history at the beginning. In agreement with this is the result of the exegesis of Matthew 16:17 ff., according to which Jesus, when he promises to Peter the power of the keys, of binding and loosing, thinks of the lifetime of Peter. What Peter will do belongs to the period of revelation, to the time of the apostles, and so to the foundation. For this reason, his exercise of the power of the keys, the power to bind and loose, is so important.

Only the original Church was led by this apostle, and he led it only in its earliest period. For as soon as the foundation for this leadership is laid, Peter will give it up. Another, James, will take it over in Jerusalem, while Peter will concentrate entirely on his missionary work and will do so, indeed, in a *subordinate role under James*.

This later subordination of Peter under James is a fact important in every respect. It confirms first of all that the leadership of the Church by Peter also has its significance for us chiefly as a *starting point*. James is the actual head of the Church from the moment that Peter dedicates himself completely to missionary work. The memory of that fact was steadily retained in the whole of Jewish Christianity, which took an interest in the ancient traditions. According to Hegesippus, "The brother of the Lord, James, takes over the leader-

17 Ph. Menoud, *L'Eglise et les ministères selon le Nouveau Testament*, 1949, pp. 25 ff., rightly distinguishes between the unique never to be repeated witnessing office of the apostle and his functions that continue to be exercised in the Church. On this see Ed. Schweizer, *Geist und Gemeinde im N. T. und heute* (*Theologische Existenz heute;* in press).

ship of the Church with the apostles."[18] Particularly important is the fact that the *Pseudo-Clementina*, which are friendly to Peter, clearly subordinate Peter to James.[19] Peter has to "give an accounting" to James, "the bishop of the holy Church." To him Peter sends his public addresses,[20] and Clement calls him "Bishop of Bishops," "leader of the holy church of the Hebrews and of the churches *founded everywhere* by God's providence."[21] Clement traces Peter's commission to him back to a commission that James gave to Peter.[22] These late reports thus agree with what we can learn concerning James from the letters of Paul and Book of Acts.[23]

It will not do, however, to make some such objection as that Peter went to Rome just at that time in order to *"transfer"* the primacy from Jerusalem to that place. In reality Peter does not leave Jerusalem in order to transfer the primacy elsewhere; he leaves rather to spread the gospel. But the significant thing, as said, is that in relation to the new leadership at Jerusalem he does not continue in some superior position, as though James were only his substitute, or were only Bishop of the church at Jerusalem, already sunk to the position of a local church. He rather subordinates himself to the authority of James as the central government. In a time, therefore, *when Jerusalem continues to hold the leading position* and all other churches—even those founded by Paul, as the collection shows—still look to Jerusalem, Peter himself is dependent on the new leadership in Jerusalem; in Antioch he has to "fear the people who come from James" (Gal. 2:12)!

---

[18] Eusebius, *Ecclesiastical History*, II, 23, 4. According to Eusebius, *Eccles. Hist.*, II, 23, 1, he receives it "from the Apostles."

[19] See C. Schmidt, *Studien zu den Pseudo-Clementinen*, 1929, pp. 108 ff., 322 ff. O. Cullmann, *Le problème littéraire et historique du roman pseudo-clémentin*, 1930, pp. 250 ff. H. J. Schoeps, *Theologie und Geschichte des Judenchristentums*, 1949, pp. 122 ff.

[20] *Recognitions*, I, 17; *Homilies*, I, 20; *Epistle of Peter* 1.

[21] *Epistle* of Clement. [22] *Recognitions*, I, 17; *Homily*, I, 20.

[23] According to Clement of Alexandria, who likewise stresses particularly Peter's special position among the disciples (*Quis dives salvetur*, ch. 21), Peter, James, and John, after the ascension of Jesus, renounced the pre-eminent position and chose James the Just as the Bishop of Jerusalem. (*Hypotyposes*, in Eusebius, *Eccles. Hist.*, II, 1, 3. See Jerome, *De viribus illustribus*, ch. 2.) Here, however, the fact is obscured that Peter had the leadership in the *earliest* period. So also among recent scholars we find the opinion represented that James had the highest leadership *from the beginning* (see H. Koch, *Cathedri Petri*, 1930, pp. 171 ff.). But to say that is to transfer back into the earliest period a situation that only emerged after some time. Correctly H. v. Campenhausen, *ZKG*, 1951–52, pp. 136 f.

One certainly must not exaggerate the importance of the clash between Peter and Paul at Antioch.[24] Nevertheless, it clearly proves something else that seems to me much more important than the rebuke that Paul gave Peter. It proves that *in relation to James*, whose representatives he fears, Peter does not take a leading role. Therefore one cannot speak of a transfer of the leadership by Peter to another place.

The Roman Catholic tradition asserts that Peter was *bishop also in Antioch*.[25] But Galatians 2:12 proves that even if this is correct, he does not in any case lead the entire Church from this centre. It thus proves that he did not transfer the leadership from Jerusalem to Antioch and then from Antioch to Rome. He exercised leadership over the entire Church only at the beginning of the Jerusalem church and thereby at the beginning of the whole Church. Then he carries out the missionary phase of his apostolic office, and does so in the service of the Jewish Christian church of Jerusalem, whose leadership is in other hands.

As far then as the church leadership by Peter is concerned, we must take seriously the fact that the rock apostle led the *entire* Church only at *one* time. That was when, in the days immediately after Christ's resurrection and in the days of the giving of the Spirit to the Mother Church in Jerusalem, he stood at its head and exercised the work of binding and loosing, the memory of which the narrative about Ananias and Sapphira has preserved (Acts 5:1 ff.). When, therefore, the history of the Primitive Church is invoked to give present significance to the primacy of Peter in relation to leadership over the entire Church, this can happen only in the following way: The Church of today recognizes the redemptive plan of God in the fact that at its initial stage—this really was true at its initial stage—stands the apostle to whom Jesus gave the name "Rock," and to whom he announced that on him he would build the Church.

*   *   *

But in addition to the honoured place in redemptive history that our present Church should give to Peter as the first and indeed the apostolic head of the Church, one may take a further step in applying to the later period Jesus' promise to Peter. We have seen that there must be leadership in the Church, even after the apostolic period when the foundation is laid and down to the present day. In this

[24] See above, pp. 46 f.   [25] See above, pp. 52 f., and below, p. 33.

respect the leadership of the first head of the Church may be example and pattern, but nothing more than this. The leader or leaders of the future Church are given an example in the leadership that is committed to Peter. But Peter himself cannot so to speak arise in every new generation. Never again will the *kepha*, the rock, himself exercise the leadership. But all leadership of the later Church built upon the apostle should know that the keys are given to it and that it has the task of binding and loosing.

It is a fact that in the beginning a single person stood at the head of the Church as a "rock" among the "pillars." But it is not necessary to conclude from this that also in all later times a single person must stand at the head of the entire Church. The entire Church is no longer identical, as it was in the first days, with one local church.

The question as to what principle is to determine the leadership of the whole in the following period cannot be answered on the basis of an almost automatically operating mechanism. With a certain blindness to the problems involved, the Roman Catholic Church regards it as self-evident that no other principle can here be considered except that of succession tied to a specific local church. It claims as decisive—in connection with its view that Matthew 16:17 ff. has in mind successors—first, the fact that Peter was bishop of a specific church, that is, Rome, and second, that this very church has actually "led" in the history of the Church.

If, in accord with all that has been said, the leadership of the Church by Peter is to be considered only as a pattern, this means that such an exclusive application to the Roman bishops is really impossible from the start. If in what follows we nevertheless examine the different arguments with which this limitation is defended, we do so only to show that on the one hand the arguments lack any foundation in the history of the historical Peter, and on the other hand that they cannot stand theologically without this foundation.

We first of all must return to the principle of apostolic succession, of which we already have spoken in connection with Peter's role as the rock. In doing so, we now have to focus particularly on the relation of the succession principle to Rome as the seat of the *leadership of the entire Church*. We have seen[26] that the idea of succession in its later form cannot be derived from Matthew 16:17 ff., even if we add to it the New Testament passages that speak of the appointment of local church heads by the apostles. Completely lacking in Matthew 16:17 ff., however, is any reference to the idea that a

[26] See above, pp. 207 ff., 219 f.

specific local church would have to carry the succession in the leadership of the *entire Church*. This, to be sure, is admitted by the defenders of the Roman claim to primacy, and they never support their argument upon this saying alone, without adding those other theological considerations of which we shall speak later. But we still must ask here whether, even if one does not hold the Scripture alone to be authoritative, it is not at least noteworthy that in the entire apostolic record, that is, the entire New Testament, not a single passage so much as mentions the name of Rome *in connection with Peter*, and therefore it is not only in Matthew 16:17 ff. that reference to the limitation to a particular local church is completely lacking. This latter fact should cause serious thought when this very saying of Matthew 16:17 ff. is limited to the Bishops of Rome and when this saying, whatever the decisive additional arguments may be, is always regarded as at least the starting-point for the proof that is supposed to justify a development of such tremendous scope.

From the historical point of view, as we have seen, we can indeed explain the *silence* of the entire New Testament concerning any relation of Peter to Rome. *Theologically*, however, we hardly can do so *if* this relation is to justify the exclusive claim that the Roman Bishops make to this saying of Jesus.[27] In our historical study we have concluded, on the basis of all sorts of indirect arguments, that Peter very probably came to Rome at the end of his life and there became a martyr. But does this suffice as the starting-point for an assertion that takes so uniquely important a theological role in the picture of redemptive history, the assertion, that is, that only *this* church that is linked with the chain of Roman bishops may appeal to Peter and that it is the only "catholic and apostolic Church"? In particular, should not the silence of the Scripture concerning Peter's episcopal office in Rome stimulate us to consider whether it is really true that for all time to come the Church is to be led by this episcopal see?

We now go on, however, beyond the Scriptural witness. What is the truth in general concerning the presupposition, assumed without any discussion, that the leadership of the entire Church in the post-apostolic period is to be determined from one and the same

---

[27] M. Meinertz, *Theologie des Neuen Testaments*, Vol. I, 1950, p. 79, concedes: "With regard to the succession to Peter, there naturally is still no supporting proof for that in the New Testament." My opposition to this statement is directly against the word "naturally." For this does not seem to me at all natural, if salvation is really to depend on this succession.

episcopal see by the chain of succession of the occupants of this see? Of certain *individual churches* we can say that by instituting local church heads[28] the apostles, in their unique capacity as apostles, thus created the first bishops of these churches. This, to be sure, says nothing at all as to who after them is to choose the subsequent bishops.[29]

The apostle Peter, on the other hand, never established a bishop as the leader of the *entire Church,* and above all he himself never gave distinction to any Church *except Jerusalem* as the seat of his own leadership of the entire Church. *For even if, after his leadership of the Jerusalem church, he temporarily as apostolic missionary was the leader of still other churches, yet so much at least is definite, that when he was there he was only the leader of those single churches, and in no case leader of the entire Church. Peter was the leader of the entire Church only at Jerusalem.*

Thus if *one* church wished to claim a special position in this respect and if the geographical principle as such were not completely arbitrary, it could only be the church of Jerusalem. In the New Testament this is the only church of which we hear that Peter stood at its head. Of other episcopates of Peter we know nothing certain. Concerning Antioch, indeed, as we shall see—and we shall return to this point—there is a tradition, first appearing in the course of the second century, according to which Peter was its bishop. The assertion that he was Bishop of Rome we first find at a much later time. From the second half of the second century we do possess texts that mention the apostolic *foundation* of Rome, and at this time, which is indeed rather late, this foundation is traced back to *Peter and Paul,* an assertion that cannot be supported historically.[30] Even here, however, nothing is said as yet of an episcopal office of Peter. But even if Peter did occupy in Rome an episcopal position, this could hold good at the most for the *local* church in Rome, for it is a fixed fact that *at that time,* in the sixth decade of the first century, Rome still played no leading role in the Church at large, and Peter did not rule the entire Church from Rome. In our present discussion, however, we are concerned with the question as to how the succession was determined, and this concerns the leadership of *the Church at large.* In that

[28] See above, pp. 219 f.

[29] Ed. Schweizer, *Das Leben des Herrn in der Gemeinde und ihren Diensten,* 1946, pp. 75 f., emphasizes here that even this installation by the apostles in the Pastoral Epistles did not take place without the presence of the congregation, and in *Geist und Gemeinde im N. T. und heute* (in press) he stresses that in I Tim. 1:18 the installation occurs only after "preceding prophetic instruction."

[30] See above, pp. 116 f., 45, 79 f.

connection we only wish to show, in an anticipatory way, that not only in the Scriptures, but also *in the history of Primitive Christianity, there is no trace at all* that the succession to Peter in the leadership at large was to be determined by the fact that he was bishop in this or that city. In the life of Peter there is no starting-point for a *chain of succession* in the leadership of the Church at large.

The fact that Peter most probably suffered his martyrdom in Rome cannot give to this church the dignity that belongs solely to the Mother Church in Jerusalem, the dignity of having once represented the entire Church and of having been led as such by the apostle Peter *in the apostolic period of revelation.*

But even Jerusalem naturally is not to be considered as permanent bearer of succession in the universal leadership of the Church. The authority of James, moreover, is not derived from Peter but from his direct relations to Jesus. He probably was regarded as an apostle who was instituted as such by Jesus himself. This is the view of Paul,[31] and the later tradition also was still able to report that he was appointed bishop by Jesus himself.[32] A chain of succession in the leadership of the *entire Church*, going back to Peter and to Matthew 16:17 ff., thus does not exist. Concerning Clement of Rome, who is so eagerly designated as the Roman Pope appointed by Peter, it cannot be proved from reliable sources either that he received his office from Peter or that he was the leader of the Church at large; to exhort a divided sister church to harmony in a letter is not enough to establish one as the pope. Peter at the beginning led the entire Church in Jerusalem. But which bishop after him is to play the leading role in each case cannot be decided by the principle of a succession determined according to the location of the bishop's seat. There is no succession that leads from Jerusalem to another city. This must be stated as a basic proposition.

---

[31] This conclusion, moreover, seems to follow from the fact that Paul reckons him among the "pillars" (Gal. 2:9), and especially from Gal. 1:19 (ἕτερον δὲ τῶν ἀποστόλων οὐκ εἶδον εἰ μὴ Ἰάκωβον: "but other of the Apostles I did not see except Peter"). H. Koch, however, in "Zur Jakobus-frage, Gal. 1, 19" (*ZNW*, 1934, pp. 264 ff.), thinks he can explain the passage otherwise: Paul saw no other apostle but Cephas, but did indeed see James. He is regarded as an apostle also by K. Holl, "Der Kirchenbegriff des Paulus, in seinem Verhältnis zu dem der Urgemeinde" (*Gesammelte Aufsätze*, Vol. II, p. 49); H. v. Campenhausen, *ZKG*, 1950–51, p. 137.

[32] According to the Pseudo-Clementine Epistle of Peter to James, V, and *Recognitions*, I, 43, James was installed by the Lord; so also according to Epiphanius, *Heresies*, 78, 7, and Chrysostom, in *Homily on First Corinthians*, 38, 5.

Moreover, there are other churches besides Jerusalem and Rome,[33] above all *Antioch*, which regard Peter as their first bishop. We have seen[34] that the tradition of the episcopate at Antioch is exceedingly hard to defend on historical grounds, even if the letters of Ignatius suggest the assumption that the monarchical episcopate developed relatively early at Antioch. It must nevertheless be emphasized that this tradition is much older and better attested than is that of the Roman episcopate. In the time of Peter the Roman church had no more significance, and perhaps even less, than did the one at Antioch. They were both local churches, and as such they were led by Peter, if the traditions in question are correct.

If one were determined to maintain the completely arbitrary principle according to which Peter's episcopal office in a church could aid in giving to its later bishops the exclusive claim to Matthew 16:17 ff., then on this basis Antioch could establish a greater claim to the primacy than Rome. Nevertheless, we have already mentioned and shall again speak of the fact that according to the judgment of most Roman Catholic theologians, even the episcopate of Peter is by no means sufficient of itself. Just as little does the interpretation of Matthew 16:18 suffice. Rather, to both arguments there must be added as the decisive criterion of the primacy the effective role that a church has played and plays in the further history. Since, however, the episcopate of the apostle and the relation of Jerusalem to Rome are regularly cited as arguments in connection with the history of Peter, we had to examine this question on all sides. We come to the conclusion: There is no basis whatever in any ancient text for the assertion that Rome inherited the legal succession from Jerusalem. Even if Antioch should be inserted as an intermediate stage, such a theory would not be any better supported. *For Peter ruled the Church at large in that period neither from Antioch nor from Rome, but only in Jerusalem and for a short time.* The history of Primitive Christianity gives no warrant of any kind for the assumption that Peter came to Rome to transfer the primacy to that place.

There are some well-known Roman Catholic theologians who, in view of the lack of any basis for such an assertion, do not make the primacy of Rome depend at all on the *stay of Peter in Rome*. Indeed, they believe that in their theological statement they can actually in

[33] The Pseudo-Clementine *Homily* 3, 53, presupposes that there is in Caesarea a *Cathedra Petri* (an episcopal "chair of Peter").
[34] See above, pp. 52 f.

principle forgo this basis, since it is only *the fact* that the Bishops of
Rome are successors of Peter—not the How—that is decisive, and
since the transfer of the succession to Peter to the Bishops of Rome
is even conceivable without Peter himself having been in the city
of this later episcopal see.[35] This view completely surrenders the
appeal to the history of the historical Peter. However, the Roman
Catholic teaching seems not completely consistent on this point, and
one can ask whether this surrender can really be reconciled with the
wording of the Vatican pronouncement.[36]

But in any case it is true that the stay of Peter in Rome has never
been the only decisive argument for the primacy of Rome. All
Roman Catholic theologians argue rather that later, from the beginning of the second century on, *Rome effectively played an outstanding
and leading role in the Christendom of that time.* One thus can say, they
contend, that the historical *development of church history* proves that
after the destruction of Jerusalem the primacy passed from Jerusalem
to Rome.

To this, however, it must be replied that from the effective historical role which a church plays in *post-apostolic times* no divine right
can be derived for *all* time if, as we have just established, this role
lacks any connection with the Apostolic Age. It will not do to appeal to

---

35 See R. Graber, *Petrus der Fels*, 1949, p. 37, and Ch. Journet, *L'Eglise du verbe
incarné*, 1941, pp. 522 ff. R. Graber cites Dunin-Borkowski, "Die Kirche als
Stiftung Jesu" (*Religion, Christentum und Kirche*, 1923, pp. 45 f.): "It is a widespread error that the Catholic apologetic must necessarily make the papacy, as
the continuation of the rule of Peter, dependent on the stay of the Prince of
Apostles in Rome and on his episcopal office there. This is not the case. Certainly
one can give such a proof, but it is by no means necessary. . . . As soon as it . . .
is established that Christ not merely fixed the primacy of Saint Peter but spoke
of this primacy as a lasting institution, there is lacking only the proof that the
Roman bishops alone claimed the special rights of the Rock man." Further,
L. Kösters, *War Petrus in Rom?*, 1938, pp. 50 f.: "It would be entirely conceivable
that Peter had appointed the chief of the Roman Church as his successor in
the primacy received from Christ, even if he himself had never been in
Rome."

36 *Vaticanum*, fourth session, July 18, 1870, ch. 2: . . . *qui* (Peter) *ad hoc usque tempus
et semper in suis successoribus episcopis sanctae Romanae Sedis, ab ipso fundatae eiusque
consecratae sanguine, vivit et praesidet et iudicium exercet* ("who even unto this time
and always lives and governs and exercises judgment in his successors, the bishops
of the holy Roman see, *which was founded by him and consecrated by his blood*").
From the significance, moreover, which is attached in Roman circles to the discovery of the grave of Peter, it seems proved that the opinion held by those
named in the preceding footnote and by many eminent Roman Catholic
theologians is not generally shared.

tradition as a source of revelation to justify this flight into later history; the sole justification for the Roman Catholic tradition rests on this very assertion of the primacy of Rome. It simply is not true that every development in church history is to be accepted without question as legitimate tradition. And one cannot prove the *foundation* of the Roman tradition by use of this tradition itself. The problem is to show that the tradition of the primacy of Rome, on which all remaining Roman Catholic tradition depends, is valid.

The flight into later history could only assure the permanent primacy to a certain episcopal see if, in the first place, Matthew 16:17 ff. justified us in seeking successors in the sense of a tie with one church, and if, secondly, the line could be drawn backwards from the later effectively exercised primacy of one church to the apostolic period and so to the historical Peter. *Neither of these things, however, is true.* That being the case, the effective role that the Roman Church has played and now plays does not prove that it has to exercise *the same* primacy that Peter exercised in Jerusalem after it was promised to him by Jesus.

The Roman church, it is true, gradually attained a pre-eminent position in the course of the second and third centuries. No historian or theologian will dispute this. The question, however, is whether the primacy promised to Peter in Matthew 16:17 ff. and actually exercised by him in Jerusalem in the beginning is therefore to be transferred exclusively to the Bishops of the Roman church. That a church occupies a pre-eminent position still does not prove that it stands in such a relation to Matthew 16:17 ff. as to give it a divine right for all time to come. The secular historian, indeed, explains that pre-eminent position by the purely "immanent" consideration that Rome was the chief city of the Roman Empire, so that the Christian church located there naturally and necessarily attained a special dignity. This reason certainly did play a strongly contributory role. In addition, the theologian will discover factors within the Church, grounded in the situation of that time, and with Ignatius of Antioch he may recognize that the Roman church of that time has also a "pre-eminence in love."[37] But even if we wish to speak here of a divinely intended *development* in the history of the Church of Christ, it does not follow from this that this historical role is a sign that it is a divinely intended *norm* for the leadership of the Church of all time. For we say once more: Matthew 16:17 ff. does not say a word as to how the succession to Peter in the leadership of the

[37] Ignatius, *To the Romans* 1:1: προκαθημένη τῆς ἀγάπης.

Church at large is to be determined. It is arbitrary to take into account *a priori* only this *one* possibility that one church, which—not in the apostolic period of revelation, but later—stands out among the other churches, must *for ever* furnish the successor of Peter. The fact that the bishops of this church in later times *make the claim* that they alone are intended in the promise of Jesus in Matthew 16:17 ff. cannot prove the legitimacy of this claim.

Moreover, *until the beginning of the third century* it never occurred to a single Bishop of Rome to refer the saying in Matthew 16:17 ff. to himself in the sense of the leadership of the entire Church. It was probably Callistus (217–222), though according to others it was actually Stephanus (254–257),[38] who first applied to himself the words "You are Peter," and this did not pass without contradiction. Tertullian protests that he intends to refer the saying only to the person of Peter and not to the bishops at all; Cyprian, on the contrary, refers it to *all* later bishops and not to the Bishop of Rome alone.[39] The appeal that the Roman Bishops made to Matthew 16:17 ff., moreover, fell far short of general acceptance even in the third century, and only much later does the exclusive reference to Rome become a self-evident axiom.

Irenaeus, to be sure, speaks even in the second century of the oft cited "more powerful and pre-eminent position of Rome" (*potentior principalitas*).[40] To support this, however, he does not appeal to Matthew 16:17 ff.[41] Rather, in accordance with the tradition principle of the rabbis and the philosophical schools, which Hegesippus, following the Gnostics, seems to have naturalized in the ancient Church,[42] he points to the particularly well-preserved apostolic tradition; this is connected only with the *foundation* of the Roman church, and indeed by both Peter *and* Paul; it is not connected with the primacy of Peter.

Moreover, the entire controversy as to whether in Rome appeal was first made to Matthew 16:17 ff. at a somewhat earlier or later

---

[38] So, for example, recently also K. Heussi. See above, p. 160, note 8.

[39] See E. Caspar, *Geschichte des Papsttums von den Anfängen bis zur Höhe der Weltherrschaft*, Vol. I, 1938. On this subject, see above, pp. 160 f.

[40] *Against Heresies*, III, 3, 2.

[41] P. Batiffol, "Cathedra Petri" (*Etudes d'Histoire ancienne*, 1938, p. 14), thinks that in the word *principalitas*, which is to be understood chronologically, the "You are Peter" is implied. His interpretation, however, does not seem to me to be sufficiently grounded.

[42] H. von Campenhausen, *Lehrerreihen und Bischofreihen im 2. Jahrhundert. In Memoriam Ernst Lohmeyer*, 1951, pp. 240 ff.

time does not have for our question as much significance as is attached to it.[43] In any case, more than one hundred years passed before the primacy of Rome was connected with the promise of Jesus to Peter. The fact that, in a time when the Roman church already had a certain consciousness of pre-eminence, it still did not justify its consciousness by reference to Matthew 16:17 ff., should certainly cause one to think. There is, indeed, a chain of succession of Roman bishops, which may have its value for the Roman church. *There is no chain of succession of leaders of the Church at large*, even though the local Roman chain was later made for this purpose. In the period after James there is a great gap. In the hortatory writing of Clement which is called the First Epistle of Clement, a bishop speaks in a brotherly way to a sister church, just as also happened elsewhere without any conclusion being drawn that such an act justifies a claim to primacy.

It is arguing in a circle, a *petitio principii*, to assert that since on the one hand the promise of Jesus to Peter exists, and on the other hand the fact exists that Rome exercised a primacy from a relatively early date, we therefore must conclude that this primacy rests on that promise, in such a way that it is the norm for all time. That this relation exists between Matthew 16:17 ff. and the pre-eminent position that Rome later occupied is precisely the thing it is necessary to prove.

In answer to these and other objections the Roman Catholic theologians are accustomed to point out that the promise to Peter had to become *visible* in history, since the Church is a visible Church and continues on earth the work of Christ. The idea of the continuation of the work of Christ in the visible earthly Church I affirm, since I find it especially in the entire Gospel of John as a central declaration. Therefore, as far as I am concerned—I do not speak here at all in the name of official "Protestant theology"—it is not true that on this point the common basis for discussion is lacking. It should be sufficiently clear from my previous writings that I really take seriously the fact that the present in which we stand, the period of the Church, belongs in the redemptive history; this history, to be sure, must continually find its norm in the apostolic period of revelation as the central point of time. The promise of Jesus to Peter was visibly fulfilled in Jerusalem in the days following the resurrection. But from this it does not result that the Roman claim to be henceforth the only

[43] It was chiefly A. Harnack, P. Batiffol, H. Koch, and E. Caspar who took part in this controversy.

legitimate visible Church is justified on the ground that Rome actually occupied a pre-eminent position from a certain time on. It should not be disputed that this pre-eminent position has some significance for the development of the gospel line of redemptive history in the period of the Church. But this position does not necessarily rest upon the promise of Jesus to Peter, in the sense that therefore for all time to come only the occupant of this episcopal see can be the leader of the true Church; such a conclusion does not follow from faith in the visibility of the Church in which Christ continues his work.

There have been and there are today, outside of the Roman Church, visible churches in other centres also, and it would be arguing again in a circle to reply that such a church is not a real church because it does not stand in succession to Peter. From Matthew 16:17 ff. and the rest of the New Testament come other criteria, in addition to the narrow criterion connected with an episcopal see, which permit us to recognize that Church *which Christ builds upon Peter the Rock*. We cannot discuss here the entire involved question of the criterion of the Church and of tradition.[44] But it should be emphasized that it is arbitrary to assert that Christ built his Church upon Peter only at the place where, at a certain date, this or that church was the leader of Christendom.

Developments of the *post-apostolic* period of church history, important as they may be for the development of redemptive history in the period of the Church, cannot give a permanent and exclusively *normative* position to any of those leading places. For one thing, the intent of Jesus leaves us no possibility of understanding Matthew 16:17 ff. in the sense of a succession determined by an episcopal see. Moreover, the history of Peter knows nothing of a transfer of the ruling seat (*cathedra*) of the Church at large from Jerusalem to another city. In the apostolic period Rome was not the centre of the Church at large. There at the midpoint of the times, the point decisive for the Christian, no hint is anywhere given that the Roman or any other bishop's seat is in the future to be the permanent centre of the Church at large. In addition to Rome there were, in the post-apostolic period as previously, other centres of the visible Church; there are now other centres and there probably will be still others, whether their name is Antioch, Corinth or Ephesus, Alexandria or Constantinople, Wittenberg, Canterbury or Geneva, Stockholm or Amsterdam.

The actual power that these centres have exercised or now exercise

[44] I hope to do this in another place.

proves nothing as to the legality of any claim they may make that they *alone* stand in succession to the first leader, Peter, whom Christ established over the Church at large. Even the fact that only one of these outstanding places has asserted and now asserts such a claim proves nothing.

The decision as to who at each time is to stand at the head of the entire Church cannot be made from the standpoint of an episcopal see fixed once for all. The apostolic quality, the connection with Peter, can be preserved in another way. Neither from Scripture nor from the history of the ancient Church can a divine right for the primacy of Rome be derived.

For this reason even the Roman Catholic Church appeals to a dogmatic utterance according to which the Bishops of Rome are the sole successors of Peter.[45] We do not need to return again to the question how far this utterance lacks basis either in Scripture or in the most ancient tradition. We should, however, ask this question: Is it not another and final begging of the question, *a petitio principii*, when this very assertion, which is so notably basic for the Roman claim, is founded only upon later dogmas? For the exclusive claim to *proclaim dogmas through the possession of sole apostolic authority* is nevertheless dependent on this very dogma of the legal succession to Peter. What is involved here is not just another dogma; it is that dogma that is meant to justify completely the exclusive right of the Roman Catholic Church to promulgate dogmas. In such a situation, can every other basis be lacking, above all the witness of Scripture, which Rome does not mention at all in connection with Peter? Can ancient tradition also be lacking? It knows nothing of a government of the Church at large from Rome by Peter, and also knows nothing of a transfer of his succession to the Roman Bishops.

We reach the following conclusion of these doctrinal and theological discussions:

In so far as Peter is the rock, he is such in the temporal sense of laying the foundation as an apostle. In every generation Christ intends to build his Church on the foundation of the apostles, and among them Peter is the most important.

In so far as he is the leader of the Primitive Church in Jerusalem, this also has chiefly temporal significance, and in this respect his bearing

---

[45] See the sentence from the *Vaticanum* cited above in note 36. The most thorough presentation of the Roman Catholic doctrine seems to me to be offered by the already mentioned work of Ch. Journet, *L'Eglise du verbe incarné*, 1941. See, especially, pp. 522 ff.

for the redemptive history of all later time consists in the fact that he held the leadership of the original Church.

If we wish to derive further from the saying that after Peter also there must be in the Church a universal leadership that administers the keys, the power to bind and loose, this cannot take place in the sense of a limitation to the future occupants of one episcopal see. This principle of succession cannot be justified either from Scripture or from the history of the ancient Church. In reality the leadership of the Church at large is not to be determined by succession in the sense of a link with one episcopal see. The significance of individual churches for the Church at large comes and goes. But the rock, the foundation for all churches of all times, remains the historical Peter. At that time he was especially chosen by Jesus from among the Twelve; he was given special distinction as a witness of Jesus' life and death and as the first witness of his resurrection. On him Christ, who is himself the cornerstone, will keep building his Church as long as there is such a Church on earth.

INDEX OF
AUTHORS CITED

ACHELIS, H., 123, 135
Actus Vercellenses, 23, 62, 108
Adam, K., 160, 161, 170
Alfaranus, Tiberius, 139
Allen, W. C., 60
Altaner, B., 77, 84, 91, 95
Ambrose, 60, 162
Apollonj-Ghetti, B. M., 138
Aristophanes, 17
Augustine, 46, 60, 84, 133, 162

BACON, B. W., 83
Bardy, G., 160
Barth, K., 184
Baruch, Apocalypse of, 84
Batiffol, P., 124, 131, 160 *bis*, 161, 234, 235
Bauer, A., 75
Bauer, W., 54, 87, 110, 116
Baumann, R., 223
Baumgartner, W., 64
Baur, F. Chr., 71 *bis*, 74, 164
Bechtel, 17
Belser, J., 37
Benoit, P., 105
Bernard, J., 60, 61
Besson, M., 13
Bezold, C., 63
Bieder, W., 201
Bigg, C., 86
Billerbeck (Strack-), 19, 84, 163, 186, 191, 205, 206
Blass, F., 17, 116
Blumhardt, 196
Bohren, R., 192, 201, 205
Boismard, R. P., 88 *bis*
Bonnell, E., 73
Bornkamm, G., 85
Brandon, S. G. F., 38
Brandt, W., 13
Braun, F. M., 40, 47, 166, 167, 169, 208

Brun, Lyder, 62
Bruston, Ed., 202
Bultmann, R., 25, 30, 61 *bis*, 67, 87 *quater*, 159, 167, 168, 173, 180 *bis*, 186, 188, 189 *bis*, 195, 196, 197, 200

CALVIN, 162, 163
Campbell, J. Y., 187
Campenhausen, H. von, 43, 58, 77, 86, 95 *bis*, 215, 225, 230, 234
Caspar, E., 160 *bis*, 234, 235
Catalogus Liberianus, 113, 124 *bis*
Cecchelli, C., 38, 79, 106, 107, 132, 148
Celsus, 63
Chapman, J., 161, 162
Charles, R. H., 112 *bis*
Cheramy, R., 132
Cheyne, Th. K., 74
Chrysostom, 46, 52, 151, 162, 230
Clemen, C., 112
Clement of Alexandria, 18, 23 *bis*, 41, 86, 117, 225
Clement of Rome (*I Clement*), 45, 51, 55, 75 *bis*, 76, 77, 83, 88, 89–109, 110, 114, 115, 116, 230, 235
Clementina. See *Pseudo-Clementina*.
Craig, C. T., 77
Cremer, H., 188
Cullmann, O., 28, 30, 35, 62, 67, 75, 99, 155, 167 *bis*, 187, 193, 196, 199, 200 *bis*, 201, 211, 225
Cureton, W., 127
Cyprian, 160, 161 *quinquies*, 234
Cyril of Alexandria, 162

DAHL, N. A., 166, 168
Dain, A., 96
Dalman, G., 19, 22 *bis*, 204
Damascus Document, 64, 197
Damasus Inscription, 134
Dannenbauer, H., 75, 94, 110, **122**
Dausch, P., 169, 171
Debrunner, A., 17, 116
Deichmann, Fr. W., 133, 140
Deissmann, A., 17, 31, 166, 182
Delehaye, H., 95, 118, 129, 130
Dell, A., 18, 19 *bis*, 165, 205
Depositio episcoporum, 123, 151
Depositio martyrum, 123, 124, 125, 126, 128 *bis*, 131, 140, 151
De Wette, W. M., 73
Dibelius, M., 37, 49 *bis*, 76, 91, 96, 97, 98, 99, 105, 165
Diehl, E., 133, 140
Dionysius of Corinth, 54, 116
Dix, G., 219

Döllinger, J., 46
Draguet, R., 76
Drews, A., 17
Dubowy, E., 98
Duchesne, L., 123, 124, 126, 127, 128
Duensing, H., 112
Dunin-Borkowski, 232
Dupont, J., 37, 38, 48
Dupont-Sommer, A., 64
Dutlin, J., 202

EASTON, B. S., 165
Eggenberger, Chr,. 90, 100, 107
Eichhorn, J. G., 73
Eisler, R., 22, 185
Eliezer ben Jehuda, 22
Ellendorf, 71
Engnell, J., 199
Enoch, Book of, 189, 199
Epictetus, 95
Epiphanius, 230
Eppel, R., 202 *bis*
Erasmus, 85
Erbes, C., 74, 118, 124, 127, 128, 129, 130
Escobar, M., 138
II Esdras, 50
IV Esdras, 84
Euringer, S., 166
Eusebius, 18, 23, 52, 54, 84, 95, 113, 114, 116, 117 *quater*, 118, 120, 136, 171 *bis*, 225 *bis*

FALLANI, G., 138
Fascher, E., 13, 43, 105
Feine-Behm, P., 105
Ferrua, A., 128, 138, 139, 144, 147 *bis*, 148 *bis*
Fick, 17
Fiebig, P., 20
Fillion, L., 13
Filocalus, Furius Dionysius, 123
Firmilian, 161
Flacius Illyricus, 73
Flemming, J., 112
Flew, R. Newton, 166, 167, 189
Foakes-Jackson, F. J., 13, 22, 50, 79
Fouard, C., 13
Franck, Seb., 72
Frey, J. B., 134
Fridrichsen, A., 37, 38, 56, 63, 75, 108, 167, 216

Fuchs, E., 17
Fuchs, H., 84 *bis*, 107

GAECHTER, P., 33, 36, 41, 42, 43, 44, 49
Gaius, 117–121, 123, 136, 137, 138, 145, 146 *ter*, 149, 151
Galen, 19
Galtier, P., 160 *bis*
Gander, G., 206
Gaugler, E., 187
Geiselmann, J. R., 159
Gerkan, A. von, 129, 132
Gibbon, E., 73
Gieseler, J., 73
Gloege, G., 163, 167, 195
Goetz, K. G., 20, 29, 57, 59 *bis*, 61 *bis*, 62 *bis*, 63, 186
Goguel, M., 25, 28, 29, 34, 49, 54, 55, 60, 77, 81, 114, 117, 120, 124, 127, 160 *bis*,
    165, 183, 185, 186, 198, 202
Goldast, Melchior, 72
Graber, R., 30, 38 *ter*, 41, 78, 175, 192, 232
Grégoire, H., 119, 150
Gressmann, H., 165
Grill, J., 165
Grimaldi, Giacomo, 141
Grisar, H., 139, 146
Grundmann, W., 36, 37, 41 *bis*, 62, 66, 67, 106
Guignebert, Ch., 74, 75, 94, 117, 118 *bis*, 124, 127
Günther, E., 86, 95

HAARBRÜCKER, Th., 63
Haase, F., 63
Haller, J., 75, 85, 94, 168
Harnack, A., 38, 41, 54, 59, 60, 61, 62, 63, 74, 85, 90, 112 *bis*, 122, 160 *bis*, 165,
    166 *bis*, 170, 185, 189, 202, 218, 219, 235
Hatch-Redpath, 18
Hauck, Fr., 86
Hebrews, Gospel of, 27
Hegesippus, 234
Heiler, F., 165, 205
Hennecke, E., 112
Herbig, R., 143
Héring, J., 178, 179
Hertling, L., 129
Hesiod, 19
Heussi, K., 71, 75 *bis*, 76 *ter*, 78, 80, 83, 85, 86 *bis*, 87, 92, 93, 94 *bis*, 95, 96, 97, 110,
    115, 118, 120, 122, 145, 150, 160, 234
Hippolytus, 160
Hirsch, E., 20, 51, 54, 65, 78, 106, 168
Holl, K., 46, 94, 105, 109, 119, 230
Holsten, C., 62

Holtzmann, H. J., 164
Holzmeister, U., 37
Homer, 19
Huelsen, Ch., 141
Huffman, N., 59

IGNATIUS, 89, 96, 99, 109–111, 113, 151, 159, 231, 233
Immisch, O., 179
Irenaeus, 116, 234
Isaiah, Ascension of, 112

JEREMIAS, J., 166, 167, 168, 186 ter, 191, 192
Jerome, 46, 52, 84, 124, 125, 128 bis, 151, 225
Josephus, 19, 85 ter
Josi, E., 138 bis
Journet, Ch., 232, 237
Jülicher, A., 105
Juster, J., 79
Justin Martyr, 19, 115, 151, 159
Juvenal, 134

KAAS, L., 138
Kahle, P., 64
Kattenbusch, F., 58, 59, 166, 167 bis, 189 bis, 190
Katzenmayer, H., 52, 54, 55, 76, 78
Kerygma Petri, 41
King, C., 77
Kirch, C., 123
Kirk, K. E., 219
Kirsch, J. P., 126, 127, 132
Kirschbaum, E., 129, 131, 138 bis, 140
Kittel, G., 58, 86, 95, 100, 159, 188, 215
Klauser, Th., 118, 140
Klausner, J., 63
Klink, J. L., 27, 45
Klostermann, E., 165, 191, 201, 204
Knabenbauer, J., 21
Kneller, A., 166
Knopf, R., 86, 90, 92, 95 bis, 99
Koch, H., 121, 160, 161 bis, 225, 230, 235
Köhler, W., 121, 160
Kösters, L., 232
Kraeling, E. G., 199
Krüger, G., 75, 94
Kuhn, K. G., 83, 188
Kümmel, W. G., 48, 49 bis, 105, 167 bis, 168, 194 bis, 200
Kurfess, A., 107

LAGRANGE, M. J., 18, 21, 80, 169, 170, 177, 188, 202 *bis*
Lake, Kirsopp, 50
Lammert, F., 118
Lampridius, Aelius, 148
La Piana, G., 134 *bis*
Leclercq, H., 129
Leenhardt, F. J., 167, 190
Lemerle, P., 138
Leo the Great, 130
Leuba, J. L., 44, 222
Levy, J., 19
Liber Pontificalis, 124, 127, 128 *bis*, 133, 143, **145**
Liechtenhan, R., 37, 168, 182
Liempt, L. von, 96
Lietzmann, H., 50, 54 *bis*, 55, 74, 75 *quater*, 76 *ter*, 78, 86, 88, 92, 95 *bis*, 106, 118,
    119, 123 *bis*, 124, 125, 126, 127, 128, 129, 132, 133, 134, 135, 138, 140, 141,
    142
Lightfoot, J. B., 95
Linton, O., 166, 167, 190
Linus (Pseudo-), 127
Lipsius, A., 127 *bis*
Lohmeyer, E., 59, 61, 66, 234
Loisy, A., 21, 90, 164, 196
Luther, 72, 132, 162 *ter*

MACARIUS MAGNUS, 121
III Maccabees, 202
Mancini, G., 132
Manson, T. W., 78, 166, 189, 215, **219**
Mariana, Juan de, 88
Marsilius of Padua, 72
Martyrdom of Peter and Paul, 127
Martyrologium (Jerome), 124, 125, 128 *ter*, **130**
Marucchi, O., 132, 140
Massaux, E., 159
Meinertz, M., 13, 201, 207, 219, 228
Meinhold, P., 99
Melanchthon, 163
Menoud, Ph.-H., 34, 224
Merrill, E. T., 75
Merx, A., 18, 19
Meyer, A., 19, 60
Meyer, Ed., 28, 54, 61, 78, 166
Michaelis, W., 81, 105, 167, 172, 173, 175, 177, 180, 186 *bis*, 188, 200, 204,
    208 *bis*
Michel, O., 86, 168, 187, 188
Miegge, G., 77
Mohlberg, L. C., 130, 131, 140
Möhler, J. A., 46

Molland, E., 75
Mommsen, Th., 123
Monceaux, P., 91, 118, 125
Moneta of Cremona, P., 72
Mülhaupt, E., 72, 73, 132, 162 *bis*
Müller, K., 58, 63
Munck, J., 77, 84, 86, 88 *bis*, 89, 99, 100 *bis*, 102, 107, 109, 110
Mundle, W., 219

Neander, A., 73
Nicolosi, 140
Noack, B., 100

Odeberg, H., 166
Oepke, A., 159, 168, 169, 186, 187, 189
Oncken, H., 72
Origen, 52, 63, 84, 117, 159, 202
Otto, R., 167
Overbeck, Fr., 46

Papias, 113, 116
Pauly-Wissowa, 13, 43, 118
Perler, O., 77, 110
Pernot, H., 20
Peter, Acts of, 42
Peter, Apocalypse of, 63, 85
Peter, Gospel of, 63, 85
Peterson, E., 108, 200, 219
Philo, 85
Pieper, K., 170
Piganiol, A., 140
Pistis Sophia, 63
Pius XII, 138, 143
Pliny, 142
Polycarp, 95, 96, 114, 119, 136, 150 *bis*
Polycrates, 120, 136
Porphyrius, 122, 123
Porter, J. R., 37
Prandi, A., 132
Preisker, H., 83, 85, 86
Preuschen, E., 20
Proclus, 117, 118, 151
Prudentius, 127
Pseudo-Clementina, 23, 41, 43, 51, 62 *ter*, 115, 159, 225, 230, 231

Quentin, H., 125, 130

Ramsey, A. M., 219
Reicke, Bo, 100

Reitzenstein, R., 165
Renan, E., 74
Rengstorf, K. H., 58, 215, 219, 220
Respighi, C., 138
Riddle, D. W., 18
Riesenfeld, H., 196, 199, 206, 209, 218
Robertson, J. M., 18
Robinson, D. F., 38
Rost, L., 64, 187, 188, 190

Sanders, L., 77, 95, 98, 99
Sasse, H., 61
Schäfer, E., 129, 135, 138, 151
Schechter, S., 188
Schermann, Th., 18
Schlatter, A., 83, 85, 165, 173, 180, 188, 201, 205
Schleiermacher, F., 73
Schlier, H., 48, 49
Schmidt, C., 108, 122, 225
Schmidt, K. L., 31, 60, 159, 166, 167 bis, 169, 173, 182, 184, 188, 189, 191, 208
Schmiedel, P. W., 74
Schmutz, St., 77
Schneider, A. M., 129 bis, 132, 133, 135, 136
Schneider, Fedor, 124
Schniewind, J., 167, 204, 205
Schnitzer, J., 165
Schoenbeck, H. von, 140
Schoeps, H. J., 43, 51, 225
Schuler, M., 77
Schulthess, F., 20
Schweitzer, A., 165, 193, 194, 200
Schweizer, Ed., 36, 205, 215, 219, 224, 229
Seeberg, E., 63
Selwyn, E. G., 83, 84 bis
Seston, W., 140, 142, 143
Shahrastani, 63
Sharbil, 127
Sibylline Oracles, 84
Sickenberger, J., 166, 170
Sieffert, F., 13, 31
Simon, M., 198
Solomon, Odes of, 202
Spanheim, Fr., 73
Speier, H., 143
Stählin, W., 219
Staerk, W., 64
Stauffer, E., 26, 29, 30, 42, 59 ter, 60, 61 bis, 64, 168, 180
Stonehouse, N. B., 60
Strabo, 85

Strack-Billerbeck, 19, 84, 163, 186, 191, 205, 206
Strathmann, H., 25 *bis*, 86, 95, 168, 186
Strauss, D. F., 27, 164
Streeter, B. H., 25
Stumpff, A., 100
Styger, P., 128, 133
Surkau, H. W., 86
Syncellus, 85
Syriac Treasure Cave, 63

TACITUS, 96 *bis*, 107 *bis*, 120, 142, 149, 151
Talmud, Babylonian, 85
Tatian, 165
Tertullian, 84, 87, 96, 117 *bis*, 121, 123, 137, 159, 160 *ter*, 161
Tisserand, E., 112 *ter*
Tolotti, F., 128
Torrey, Ch. C., 50
Tricot, A., 13

USENER, H., 124

Vaticanum, 232, 237
Venelus Minhoniensis, Ulricus, 72
Vielhauer, Ph., 188, 192
Vischer, W., 47, 201, 204
Völlmecke, A. M., 46
Volz, P., 190

WEISS, B., 182
Weiss, Joh., 165
Wellhausen, J., 22, 61
Wendland, H. D., 167, 195
Wendland, P., 98
Wilpert, J., 129, 134
Windisch, H., 83, 85, 86

ZAHN, Th., 18, 81, 84, 85, 163, 165, 177, 180, 188, 202, 203, 204
Zeiller, J., 54, 72, 113
Zeller, E., 112
Zoeller, W., 219
Zwingli, 163

INDEX OF
BIBLICAL PASSAGES

Genesis
17:5 ....177n.
17:5 ff........................19
17:15 ....19, 177n.
32:28 ....19, 177n.

Numbers
12:7........................192
16:3 190

Deuteronomy
7:6............................190
19:15 62

Ruth
4:11 192

Nehemiah
9:7........................50

Job
30:6........................18
38:17 ....202, 202n.

Psalms
9:13........................202
107:18 202

Isaiah
7:3............................188
10:21 188
22:22........................203 *bis*
38:10 202
43:14 83
52:13 67
53........................186n.
62:2........................19
65:15 19

Jeremiah
1:18 f.........................192n.
4:29........................18
50–51........................83

Ezekiel
12:3........................37n.

Daniel
2:34 f...................191, 192n.
2:44 f...................191, 192n.
3:12........................100n.
7:9–28 189
7:18 189
7:27 189

Amos
9:11........................192
9:11 f.........................192

Ecclesiasticus
14:18.... ....185n.

Wisdom of Solomon
2:24........................101
16:13........................202
17:17........................19

Matthew
1:21........................177n.
1:25........................177n.
2:23........................177n.
4:10........................174, 174n.
4:18........................23
8:11........................65
8:14........................23
9:36........................197

Matthew—*continued*

9:37 f. 196
10:2 . . . . .24, 26
10:4 . . . . .22n.
10:6 . . . . .64, 190, 192
10:7 f. 196, 203, 205
10:23 196
11 176
11:4 f. . . . . .194, 196 *bis*
11:4 ff. 205
11:7–9 186
11:25–30 .186
11:27 179
12:28 194
13 176
13:41 . . . . .191n.
13:47 ff. 196
14:28 . . . . .23, 61
14:28 ff. 26
14:33 175
15:15 24
15:24 . . . . .190, 192
16 20
16:13 . . . . .20n.
16:16 ff. 21, 30, 34, 53, 56, 57
16:17 . . . .20, 21, 160, 177, 178, 179,
    182, 191
16:17 f. . . . . .61, 202n.
16:17 ff. . . . . .25, 26 *ter*, 57 *ter*, 70, 155,
    158, 159 *bis*, 160n., 161, 162 *bis*, 165,
    167, 170n., 178n., 180, 181, 182 *bis*,
    183 *quater*, 184 *ter*, 190 *bis*, 194n.,
    198 *bis*, 198n, 199, 200, 201, 207,
    208n., 210 *ter*, 211, 213 *bis*, 214 *ter*,
    217 *ter*, 220, 222, 224 *bis*, 227 *ter*,
    228 *bis*, 230, 231, 233 *quater*, 234
    quinquies, 235 *bis*, 236 *bis*
16:17–19 . . . .7, 18, 25n., 158, 159n.,
    168n., 170, 173n., 175, 176, 179 *bis*,
    200n.
16:18 . . . .20, 26, 121, 155 *bis*, 159n.,
    165, 169, 179, 184, 199, 209, 217, 231
16:18 ff. 71
16:19 . . . . .203, 204
17:24 24
18:17 186
18:18 .205 *bis*
18:21 24
21:20 . . . . .24, 25

Matthew—*continued*

21:42 . . . . .206, 217
21:42 ff. . . . . .192n.
23 176
23:13 . . . . .204 *bis*
23:15 204
23:37 . . . . .88n.
24:10 107
26:31 197
26:40 24
28:19 216

Mark

1:16 . . . . .23 *bis*
1:16 ff. 60
1:17 196
1:29 23
1:29 ff. 23
1:36 24
2:18 ff. 201
3:16 . . . . .21 *bis*, 24, 177, 177n.
3:17 20
3:18 . . . . .22n.
3:33 ff. 197
5:37 23
7:17 24
8 26
8:27 . . . . .20n.
8:27 ff. . . . . .20, 171 ff., 178n.
8:29 ff. 24
8:31 f. 173
8:32 67
8:33 24
9:2 23
9:2 ff. 24
9:5 24
10:28 24
11:21 . . . . .24, 25
13:2 198
13:34 . . . . .203n.
14:28 . . . . .59, 201
14:29 24
14:33 23
14:37 .21n., 24
14:57 f. 198
14:62 . . . . .189, 200, 201
15:10 108
16:7 . . . . .25, 59

Luke

1:13	177n.
1:31	177n.
1:59–63	177n.
2:21	177n.
5:1 ff.	23, 26, 61
5:2 f.	23
5:8	68
5:10	23
6:14	24
6:15	22
8:45	24
9:32	24
10:1 ff.	216n.
12:32	197
12:41	24
12:42	203n.
16:1 ff.	203n.
20:17 f.	191
22:8	24
22:31	26
22:31 f.	30, 57 *bis*, 155, 190
22:31 ff.	182, 183, 184
22:31–34	183 *ter*, 184
22:32	61
24:34	58 *bis*, 59, 60, 181

John

1–20	29, 29n.
1:35 ff.	23
1:41	28
1:42	19, 21 *ter*, 29, 177, 177n.
1:44	17, 22 *bis*
2:19	198
4:38	36
6:66	182
6:66 ff.	27n., 29 *bis*
10	64
10:1 ff.	197
10:16	64
12:21	22 *bis*
13:24	27
13:36	27n.
13:36 ff.	87
17:20	209, 220, 221
18:15	27
20	28
20:4	28
20:8	28

John—*continued*

20:23	204n., 205 *bis*
21	29, 30n., 58, 60, 60n., 63 *bis*, 64, 87, 181 *ter*, 183
21:3	23
21:13	181
21:15 f.	21
21:15 ff.	30, 181, 183 *quinquies*, 184, 218, 218n.
21:16	155
21:16 f.	122
21:16 ff.	63, 197, 208, 212, 216
21:18	87 *bis*, 94, 117n.
21:18 f.	87n., 117
21:18 ff.	86, 87n., 113

Acts

1–12	38, 39
1:13	22, 24
1:15–16	33n.
1:15 ff.	33
1:21	216
1:22	58, 216
2:10	79n.
2:14	33
2:37	33, 41
2:42	35
3	33
3–4	67
3:4	34
3:13	67
3:26	67
4:1	34
4:8	34
4:13	22, 34
4:25	67n.
4:27	67
4:30	67
4:33	35
5:1 ff.	34, 57, 226
5:1–11	34n.
5:2	34
5:12	35
5:15	35
5:29	34
6:10 ff.	198n.
7:38	187
8:1	35, 52
8:4	35

Acts—*continued*

8:12...........................35
8:14........................35, 40
8:14 ff.........................53
8:16...........................35
8:17...........................35
8:18 ff.........................34
8:26 ff.........................66
9–10........................36, 40
9:31..........................192
9:36 ff........................85n.
10–11...................22, 62n.
10:41.........................216
11:4–18.......................37n.
11:19..........................52
11:27..........................48
11:27 ff.......................49n.
12.................37n., 41n., 47
12:1–19.......................38n.
12:9..........................62n.
12:17........37, 38, 39, 41 *bis*, 53, 80
13–28..........................38
14:23.........................219
15....39, 47 *ter*, 48 *ter*, 49 *quater*, 52
15:1 ff....................47, 49n.
15:7........................49, 50
15:7–11.......................37n.
15:14......................17, 17n.
15:19 f........................48
18............................53
20:17 ff......................219
20:28....................197, 220
21:25..........................48
28:14..........................38

Romans

13:13.........................99n.
14:19........................192n.
15.........................106 *bis*
15:2.........................192n.
15:16 f.......................44n.
15:20....45, 79, 105, 113, 192n., 209, 217 *bis*
15:20 ff......................106
16............................78n.

I Corinthians

1:12.......................18, 53
1:14 ff........................53

I Corinthians—*continued*

3:3...........................99n.
3:6........................53, 116
3:10.....................209, 217
3:11......................47, 217
3:22...........................18
4:1..........................203n.
4:15.......................53, 116
8:1–10.......................192n.
9:1.....................54, 58, 216
9:5.........18, 23, 42, 53, 77, 81
9:7..........................197
10:4.........................217
15:3 ff...................58n., 63
15:5....18, 29, 58 *ter*, 59, 59n., 60, 63, 67, 180
15:5 ff.......................216
15:6.........................58n.
15:8.........................59n.
15:32........................109
15:50.......................185n.

II Corinthians

11:26....................103, 109
12:20........................99n.

Galatians

1:12..........................69
1:12 ff......................220
1:16....................185n., 216
1:16–18.....................186n.
1:18.....................18, 222
1:18 ff....................39, 41
1:19......................230n. *bis*
2:1................46n., 47, 52n.
2:1 ff.....42, 47 *bis*, 48 *ter*, 49 *ter*, 52
2:4..........................105
2:6.......................47, 78n.
2:7 f................18, 42n., 43
2:9....18, 34, 43, 44, 46, 79, 92, 106, 110, 186n., 209, 217, 230n.
2:11...................18, 18n., 38
2:11 ff.........40, 46, 51, 52, 53, 106
2:12.....................43, 225
2:14................18, 46n., 50
4:26...........................83
5:20.........................99n.

Ephesians
2:20................209, 217 *quater*
2:22...........................192
6:12..........................185n.

Philippians
1:15 f.........................105
1:15–17.......................104
1:17.........................105n.
3:2...........................105

I Timothy
1:18.........................229n.
3:15..........................192

Hebrews
2:14.........................185n.
3:2 ff.........................192
10:21.........................192
12:22..........................83

I Peter
1:1........................52, 83
1:3............................61
2:4 ff.........................217
2:5...........................192
2:5 ff.........................199

I Peter—*continued*
2:11...........................83
2:21 ff.........................68
4:10.........................203n.
5:1......................86, 87, 94
5:13....73, 83, 83n., 84, 85, 89, 113,
    117

II Peter
1:1.......................17, 17n.
1:14........................82, 87
1:16 ff.........................61

Revelation
1:18..........................203
3:7...........................203
11:3.........................109n.
11:3 ff......................88, 120
11:3–13........................77
11:8........................84, 86
14:8...........................84
16:19..........................84
17:5...........................84
17:5 ff.........................84
18:2 ff.........................84
21:14..................209, 217 *ter*
21:19.........................209
21:25.........................203